CRITICS LOVE
GROWING UP BRADY:

"It's a delightful behind-the-scenes look at this popular show."
—*Bookviews*

"The behind-the-scenes look at the show chronicles power struggles, script disputes, greed and teenage lust."
—*Daily News* (Atlanta)

"Brady fans are shocked!"
—*Washington Post*

"Barry Williams and his co-author, Chris Kreski, have concocted a lighthearted tell-all about Williams' years on the show."
—*Entertainment Weekly*

"A fond look at the people and the show that sated the appetite of a TV-watching generation hungry for 'wholesome' programming."
—*Tribune Revieu* (Greensboro)

"All 116 episodes—not to mention the reunions—are given their due, so if you're curious you'll find them here."
—*Dayton Daily News*

"Williams . . . strips the saccharin veneer off one of TV's legendary families and reveals the hardwood hijinks underneath."
—*Rockland Journal*

GROWING UP BRADY

I Was a Teenage Greg

Barry Williams with Chris Kreski

HarperPaperbacks

A Division of HarperCollins*Publishers*

HarperPaperbacks *A Division of* HarperCollins*Publishers*
10 East 53rd Street, New York, N.Y. 10022

A trade paperback of this book was published in 1992 by HarperCollins*Publishers*.

Front cover photographs © Paramount Pictures, Inc.
Back cover photograph courtesy of Barry Williams

First HarperPaperbacks printing: February 1993

Printed in the United States of America

HarperPaperbacks and colophon are trademarks of HarperCollins*Publishers*

❖ 10 9 8 7 6 5 4 3 2 1

Contents

Foreword

How Barry grew up to be sane, I've no idea, bearing in mind that "sane" in the acting world is a relative term. Considering the pressures, conflicts, and stresses involved, how Barry grew up at *all* might be a more pertinent question.

But this book is a testament to the fact that he has at least survived, and apparently survived to tell about it. It might be said that at best he speaks with veracity and can lay to rest some of the semiaccurate trivializations that have recently found their ways to the booksellers. And yes, alas, it is possible to trivialize the trivial.

The question of adjustment for a young performer is a serious one. Despite the common belief, no child is a born actor. No youngster left to his own devices conceives of learning a text or a song with the notion of staging it before a group of adults.

Children can be instinctive mimics (as anyone knows who has seen a toddler bounce to a video beat or imitate the characters on "Sesame Street"), and they can readily role-play in invented games with their peers. In no way, however, do they perceive this as entertaining others, but quite simply as entertaining themselves.

Some outside conditioning must take place before a potential thespian emerges from the child and transforms simple self-amusement into attention-getting behavior. It can start with something as simple as a lauded patty-cake or parental applause when little Johnny is able to find his nose with his finger. Little Johnny, of course, knows nothing of performance at this stage but simply reads his actions as a method of receiving love and approval. As Dr. Joyce Brothers points out, it is when little Johnny begins to point to other parts of his body that the confusion begins. He quickly learns that not *all* performance brings praise, nor will it necessarily amuse *him*.

If confusion is not the quintessence of prepubescent acting, it is almost surely the result of it.

Duke University inaugurated a study to attempt to determine the most stressful situation in which a human being could find himself short of anything life-threatening—that is, outside of going to war or having a pistol pointed at one's head, what was it in normal life that could create the most intense strain and pressure?

They found that by far the surest way to induce perspiration, loss of voice, and trembling of the extremities was the simple act of arising before a group to speak or perform in some manner. More than social problems, work-related stresses, marital difficulties, school demands, the thoughts of having to stand in a spotlight can cause laryngeal stricture and turn the brain to mush.

It requires little to imagine the effects of being hired to appear on a motion-picture set, where thousands of watts of light and sixty or seventy pairs of judgmental and demanding eyes are focused directly on you. Add to that the knowledge that when "Action!" is called, virtually everyone around you is practiced and competent, time costs thousands of dollars an hour, and the competition for your job is more intense than in any other vocation.

In this most exacting profession, it becomes a matter of the pressure not just of standing up and performing but of having to perform perfectly.

Even recompensed with parental love and approval, Little Johnny is hardly immune to this kind of stress.

In the course of his development, a child routinely risks failure; it is part of his learning. If he falls off his bike, he simply gathers himself up, remounts, and tries again until he gets it right. He has no one to satisfy but himself. In school, failure is normally met with nurturing, and time is allowed for progress; and parental teaching is for the most part grounded in love. Bruised sensitivities are given time to heal. Little or none of this occurs in the milieu of professional television. Success is demanded on the spot. That same little Johnny who only recently learned to point to his nose now has a much more complex and demanding task of achieving approbation.

A parent or guardian is required to be with the child on the set and can now witness failure magnified to its larger consequences. While some of the adult actors around him may offer gentle indoctrination to a point, the director, and ultimate authority figure, is far less likely to do so. And whether or not the child is successful, fear of failure is a constant.

How often in the supermarket do we see the results of these pressures on young actors displayed in tabloid excess? Deprived of a constancy in education, normal interaction with their age group, and an overload of attention that would dilate the ego of a saint—added to the unfortunate fact that a series' end may also coincide with the end of a young career—so many of them have found their last splurge of publicity in the scandal sheets, blaring their stories of substance abuse or felony.

The questions of confusion in purpose, love and approval and rejection are now major problems.

After forty years in the theater, my conclusion long has been that the stage is no place for a child. For him to act naturally is difficult enough; for him to grow up naturally in this environment is too much to expect.

It seems to me that for us adults in the profession, there is a responsibility beyond just gentle indoctrination: in these ersatz television families we create, we are forced, like it or not, to assume some of the role of parent simply in order to prevent the most blatant exploitation of the child. Even so, we offer only a semi-solution, not without its own complexities and problems.

Surrounding the child with further authority figures is problematic, considering that he already has in attention a parent, a producer, a director, a crew, a dialogue coach, and a welfare worker. Investigation, risk taking, and challenging, normal parts of a child's development, are rarely countenanced. But at least the actor playing a parent, having already established a relationship within the text, has an opportunity to extend those bonds into reality, and because he is faced with exactly the same professional obstacles as the child, he has an open window for lessening of tension. The fact that we are doing the same thing gives us commonality and affords the adult a chance to show that failure and experimentation not only can be allowed but are part of the honing process. He is also in a perfect position to offer a pat on the back when a hurdle is crossed.

Having painted a picture of the gentle art of acting

as a black hole for the young psyche, a pit at the bottom of which is developmental disorder and lost youth, am I not denigrating my task at hand? Am I not supposed to be creating an introduction to the thoughts and remembrances of someone for whom I care a great deal and who has my respect as a man and as an actor? Presumably the text you are about to read is not a tragic thesis on the life and declining times of Barry Williams. Have I not ended up with an inaccurate depiction of a dichotomy of purpose? No. My digression into the darker possibilities of theatrical life is only to underscore the fact that "The Brady Bunch" was virtually atypical.

Is the reader then expected to believe that of the plethora of sitcom children spawned from 1965 to 1985, these, my syndicated brood, were incomparable? Yes. Sound like a father speaking? Maybe. Self-aggrandizing? Perhaps. But in retrospect at least, I think I am fairly objective. The show was what it was, no more, no less.

After a career of eighty-three theatrical productions, five television series, and enough film to girdle the earth, I am willing to go on record. Having personally met, known, or worked with the vast majority of other young actors in the popular television shows during that twenty-year span, I can un-abashedly say that the six faces that appeared in the squares of the opening credits of "The Brady Bunch" were almost without equal.

I don't know to what to attribute not ending up with at least one bad apple in the kid department. I am obliged to say, however, that for everything Sherwood Schwartz, the *pater generator* and producer of the series, would willingly accept credit, the one to which he could lay uncontested claim is the casting of the children. Several hundreds were auditioned, and he gleaned the very best of the lot. Also my guess is that Sherwood had as good an eye for parents as he had for their offspring. In some ways they were as atypical as their children.

Second, the general tone and good nature of the scripts themselves, coupled with an effort to keep them within the bounds of reality and morality, tended to engender a positive influence. Third, a cast and crew not unmindful of maintaining a suitable atmosphere. And perhaps the most important of all, a teacher/welfare worker who was one of the dearest and most proficient in the business.

There were occasions when the kids were predictably kids, and attention spans weren't quite as long as hoped, but the minor problems that occurred were not actors' personality problems, they were the same generic difficulties everyone has at home.

The best accolade I can give them is to say that they came into the show with a certain innocence and naïveté, and five years later they left the show with an appropriate amount of both qualities. They are now men and women of substance, ease, and grace, whom I very much consider family.

To me, "The Brady Bunch" *was* the kids. Their gentle personalities, vulnerabilities, and ability to remain identifiable to those their own age were its success. For adults to play familial love is relatively easy; for children to do it convincingly is remarkable. That the show is now playing to a third generation of viewers speaks for itself.

I believe that what you are about to read, both in the lines and between them, will give some insight into the qualities that Sherwood must have seen.

ROBERT REED
Pasadena, California, 1992

Acknowledgments

The authors wish to thank the following people for their encouragement, support, assistance, and tolerance in the writing of this book: Fifi Oscard and her able team; Kevin McShane; Judy McGrath; Larry McCallister; Abby Terkuhle; Sherwood Schwartz; Howard Barton; Michael Dugan; Robert Reed; Florence Henderson; Geoff Whelan; Karen Lipscomb; Ann B. Davis; Vanessa Vassar; Maureen McCormick; Christopher Knight; Eve Plumb; Patrick Netter; Michael Lookinland; Susan Olsen; Frances Whitfield; Lloyd Schwartz; Craig Blenkhorn; Scott Blenkhorn; James Pettit; Darlene Schwartz; Jack Rosenberg; Beverly Kitaen-Morse; Matthew Martin; Peter Murray; Ira Bernstein; Robert Lydiard; and Pat Mullens.

A special thank you to our editor Craig Nelson and to Jenna Hull for their unflagging perception and flexible deadlines.

And my wife Diane for her love, caring, and patience while sitting through all those episodes.

1
Through the Clouds

Spring 1990. Somewhere over Texas.

The DC10's first-class cabin is crammed full of unruly passengers, and the stewardess is frazzled, near tears.

A young woman in the second row loudly orders her third Jack Daniel's. The young man sitting beside her is matching her drink for drink with his Jim Beam. With rowdy enthusiasm, they laugh as they sip, comparing and extolling the virtues of their respective brands along the way.

Word comes up from the back of the plane that a young, expectant mother, traveling alone, is going into what appears to be premature labor. Frantic, several passengers tug on a man they recognize from television as an ob-gyn, asking if he might be of some assistance. He declines, explaining that he's *not* a doctor, but he plays one

TV doctor meets real-life Mom-to-be.
(Barry Williams)

on TV. Luckily, the labor turned out to be false.

On the "doctor's" left, an attractive middle-aged woman is having a terrific time, entertaining, and signing autographs for a raucous posse of enamored fans.

Then a delicate situation arises. That young woman from the second row, still animatedly defending the superiority of Mr. Daniel, lights up a cigarette. Quickly, the put-upon stewardess with the "type A" personality makes her move to head off this transgression by approaching a familiar-looking older woman, sitting by herself in the last row of the cabin quietly working on needlepoint.

"Excuse me, Alice," the flight attendant inquires, "would you mind asking Cindy to extinguish her cigarette? This is a nonsmoking flight."

Looking up from her in-flight stitchery with a furrowed brow, the woman replies, "First, *my* name is not Alice, it is Ann B. Davis. Second, I'm *not* their maid. And third, their behavior is not my responsibility, it's yours."

Finally the light dawns upon the unsuspecting attendant, and she realizes that this woman is not really the loyal "Brady Bunch" housekeeper that she's known, loved, and watched on TV hundreds of times. Having watched us file onto the plane together, she's made the very common mistake of simply assuming that this group of familiar faces do indeed somehow belong to a biologically entwined family.

After all, there's Cindy settled into the second row with Bobby beside her. Carol Brady and Dr. Greg fill the opposite row, with Jan and Peter just behind. With that in mind, the stewardess came to the perfectly natural assumption that Alice might be of some assistance in this situation.

Slapping her forehead in belated recognition, the stewardess walks over to Susan Olsen (as opposed to Cindy) and says, "Excuse me, you'll have to put that cigarette out right away, or be arrested upon our arrival in Los Angeles." Susan, who by now is nearly finished anyway, frowns, takes a long last drag on her Marlboro, and grudgingly crushes the butt.

The kind of confusion our flight attendant experienced is

not at all uncommon around the "Bradys." That's because for more than twenty years our fantasy family has been beamed into living rooms all over the world. Through four successive decades, on all three major networks, in six separate reunions and in countless thousands of reruns, the Bradys have woven themselves into the fabric of Americana. Generations have grown up watching our harmless, pleasant, moralistic tales. Children have identified with the oldest, youngest, or middle sibling, and *always* the question has been asked: "Why can't *our* family be more like the Bradys?"

In short, when you're dealing with the public perception of the Brady Bunch, the blurring of reality should come as no surprise.

Back to the plane. I should explain that we almost *never* behave this badly (we are *not*, after all, the cast of "Diff'rent Strokes"). However, on this *particular* occasion, we were sort of whistling past the graveyard, and our emotions got carried away. Stated simply, "The Bradys," 1990's horrendous attempt to take the "Brady Bunch" characters seriously, was dying, waiting pitifully for someone to come along, pull the plug, and put it out of its misery. Our ratings and our spirits were both abysmally low when CBS, desperate to bail out its quickly sinking ship, came up with a solution to raise them both: they requested (i.e., *demanded)* that we all go on a nationwide promotional spree.

So, with bags packed and stories straight, we hit every talk and news show that would have us. We put on our best Brady faces, told the truth about each other, and lied about the show. We said it was "a lot like 'thirtysomething'," "terrific," and "a return to good solid family entertainment." We answered the same old questions a hundred times each, and soon, as you might expect, we were exhausted—and more depressed than ever.

Finally, there was a light at the end of the tunnel, and we had just one more TV appearance to sit through, "The Sally Jessy Raphaël Show."

Little did we know, the worst was yet to come.

Sally was on location for a week, having abandoned the

show's comfortable New York studios for a large converted outdoor parking lot in Miami. The set was simple, consisting of an uncovered stage, equipped with one folding chair for each "Brady." I remember arriving and thinking that even though we were exhausted, it might be relaxing to close out the week by fielding Sally's questions, sitting in the sun and dreaming about a nap on the flight home to L.A.

We got dressed, made up, miked, and walked onstage to find about three thousand people cramming the parking lot, overflowing the portable bleachers of the audience area, and waiting anxiously to see us. The sight was simply overwhelming, and really seemed to recharge our batteries. I can even remember thinking to myself that this one last "chore" might actually turn out to be fun.

We took our places, started taping—and it *was* fun. The audience was packed with fans, some expert in the area of Brady trivia; and as Sally passed her mike among them, we Bradys had a great time together, meeting our fans, talking with them, and of course doing our best to answer their questions.

Twenty minutes later, as things were really starting to roll along, the weather stopped cooperating. All at once, with a meteorological fury unique to Florida, our blue sky passed right by gray and turned black. The winds picked up and it started to rain—hard.

It quickly became obvious that *this* was no spring mist and that we were fast approaching full-blown typhoon status. So what do we do? You guessed it: in that age-old show-business tradition of "the show must go on," we defied logic *and* sanity by continuing to roll tape. Sally's big red glasses were fogging up, and her hair spray was melting into a congealed mass of sticky goo. Chris Knight's brand-new snakeskin boots got soaked, and Florence Henderson's mascara began etching a smudgy black trail down the left side of her face.

At the same time, the microphones clipped onto our now soaking shirts were beginning to short out, and the tech crew was frantically replacing them whenever they could sneak onto the set without being seen by the cameras. Production assistants seemed to rise up out of nowhere, handing us umbrellas that they hoped might shield us from the deluge.

Now it gets weird, because while we probably *should* have been irritated, we were instead somehow taken with the absurdity of our sopping-wet situation and started getting giddy, laughing in the downpour, and going with the flow, so to speak.

Gamely, we kept right on taping . . . that is, until a coupla quick cracks of lightning scared us into sprinting toward the nearest trailer. Time to call it a wrap? No way. Y'see, all of us were due back on the Brady set in less than twenty-four hours, and in order for that to happen, our travel schedule was *very* tight. In fact, even *before* our "rain delay," we had been slated to go directly from the "Sally" set to the airport. With that in mind, we couldn't rearrange our flight plans, and simply had to huddle together, shiver, and wait the storm out.

After a few moments, another merciful contingent of PAs arrived, bearing towels and dry T-shirts. Hoping the storm might pass quickly, we changed, and cranked our blow-dryers into overdrive, aiming them not only at our hair but at our pants, shoes, socks, and various body parts as well. Finally, after about thirty minutes, we were able to roll the cameras once more. The sky was still a threatening gray, and it was still raining, but now at least the downpour had been downgraded to a moderate rain.

With a plane to catch, we agreed to leave the relative comfort and safety of our trailer and finish taping. That's when we noticed an amazing thing: those three thousand Brady fans were *still* in place! They had withstood the buckets of rain, the wind, and the lightning, just to see us return! I was astonished, and simultaneously touched. The crowd cheered loudly as we resumed our positions, and as we dripped our way through the rest of the taping, we found ourselves having a terrific time. In the end, the afternoon had reaffirmed my belief that while most of our little seventies sitcom may have been trivial, it *had* somehow managed to strike a chord, touching the hearts of a lot of people—so much so that this particular group was willing to show their appreciation by enduring a monsoon.

Once finished, we Bradys soggily trudged toward the airport, boarded our plane, and took off. Punchy, tired, cold, and still damp, we were determined to get some transcontinental shut-eye but try as we might, none of us could sleep.

Perhaps due to the close quarters of a six-hour flight, perhaps due to fatigue, and perhaps due to the fact that our defenses had been worn down, we began to really open up with each other and share our experiences, not just of the past few hours but also about our more than twenty years' worth of communal experiences.

We started talking, laughing out loud, and sharing the stories and feelings about each other that we'd either never before told, long since forgotten, or simply denied. There was plenty to share, and it wasn't long before we got a bit rowdy, unruly, and just plain "un-Brady-like." Susan "Cindy" Olsen (who *never* minces words) remembers it this way:

"Basically, we got smashed. So here's little Cindy and Bobby swilling Jack Daniel's and Jim Beam, and taking complete advantage of the fact that we were in first class, so it was free. We were lucky that the *National Enquirer* wasn't there to get pictures of the tragic adulthood of TV's cute little Bobby and Cindy Brady.

"But can you imagine seeing the whole Brady family together on your airplane? People were looking at us like 'Wow, they must really be related!' And here's little Bobby and Cindy kinda challenging each other to see who could get the drunkest, and just like when we were kids giving each other a dare, we were giggling and going 'Yeah, let's do it,' and driving that poor stewardess insane asking for full glasses of 'Jack' and 'Jim.'

"Soon the stuff starts to kick in, and Michael and I start saying things like 'Oh, jeeesh, I reeeeally used to looooove you.' And I told him how I'd had like a million crushes on him, and he just kinda went 'Huh?'"

So here we are, thirty-two thousand feet up, twenty-two years older than we were when we shot the pilot episode of "The Brady Bunch," and we're using the cramped confines of a DC10 as a sort of makeshift conference room, in which we're catching up with one another, rehashing our common history, and using our now grown-up perspectives in getting to know each other again . . . maybe for the first time.

We talked all the way across country, discussing our different "Brady" experiences, our expectations, our disappointments, our reflections, and finally came to the conclusion that while growing up presents all kinds of challenges, the multitudinous advantages *and* drawbacks of growing up Brady complicated that process immeasurably.

As I watched my TV family reminisce and listen and learn and share, I was absolutely fascinated. I also realized that *these* stories, the real ones that took place behind the cameras and away from the carefully groomed facade of network public-relations departments, were all but hidden from the kind of fans who'd just greeted us so warmly in the freezing rain. It occurred to me that they deserved to be told.

As you'll see, this isn't a "trivia" book about "The Brady Bunch." Instead, it is a book about the relationships, the behind-the-scenes stories, and especially the *people* who made it all happen, and who made it so special to an entire generation of Americans.

Above all else, it is a book about the unique challenges of growing up in show business *and* growing up Brady.

Soaked on Sally.
(Courtesy Multimedia Entertainment, Inc.)

2
In the Beginning . . .

Just after my fourth birthday, I became one of those annoying kids who are bound and determined to get into show business. Saturday movie matinees and late-fifties television (the schlockier the better) held a magical, almost hypnotic fascination for me. I bought into it all—the excitement, the adventure, the magic, and while my friends were dreaming about becoming the next Willie Mays, clocking fastballs over center-field fences, *I'd* dream about "The Fabulous Barry Williams Show." I'd sing, dance, tell jokes, schmooze with my incredible imaginary guest stars—and let me tell you, I was *great!*

Now, a lot of kids dream about moving to Hollywood and becoming TV stars, but I knew that I had an edge. Y'see, I already lived in the L.A. suburb of Pacific Palisades, and a bona fide TV star lived right on my block.

The star was Peter Graves, and in 1958 he was still nine years away from becoming "Mission: Impossible"'s white-haired good guy, Mr. Phelps. Instead, he played the hero on my absolute favorite TV show, "Fury."

It was a western type show set in the 1950s. A man (Peter Graves) adopts an orphaned city kid and brings him out to live on his country ranch. It was standard western fare with the good guys in white hats and the bad guys in black, and of course one great horse . . . Fury. Still, I loved it, and thought Mr. Graves was just about as cool as a human being could get. Often, I'd spend my Saturday mornings watching him tie up the bad guys, and my Saturday afternoons watching him tie up his garbage or mow his lawn. He was my idol, the grown-up embodiment of everything I wanted to be.

Turns out Mr. Graves had a daughter. Her name was Claudia, and she was a babe . . . literally. We met in nursery school (I swear), hit it off; one thing led to another, and pretty soon three-year-old Claudia became my very first girlfriend. We were inseparable, and crazy enough about each other to perform the most hallowed of all preschool love ceremonies. We exchanged ABC gum.

In case your pre-pubescent memory fails you, "ABC" stands for "already been chewed," and to exchange it makes a toddler couple about as committed as they can get. Anyway, on one particular Sunday afternoon, my "girlfriend" and I were swapping Bazooka and playing in the Graveses' living room when a thought struck my nearly fully hardened skull: "If I ask Mr. Graves how *he* became an actor, maybe I can do it the same way."

I summoned up all the intestinal fortitude my teeny-tiny gut could bear, marched into Peter's office, and spit it out. "Mr. Graves," I squeaked, "how did *you* become an actor?" With

What ... me worry?
(Barry Williams)

which he smiled what seemed like an all-knowing smile, stood up, towered over me, and put a hand upon my shoulder.

Anxiously, I awaited his pearls of wisdom, the magical advice and secret information that would instantly transform me into a successful working actor with a big hit series just like his. I remember wishing I had a tape recorder so I wouldn't forget anything he'd say.

Finally, after a long, pensive pause that could have used a drumroll, Mr. Graves drew a breath, looked down, and said, "Well, Barry, I just thought about it."

"Huh?"

Not exactly the kind of response I'd hoped for, but I said to myself, "If it came from Mr. Graves, it *has* to be good advice." I was a dumb kid, what can I tell you.

Anyway, determined to follow in Peter's oversized footsteps, I ditched Claudia, marched home, and thought. I sat still in the kitchen, stared off into space and thought for days on end, until finally I began to really bug my folks. However, by this time, they were used to my odd thespian tendencies, so they just smiled, and passed off this latest bout of bizarre behavior as simply another passing phase.

After about a week, I gave up on Mr. Graves's abstract-thought route, but was still bound and determined to act. My parents, on the other hand, weren't nearly as enthusiastic. Dad was a nose-to-the-grindstone businessman who didn't know much of anything about Hollywood, except that it was full of nut cases and worse yet "show people." Mom was slightly less negative, but had absolutely no idea how a kid might go about getting his foot into Hollywood's door.

With two less-than-eager parents to soften up, I knew that getting started was going to take a while, and with formal acting lessons out of the question, at least for the moment, I did a lot of pretending, practicing, and rehearsing on my own.

The bulk of my informal training came a few years later, while serving as club mascot for the neighborhood gang which already counted among its members my two brothers, Craig and Scott. We weren't *anything* like the horrifying gangs of today, but we also weren't a Wally-and-Beaver-esque boys club either. Most of the guys were between thirteen and fifteen years old and, basically, were the kind of kids whole neighborhoods love to hate—real egg-throwing, class-cutting, hitchhiking, tit-squeezing bastards. I was seven years old and wanted desperately to fit into this motley assemblage of older guys.

Guess who became the gang's designated guinea pig.

One of my first "duties" as club mascot involved a vacant lot, a hollow tree, an enormous swarm of bees, and the granddaddy of all firecrackers, the cherry bomb. It seemed that a swarm of bees had moved into our favorite vacant lot, found themselves a hollow tree trunk, and were busily converting it into a sort of buzzing bug condo. Curious and very much against overdevelopment, one particularly demented gang member began to wonder out loud about what might happen should a lit cherry bomb just happen to fall out of the sky and into the hive. Being the youngest and still the dumbest, I was elected.

Everyone took up safe positions about a hundred and fifty feet from the nest, except for me. Scared to death, but wanting desperately to act cool in front of the gang, I slowly—*very* slowly—inched my way toward those industrious but unsuspecting little insects. Matches in one hand, cherry bomb in the other, I finally got within tossing range. Shakily, I lit the wick, and as it sputtered orange, I tossed.

Bull's-eye! I had done it, a perfect sky-hook swish that dropped effortlessly into the half-rotted husk of the tree. My heart swelled with pride at my accomplishment . . . for about one second.

KA-BOOM!

At once, dead wood, honey, and about a half-trillion bees filled the sky. Now, as pride in my heart was replaced by terror in my gut, I ran screaming for my life, but wasn't exactly successful in my getaway.

I learned three things that day:

1. Bees don't like it when you blow up their house,

2. I'm allergic to bee stings, and

3. I absolutely *love* being the center of attention.

Even with twenty-three bee stings and a face that resembled a rather large, misshapen cantaloupe, I was ecstatic. I had proven that I could be every bit as mindlessly destructive as the big guys. I had gotten stung for it, literally, but in the aftermath, my parents doted on me (I made up a story for them about a terrible swarm of bees that attacked me for no reason at all), the guys in the gang looked at me with newfound respect, and even my brothers were (reasonably) nice to me.

I was in terrible pain, swollen up like a sort of prepubescent Elephant Man, nauseous, and the happiest multiple-sting victim my doctor had ever seen.

For the first time in my life, I was a star.

Eager to please, and having now had a taste of the spotlight, I was more willing than ever to pull off whatever ridiculously dangerous stunt the gang could think up. They took advantage of my enthusiasm . . . a lot.

In the months to come, my body would become a sort of crash dummy, testing gravity, electrical current, and on one occasion alcohol.

Ah, my pals. Funny how we never got together as a group unless we were sure that there were no adults around to spoil our fun. For example, on one particularly destructive Saturday night in 1963, my parents made the enormous mistake of going out to play bridge and letting us know that they wouldn't be home until well past midnight.

My brothers asked if the gang could come over to hang out, and that's when my parents made an even more enormous mistake: they said yes. Mom and Dad left the house with smiles on their faces, oblivious to the evil doings that were about to occur. The gang showed up almost immediately, barreled into the living room, and decided to rummage through the old folks' stuff. First stop was the liquor cabinet, and as it turned out, it was the last stop as well.

Y'see, the gang's unofficial leader was Bret (the *big* kid), and he had an idea. He thought it would be great fun for one of us to get rip-roaring, stinking shit-faced and entertain the others.

Guess who got the part.

In *this* case I was a fairly *reluctant* volunteer. I didn't want to lose my status as chief mascot/guinea pig, but I was also aware that *this* time, we were dealing with some *big* unknowns. Still, with the chance to be star for a night, and the gang shoveling on their enthusiastic support and encouragement, I could hardly say no.

We took inventory, and since my dad's liquor cabinet was stocked with more vodka than anything else, we figured it stood the least chance of being missed later on. *That* became my poison. None of us had any idea how much liquor it took to get somebody drunk (remember, this was 1963), and so we guessed. We decided that since my dad's Kamchatka *looked* an awful lot like water, we should probably start with a full, 8-ounce water glass—and see what happened.

The stuff smelled like gasoline, so I killed the taste by holding my nose and gulping it all down without breathing.

Now the guys huddled around me, staring as if they thought I was about to metamorphosize, like Jerry Lewis in *The Nutty Professor*. And while I enjoyed their attention over the next several minutes, my performance left them less than thrilled.

"How do you feel?" they asked repeatedly.

"Uh . . . fine, I guess."

"You don't feel drunk?"

"Uh . . . nope."

Hmmmmm . . . the more sober I stayed, the more disappointed they became. After a coupla minutes, they tested me once more, this time by having me recite the alphabet. I did it . . . perfectly, then sang it for them too.

That did it. The guys decided that they must have underdosed me. The solution? "Have the kid drink some more." Again they poured; again I held my nose; and again I gulped down the high-octane concoction.

"Sobriety" quickly became a thing of the past. *Severe*

motor-response impairment set in, and the gang finally got its yuks. *They* thought my wobbliness was hysterical, and used it as their cue to begin pushing me, poking me, teasing me, testing me, and laughing at me. Not my idea of a great time, but they seemed to enjoy it—until the floodgates opened.

Without warning, a massive wave of nausea overwhelmed me. I erupted with all the unleashed ferocity of Vesuvius, and the barf hit the fan, the couch, the carpet, the stereo system, and just about every piece of furniture that shared the misfortune of getting in my path. No room was spared from the wrath of my inebriated guts.

Thankfully, once I was empty, the show was over, and I was able to pass out.

No one ever said being a star was easy.

After that particular episode, the gang and I finally started to wise up. We stopped being mindlessly destructive and instead became deceitfully *constructive*. Now, instead of *exploiting* my flair for the dramatic by having me do something stupid like jump off a pedestrian overpass, we'd *harness* it, work up a plan, and score some ill-gotten booty. Our greatest scam ever was built on just such a foundation.

As any grown guy can tell you, the most alluring of all adolescent vices isn't cigarettes, or beer, or fireworks, or even rubbers. It's girlie magazines—the sleazier, the better. A dog-eared full-frontal "beaver" mag is in fact an adolescent-male equivalent of the Holy Grail, endlessly appealing yet hopelessly out of reach, unless, of course, your dad subscribes. None of us were that lucky, so we got our stag mags the old-fashioned way. . .under false pretenses.

Bret (the ringleader) had some very adult-handwriting and a plan for how it could score us some copies of *Playboy* and its more explicit low-rent cousin *Cavalier*. His plan involved deceit, lying to grown-ups, forgery, and my budding acting skills. It was perfect.

We swiped some of his dad's grown-up-looking stationery and one of his fountain pens, and we were ready to roll. Together, we composed a note to the counterman at the "Palisades Pharmacy," and then let Bret's grown-up penmanship put it on paper.

The result was absolutely beautiful, and at least to us, seemed unrecognizable as counterfeit. It read like this:

Dear Pharmacy Clerk:
Please give my nephew one copy of *Cavalier,* one copy *Playboy,* and two cartons of Camel cigarettes.
Thank You.

We forged a phony name on the end, and it was done. All we needed now was somebody crazy enough to risk an assault into the front lines of the drugstore while playing the role of nephew.

By now you know that I couldn't resist that challenge.

I took the responsibility of my role very seriously, and dove into it with head-first, Stanislavskian glee. I even went so far as to create a history for my fictional uncle, which I was more than happy to share with the pharmacy counter man. I told him about my "uncle," the "war hero" who'd been badly injured in Korea—so badly injured that he could no longer leave his house. I also stated that in fulfilling his shopping list, I could present him with the few simple pleasures in his otherwise unbearable life. I laid it on so thick that for the clerk to deny my request would seem nothing less than unpatriotic.

Basically, I lied—and acted—my ass off . . . and it worked!

Unbelievably, the unsuspecting clerk bought my story, packed up my ill-gotten gains, and sent me on my way.

Later that afternoon, with an unfiltered Camel in one hand and a pair of Kodachrome breasts in the other, I felt smugly content. I had finally proven myself to the gang *and* I had proven myself as an actor.

My brothers punched me in the arms and told me that what I did was really cool. No good review has ever made me feel any better.

Even after my unbridled theatrical success in my brothers' gang, my parents still loomed as a sort of Berlin Wall between me and an acting career. *Years* went by, and they didn't budge. Still, the seed had been planted, and was growing quickly. I'd even created a great new "stage name" for myself. Instead of Barry William Blenkhorn, I would add an "s" to my middle name, blow off the Blenkhorn, and become "Barry Williams" . . . yeah that's it. Needless to say, dumping the family name didn't exactly help my cause with the folks, but I wouldn't give up. I wanted my "chance" and eventually became pretty vociferous about getting it.

Finally, one weekday after school, I marched into the kitchen and launched into my *finest* performance. "How can you stand in my way?" I asked, shooting an eleven-year-old's angriest glance toward my folks. "How can you not give your own child a chance to fulfill his dream?"

I had stated my case, and to my surprise the folks buckled. My figurative Berlin Wall had caved in a full twenty-four years before the real one would. My Dad still wasn't thrilled with the idea, but I was allowed to begin taking acting lessons.

"Don't jump right in," he advised. "Instead, why not *study* acting for a while and see if you *really* like it?" To this day, I believe he thought this idea of mine would just sort of fizzle out, allowing me to rejoin the real world.

So where to turn? There was one neighborhood kid who had done a few commercials and a couple of small movie scenes. His name was Donny Carter, and when my Mom called his, we came away with the name of my first acting coach.

Her name was Lois Auer, and she taught "scene study" courses out of her home in Sherman Oaks. She also specialized in film and television techniques, which made me happy, because in my electronic, baby-boomer's mind TV was the place to be. Stage actors somehow seemed bush league. (I've since changed my tune.)

I signed up immediately. Monday night soon became acting night and the happiest time of my week. There were ten of us in the class, and we'd learn lines, blocking, stage directions, and inflection. We'd also perform scenes, and talk about acting. I was in heaven.

About six months into my lessons, I got my first big break. Mrs. Auer told my mom and me about a school documentary that was being cast in Hollywood. My first audition! At once I was both thrilled and terrified. The film was called *Why Johnny Can Read,* and it was one of those dull "English class" 16mm things that put you to sleep all through grade school. Still, I was awestruck.

I auditioned with about thirty other kids—and I got a part! In fact, not just *a* part, but *the* part: I played Johnny. My "class-mates" were each paid twenty-five dollars, but I got fifty. "Fifty bucks!" I thought. "This is gonna be a great career!"

Buoyed by my first professional gig, I started stepping up my study program with Mrs. Auer before too long. Now, in addition to my beloved Monday-night classes, I began taking a one-hour *private* class each Saturday. Now I could really progress. With *Johnny* under my belt, and with all this study-ing, I thought, "I should have my first Oscar in *no* time."

Well, *that* didn't happen; but I did get better—good enough, to try and snag an agent. Mrs. Auer set up a meeting for me with a woman named Toni Kelman, who owned a pretty good-sized kids' talent agency. Once again, I was thrilled, because to me *this* represented a genuine step into the "business" of show business. You really can't prepare for a meeting like this; you just have to cross your fingers and hope something clicks.

Something *did* click, and the meeting went very well. Toni was really pleasant, and while my mom waited outside with the receptionist, I fielded about a dozen of her "Let's get to know each other" questions. Next, Toni and I read a scene from the script of a Disney movie.

Twenty minutes later I had signed a one-year deal with her company and was off and running. To this day, I'm not sure whether she liked my reading or if she just needed a brown-haired, blue-eyed, eleven-year-old guy in her stable of kids. Either way, however, I was ecstatic.

Flash forward a coupla months and I'm auditioning for parts on an average of once a week. Nothing materialized for a while; but at just about the time I was starting to feel the first real pangs of rejection, it hit: I landed a commercial for Sears, Roebuck. It was a run-of-the-mill, "Oh, gee, isn't Sears a wonderful place to shop?" kinda thing, but it gave me my first real taste of being a kid on a union set.

First and foremost, there's the issue of school. I was told to ask my teachers for all the work I'd miss while away on my two-day commercial shoot. I was also told to take my regular school books with me to the set, where, a "production welfare worker" would assist me with my studies.

At eleven-years-old, that sounded like a death sentence. I pictured the welfare worker as an enormous, foul-smelling, mole-covered, vaguely Nazi-esque old bag, with a name like Bertha, or Hortense, and was sure she'd turn our one-on-one student-teacher relationship into a hellish scholastic nightmare.

Boy, was I wrong! School on the set turned out to be great. The union's time restrictions provided that I had to accumulate three hours of schooling per day, broken up into segments that were each about twenty minutes long. I wasn't allowed to be on camera for more than four hours or to work more than a ten-hour day, with a one-hour lunch break. Even my welfare worker turned out to be quite a babe; and with one-on-one instruction, I could knock off my daily assignments in less than half the time they'd take back at school.

Actually, my abbreviated school schedule *did* leave me with one problem: what to do with all my leftover time.

Being on a full-blown commercial set took care of that. The place was crammed full of so many technicians, lighting specialists, cameramen, prop guys, and production types, that I couldn't have been bored if I tried. I remember that *everyone* seemed to have whistles and clipboards, and that they all seemed to take this commercial shooting stuff *very* seriously. I loved that, and made the most of my every second of set time. I asked questions of everyone, never stopping until I became a pest. I snooped, I eavesdropped, and I just tried to soak up every bit of ambience the location had to offer.

I even had time to make friends with my co-star in the spot, Butch Patrick. Yep, I was working with a bona fide child star—"Eddie Munster" himself! I can remember pumping him for information, and cockily thinking to myself, "I'm a *much* better actor than he is—how come *I'm* not on TV?"

Well, within a year, I *was* on TV, having landed my first guest shot in episodic television. I was gonna be on "Run for Your Life," a mid-sixties drama that starred Ben Gazzara as a terminally ill hero "trying to cram thirty years of living into his final two." I was to play a tough New York City street kid, a real rotten little punk. My first scene took place on an apartment stoop, and consisted of me talking to Mr. Gazzara while I lit matches and used them to burn up some ants. I remember thinking to myself that even the guys in my brothers' gang weren't *that* twisted. Still, this was to be a magical day.

It started *ridiculously* early, for two reasons. Number one, I had an eight o'clock call time at Universal Studios, which entailed an hour-and-a-half drive even *without* L.A. traffic. Number two, "Run for Your Life" was my Dad's *favorite* show. This time his inherent dislike of show business melted under a wave of unbridled fandom. He volunteered to be legal guardian for a day (up until now it had always been Mom), let his employees run the business, and, with genuine excitement, made sure I got to the set *plenty* early.

At *six-fifteen* A.M. my dad and I were on the lot, parked, checked in, eating breakfast, and *more* than ready for my eight o'clock call. I read the paper, dawdled over my donut and juice, and still had time to get into makeup and wardrobe by seven-twenty.

At nine o'clock, I was called out of the studio schoolroom and onto the Universal back lot, where we'd be shooting on one of those nondescript could-be-anywhere make-believe streets. The dialogue director approached and told me that he wanted to go over my lines with me—kid actors are notoriously bad with their lines. I assured him that I was so happy to get this job, I'd not only learned my lines but Mr. Gazzara's as well. He was pleased, and seemed to relax.

Nine-thirty came and went without a sign of Mr. Gazzara. Ten o'clock and ten-thirty also passed without him. Finally, at about five of eleven, with the director fuming, and with production types gulping down fistfuls of Rolaids, the longest, blackest limousine I'd ever seen pulled up and glided silently to a stop. My first thought was that maybe the President had come to visit, but that theory was quickly shot down when Ben Gazzara slowly and deliberately exited his stretchmobile.

When you've only seen someone on television, it's a bit of a shock to meet him in person. Mr. Gazzara was no exception. He was larger than life, imposing, and had an almost regal air about him. He was also late, but made no excuses or apologies, and I remember being impressed at how his simple request for a chair was passed down through the pecking order of stagehands.

"Get Mr. Gazzara's chair!" yelled the biggest, fattest, most important prop guy.

"Get Mr. Gazzara's chair!" his assistant chimed in.

"Where the fuck is Gazzara's chair?" a teamster belched.

Finally, they reached the bottom of their clan's totem pole, and the guy at the bottom fetched the chair, running about a hundred and fifty yards in order to gently place it within plopping distance of Ben Gazzara's butt.

The out-of-breath lackey smiled and then watched Mr. Gazzara light up a cigar and sit down without saying "Thank you."

I was impressed—mightily, if not favorably.

Eleven-thirty arrived, and *still* Mr. Gazzara wasn't ready to work. He hadn't changed into his wardrobe, hadn't shaved, and hadn't visited the makeup man. It goes without saying that he hadn't come close to memorizing his lines. In fact, as I watched him look over his script, I became convinced that he was reading it for the first time.

High noon came. It was time for rehearsal, and an amazing shift occurred. Even on our first walk-through of the scene, Mr. Gazzara was tight with his lines, and really seemed to *listen* as I spilled out my own. His reactions and responses seemed genuine, and affected me so much that I actually managed to *forget* I was acting. He so totally absorbed us both in what we were doing that I forgot to be nervous, forgot the numerous technical tasks we were performing, and nailed the scene in just two takes. *This* was a powerful lesson.

Later, we knocked off my close-ups, and out of the corner of my eye I saw Mr. Gazzara approach my dad and tell him something. Later, I badgered my dad mercilessly, until he finally smiled and confessed that Mr. Gazzara said that he thought I had done a *really* good job.

What a day!

On "Run for Your Life."
(Barry Williams)

3
T.V.–Inside Out

Once you've appeared on *one* television show, future acting jobs start getting a lot easier to grab. Casting directors start recognizing your face and stop treating you like pond scum; the credit list on the back of your head shot gets longer; and you find that you're no longer an outsider but a bona fide actor, and a member of that legendary, glitz-enshrouded private club, the "show-business community." Once you're "in," things start snowballing. At least that's how it happened for me.

After my experience on "Run for Your Life," I was astonished to find that I'd actually started to get *busy*, making the rounds as the troubled kid on a good handful of TV cop shows. For about six months, if a series needed a runaway/punk/delinquent/from a dysfunctional family/with a heart of gold, it was me.

First up was "Dragnet." I had about four or five scenes in a special "Christmas episode" whose plot was corny even by "Dragnet" standards. It revolved around a misguided resident of L.A.'s urban jungle who swipes a plaster baby Jesus out of his comfy churchyard manger. I played an eyewitness, and my task was to inform Joe Friday about what I'd seen.

Even as a twelve-year-old kid, I was embarrassed by the

script, but it *was* a job, *and* a decent-sized part, so I decided to try and make it work. I studied my role as never before and had my lines down forwards, backwards, and sideways by the time I got to the set.

I met Jack Webb and was immediately struck by the fact that there was no perceivable difference between him and Joe Friday. They had the same speech mannerisms, the same slouching posture, the same no-nonsense/no-sense-of-humor approach to life, and of course they had the same bad haircut.

It quickly became apparent that Mr. Webb, who also produced and often wrote the show, was not a man who could stomach the wasting of time. He'd kept the "Dragnet" crew hopping, saying that he liked to move fast to "maintain spontaneity," but he wasn't fooling anybody. As the show's producer, he was *really* just trying to keep his production costs down by every means possible.

The oddest of those means was revealed to me as we got ready to start shooting my first big scene. I was hanging in the schoolroom down the hall from the set when one of the show's assistant directors showed up and asked me where I wanted my TelePrompTer.

"What's a TelePrompTer?" I asked, trying not to sound like a dope.

"You've never worked with a TelePrompTer?" the AD sputtered back, while visions of blown lines and blown budgets danced in his head.

At this point I wasn't sure whether to be insulted or embarrassed, so I answered truthfully by saying "No."

The AD trudged out of the schoolroom like a man walking the fabled last mile.

As you probably know, a TelePrompTer is a televisionlike box that's placed very close to the camera lens. Someone sits nearby and scrolls your lines onto the screen as you read them on camera. It was sort of like electronic cue cards, and was really only used on TV newscasts—and, of course, "Dragnet."

A couple of minutes later I was on the set, with that

same AD nervously demonstrating the TelePrompTer for me. I thought it looked kinda weird but that maybe it was some new kind of acting accessory that would work even better than line memorization. Not wanting to seem amateurish, I bit my tongue and never let on that I already had my lines down cold. Instead, I said that I was sure I could learn how to use the thing quickly, and would do my best. The AD smiled at me patronizingly, convinced I'd blow his shooting schedule all to hell.

We got ready to rehearse. I squeezed in next to Joe Friday, and the two of us stared into that little black box and delivered our lines. Immediately I knew why "Dragnet" always had that brusque, flat, unnatural air about it. It wasn't acted—it was *read!*

By the time we had the cameras loaded up and ready to roll, I had come to the conclusion that I didn't like the TelePrompTer at all, and that no matter *what* the AD said, I was going to deliver my lines from memory, the way I knew best. When the cameras finally rolled, I listened, looked Mr. Webb in the eye, and delivered my lines pretty well. We finished the scene in just two takes, and Mr. Webb was impressed. "Hey, kid, how'd you learn all those lines so fast?" he asked me, with Joe Friday's every vocal nuance.

"Well, we *did* run through it twice," I replied, giving him a grade-A snow job that practically made me seem like a genius.

"That's fantastic," said Mr. Webb. "I'm gonna have to remember you."

And he did. Two months later I appeared on another show he produced, "Adam-12," and from what I heard on that set, Mr. Webb had requested me by asking for "that egghead kid from the Christmas 'Dragnet.'"

Next came "The F.B.I.," another of those hokey, right-wing, badly written "real-life dramas" wherein all the problems of the world could be traced back to one of two causes, communism and "those damn hippies." I came onboard as yet another member of America's misguided but inherently good-natured youth, and collected another check.

But my proudest early achievement was probably an appearance on a show called "The Invaders," a schlocky sci-fi thriller starring Roy Thinnes and guest-starring a sultry (and not yet basso) Suzanne Pleshette. I was to play an evil young space alien bent on global domination, and was really thrilled at getting the part. For one thing, this marked my first appearance on a show that I actually watched; and it would also mark my first time shooting on location—until now I'd just been on soundstages, squirreled away on studio back lots.

My task was to pedal a bike to the top of a hill, whip out my interstellar walkie-talkie/radio thing, call up my home planet (collect), and in a nutshell, plot the destruction of the earth. Sounds simple, right? Wrong. That one scene took longer to shoot than all my other acting experience *combined.*

I learned that day about how shooting on location is *nothing* like being on a studio set. On a soundstage, noise, light, weather, crowds, and basic film-making essentials are all easily—and artificially—controlled. You need a little more sun? Flip a switch. You want rain? Turn a knob. Outside, you're at the mercy of the gods . . . and the gawkers.

Anyone who's ever hung around a movie crew knows that even the most straightforward shooting requires a veritable mountain of equipment, and an army of big guys in flannel shirts and work boots who eat bagels, complain, and schlepp stuff around. Teamsters multiply like rabbits; generators, cables, lights, and cameras start to appear; and before long, the locals start showing up to watch—especially in suburbia. "The Invaders" was shot in a little town called San Pedro, and by the time I showed up, the crowd was closing in, and getting huge.

I was, as always, early. I hooked up with the gawkers and passed the time by watching the carpenters swear and whack the set into shape. I had been watching for about an hour when an assistant director tapped me on the shoulder and told me it was time to get ready. I went with her, and I remember hearing the neighborhood crowd whisper as she led me away, "Who was that?" and "Is *he* anybody?"

Were they talking about *me?*

I didn't have much time to ponder the question, because it was time for the effects guys to turn me into an evil space spy. Luckily, the script called for me to be masquerading as a human, so the green paint and latex were spared. This alien did, however, carry an interstellar walkie-talkie, which had to glow and beep and blip on command. In short (bad pun intended), they had to run wires through my underwear.

The wires, batteries, tape, clips, bulbs, and hardware started at my leg, ran up my pants, through my Jockey juniors, up my back, through my shirt, down my sleeve, and into my little round flashing "communicator." When they got through with me, I could barely move, and was sure that with all the junk attached to this thing, it ought to really work. I mean, it looked like I should have been able to turn the thing on and call up Captain Kirk on the Enterprise, but all it really did, under all that Vegas-like glitz, was blink, lamely, on command.

Finally, the communicator and I were ready . . . and as if on cue it started to rain. Immediately I pictured tomorrow's L.A. *Times* headline: CHILD STAR ZAPPED BY MARTIAN RADIO—TESTICLES FRIED.

The assistant director assured me that I'd be okay (they always do), but I wasn't happy.

Adding to my now soaring stress level was the fact that my scene called for me to ride a bike up a hill, around a corner, and stop on a pinhead-sized mark. Then I was to pull out my blinky communicator, lift it into the camera frame, and spew out a half-page monologue before pedaling back out of frame. That would be tough under any circumstances, but I was gonna have to do it in the rain, *and,* as my pal the assistant director was kind enough to point out, it had to be done in one *take* or we'd lose the light level necessary to shoot (prepping my communicator had taken so long that now the sun was going down).

"Wonderful!" I thought. "I have to be perfect, in the rain, or ruin an entire day's shoot . . . *and* my gonads are going to fry."

They got set up. I got my instructions from the director, had my clothes, props, and makeup fixed, and in the process was elevated to VIP status among the hundred and fifty or so gawkers who were still standing out in the rain, staring at the goings-on.

To my great relief, we *did* nail the scene in one take, my genitals survived intact, and I was through filming for the day. I left the set, heading back toward my trailer to change out of my now waterlogged costume, and was surprised by several people who came up to me asking for an autograph. With pens and paper ready, they ran toward me on the set, and I had absolutely no idea what it was they wanted. Far from being flattered, I was basically scared.

Finally, I put two and two together and figured the situation out. Now, I knew what they wanted, I just couldn't figure out *why*. I mean, just that morning I had been hanging on the sidelines with these same people; and now that they had seen a camera pointed at me, they wanted a piece of paper with my signature on it. It was a strange feeling, but I did manage to smile, and sign 'em all, "Be groovy . . . Barry Williams."

Twenty-five years later, I *still* shudder when I think of that phrase.

With a solid handful of bona fide acting credits under my belt, I started auditioning for every role imaginable, and after a month-long dry spell I got lucky.

I had landed a job on a two-part episode of Robert Wagner's show "It Takes a Thief," playing a world-class-genius kid—typecasting? My character was working on a complex and sophisticated mathematical formula with enormous military potential; and, of course, a horde of bad guys with affected accents were out to waste me. Robert Wagner's assignment was to save me from the evil foreigners and reunite me with my sister—Joey Heatherton. Before I go any further, please know that when you're twelve, it's not easy working with a white-hot, vaguely slutty-looking sex goddess. At twelve, even the wallpaper can make you horny, so you can imagine how my raging adolescent hormones and overactive imagination conspired to make my blood pressure rise whenever I got near her.

Anyway, my role on "It Takes a Thief" was the biggest I'd ever landed, and the most challenging. Until now, my jobs had called for only a day or two on the set, playing characters who didn't really have to change during the course of the show. Now I was going to spend two hours on network TV, playing a *featured* character whose entire personality undergoes a makeover. I was scared, with no idea how I'd ever pull it off.

That's where Robert Wagner comes in.

On our first shooting day, I told him about my concern, and he immediately came to my rescue by sharing some of the "homework" he'd done in creating *his* character. He told me about creating a background for him, including where he grew up, where he went to school, how and why he became interested in a life of crime, and how long he'd spent in prison as a result of his chosen profession. He said that while he actually used little of this information in the series, it nonetheless gave him a real and grounded sense of who his character was. He also suggested that I try to apply these ideas to my kid genius.

Skeptical but desperate, I gave it a shot, and was thrilled to find that it worked. The technique was a godsend, because once I got a handle on my character, it was easy to figure out how he'd react in different situations, and also how he might grow and change throughout our double episode.

I spent two weeks on that set, and throughout the experience, Mr. Wagner was patient, generous, and very helpful. He even tested my newly acquired acting techniques with the cameras rolling. For example, during one close-up, R.J. (we were pals now, so I could call him that) delivered his lines from off camera, but changed his line readings and inflections during each take. In turn, I employed the skills he'd taught me and responded appropriately (i.e., differently) through the five takes it took to get the shot. Later, R.J. explained that as a pop quiz, he'd changed the inflection of his lines to see if I'd respond robotically or spontaneously. Fortunately I passed.

But acting lessons aside, the best part of the entire shoot was the final scene. Sitting in a golf cart and driving away into the sunset with Joey Heatherton's arm around my shoulders, I was in heaven. By the way, if you ever happen to bump into this particular episode of "It Takes a Thief," look closely at this final shot. You'll notice that as Joey and I drive away, I'm smiling warmly, sighing a contented sigh . . . and *desperately* trying to look down her blouse.

I learned a lot from Robert Wagner. But the strongest, most painful, acting lesson I ever received took place on the set of the cult classic film *Wild In The Streets*. It was a psychedelic, rebellious, heavily sixties movie wherein the basic message was "Never trust anyone over thirty" and the plot revolved around a plan to poison America's water supply with LSD, drive all the over-the-hill people insane, and put the country's young people in charge of the government.

The film starred Christopher Jones as the organizer and ringleader of the chemical warfare, with Shelley Winters as his mother. My job was to appear in several scenes playing Mr. Jones as a nasty, foul-mouthed, incorrigible kid—the stereotypical bad seed. My big moment in the film involved arguing with Shelley Winters—and then recoiling in anger and pain as she slaps me across the kisser.

The scene would mark the only time in my career that I wished for a stunt double. While I may be the only actor in Hollywood who hasn't slept with Shelley Winters, I *can* lay claim to having had her smack the daylights out of me.

As we prepared to shoot our scene together, Ms. Winters pulled me aside and explained that to make the film more realistic, she wanted to really slap me, not just pretend. It would make for a more honest reaction, she explained. Not wanting to offend her, and with my budding adolescent machismo assuring me that I could easily take her best shot, I agreed. "Besides," I thought, "How hard can the old lady hit?"

POW!

On our first take she hit me so hard that I saw stars, got dizzy, and nearly went down for the count. Mind you, I may have been just twelve years old, but I was no wimp. This woman just plain *pounded* me. The force of her blows caught me so completely off-guard that I forgot my lines, my blocking, and probably my *name* for that matter. Mercifully, the director yelled "Cut."

Nobody had bothered to explain to me that Ms. Winters was an esteemed alumnus of the Lee Strasberg school of Method acting, which can be helpful in portraying honest emotions, and reactions. It can *also* be taken to extremes. For instance, if a scene calls for you to drink beer, and you *insist* on *real* beer, you may be fine for the first couple of takes, however, come take 36 you've got a problem. Ms. Winters was one of the Strasberg school's most devout disciples *ever*. Legend has it that during one of her class acting exercises, she was asked to act out a private moment, and her contribution was to get up in front of the class, hike up her dress, and actually take a dump . . . on stage. She then got up, pretended to flush, pretended to wash her hands, and left, leaving her mound of do for someone else to clean up.

I had not heard of Method acting, and my gut feeling was "I may be dealing with a crazy woman."

Anyway, we did take after take of this thing. I took my whacks, and after each shot it took a little more makeup to cover the red handprints on my cheek.

Finally, after we'd shot the thing eight ways to Sunday, I was convinced that we *must* be finished. I was wrong. Instead, the director was so happy with my pained expressions that he wanted to film one more angle—an extreme close-up. The camera was to zoom in, catch the slap, then zoom even tighter to focus on the horror in my eyes. I was told *this* would be a powerful moment, a break in my blossoming career, and that it was no time to think about pain. I figured this was to be the actor's "sacrifice" I had heard so much about.

Boy, did I sacrifice! Ms. Winters pounded me with tooth-loosening ferocity, until finally we got it perfect: just the right reaction, the right look, the right amount of pain, and hurt, and anger. Surely, I was on my way.

But no. Turns out, long after I'd completed impersonating a punching bag, the film editor noticed that Chris Jones, playing the grown-up version of me, had brown eyes. Mine are blue. That led him to ask the obvious question: "How does a maniacal kid with blue eyes grow up to be a maniacal adult with *brown* eyes?" No one could offer a logical explanation for the oversight, so all of the excruciating close-up footage that I'd painfully endured ended up on the proverbial cutting-room floor.

In retrospect, I learned a couple of things on that shoot. One is that acting can be a great deal harder than it looks. And two, Shelley Winters packs a *mean* right hook.

Over the course of the next few days, the red handprints disappeared from my cheeks, and though I was still a bit traumatized, I *did* manage to survive. In fact, all it took was one very exciting phone call to slap a smile back on my face.

Y'see, everybody has a favorite TV show, and having grown up as a Peter Graves maniac, mine was of course "Mission: Impossible." You can imagine how thrilled I was when its producers chose *me* to play the young king of a fictional Middle Eastern country known as Sardia. In the episode, those closest to me were taking advantage of my youth and trying to gain power for themselves before killing me off. Mr. Phelps's mission, should he decide to accept it, was to prove that my "friends" were in fact deadly enemies and allow me to retain my rightful position as king.

The role was farfetched, even dumb, but of all the roles I had played, it was the most challenging, the most dangerous—and the kinkiest.

Challenging, because I wasn't just playing some street punk or beach bum but the king of a faraway country. It required an accent which I'd had to be determined, then studied. And the character would have to undergo major changes within the span of an hour.

Dangerous, because at the end of the show, my "friendly" uncle, proves himself to be a traitor by trying to (get this) shoot me in the face—*three times!!!* Nice guy.

Now, to shoot that scene you obviously employ special effects, and on "Mission: Impossible" the goal was to be as realistic as possible. Thus, the old water pistol schtick was out of the question, and even blanks were deemed too phony. In short, the "Mission Impossible" effects guys decided to really shoot at me.

I'm *serious!* These guys were obsessed with perfection and determined that the *most* realistic way to shoot me in the face—short of actually killing me, which they probably considered—would be to get hold of a large, hand-held pellet gun (it actually shot big ball bearings), aim it at my face, pull the trigger 3 times, and have the projectiles stopped at the last second by a thick double pane of glass that would separate me and death by about six inches.

In theory, the ball bearings were designed to crash

through the first pane of glass and be stopped by the second. My response to the situation was the perfectly normal one—sheer, gut-wrenching, lunch-losing terror. Once again a production-conscious assistant director assured me that I'd be all right, but I wasn't happy.

The effects guys tested their theory and it worked perfectly, so now it was time for me to stick my face where it didn't belong, and film the scene. I was horrified, but I promised God that if I survived, I'd be a changed kid, and went ahead with it. Luckily, everything came off as planned; the effect worked, my face survived, and only my promise to God was broken.

Kinky, because a good portion of the episode revolved around my escape from Sardia disguised as a young, guitar-strumming gypsy . . . girl! The kind of thing that creates *Enquirer* headlines like BARRY WILLIAMS A TEENAGE TRANSVESTITE! Anyway, here I was, in full cross-dressed regalia, complete with skirt, lipstick, rouge, false eyelashes (how did women ever *wear* those things?), and long flowing brunette wig. It was uncomfortable—and only got tougher when, a couple of hours later, I desperately had to use the bathroom.

First, I had to decide which facility to use. At first I thought it might be wise to use the ladies' room, but when push came to shove I just couldn't go in. Finally, when my bladder threw up a white flag, I was forced to hike up my skirt, throw out my pride, and, in my most macho posture, march into the men's room.

Naturally, Murphy's law was running rampant, and the men's room was packed, loaded with big, burly crew members. They looked at me first in surprise, then in disgust. Homophobic anger was rising in their eyes. I nervously muttered something at them like "How 'bout them Rams?"

With that, I flicked my long hair back and locked myself in a stall.

*   *   *

In the weeks that followed I was working pretty steadily, auditioning for parts about twice a week, with the entire process becoming fairly routine. Usually I could count on a day or two's notice before an interview, but once in a while they'd just pop up out of nowhere at the last minute. I'd ride the bus home from Paul Revere Junior High, change, and bound back out of the house only to have my Mom track me down in the family station wagon. I'd hop into the backseat, and she'd haul me off to an eleventh-hour meeting.

On *one* hectic occasion, we ran off for not one interview but two, both at Paramount Studios. We sped to the studios, arrived at the gate, and as I frantically tried to spit-fix my hair and tuck in my shirt, found out that my first meeting would be for "Gomer Pyle, U.S.M.C." and the second for "That Girl." In an odd coincidence, both shows needed a kid to play the part of an overzealous fan. In an even odder coincidence, I got both parts.

Two meetings, two successes—pretty lucky, especially since there isn't much you can do to prepare for them. Basically, you show up, meet the producer and the director, lay the energy and enthusiasm on thick, read a scene, and if they like you, you're in. Still, that doesn't stop *anybody* from trying to stack the odds in their favor.

My own tricks of the trade included wearing my lucky shirt (white with fat red stripes) and trying to intimidate the fifteen or twenty guys who made up the competition. I'd stare them down, then haul out the big gun. "I was talking to R.J. the other day when I was doing 'It Takes a Thief,'" I'd say, planting the seeds of self-doubt in anyone who could hear, "and he gave me some really great character-building tips. I think I'll try them out today." Yes, Mr. Wagner's advice was helpful in more ways than he'd known.

The "Gomer" meeting came first. It went smoothly, and I left very encouraged by the producer's comments. Twenty minutes later I was on the opposite end of the Paramount lot, doing my "meet and read" for "That Girl." Some more energy and enthusiasm, a little more intimidation, and I left feeling good once more.

Mom and I arrived home, and my hunch was soon proven correct by a dinnertime phone call from my agent.

When it came time to shoot the episode of "Gomer Pyle," I was less than thrilled. My cocky thirteen-year-old's all-encompassing sense of "cool" had convinced me that Jim Nabors was going to be a complete and total geek. I mean, anyone who could make a living playing Gomer Pyle has got to be a world-class nerd, right? Wrong. Mr. Nabors turned out to be a nice guy. Friendly, pleasant, and *very* funny, he seemed completely unaffected by his celebrity. My definition of "cool" expanded that day.

"That Girl" was another story. Much less accessible than Gomer, Marlo Thomas made it abundantly clear that her *hair* was the most important entity on the set. Between each camera shot, we'd stand around wasting time, waiting for her personal hair stylist to lacquer up that big do until it looked like she could hammer nails with it. Over and over again the hair spray flew and the hair got bigger and bigger. Global warming may in fact be directly traceable to Marlo's head. Next time you watch an episode of "That Girl," notice how the size of Marlo's hair changes from shot to shot. It's often much funnier than the show.

Anyway, the most significant part of working on this doubleheader would be meeting director John Rich. Mr. Rich directed *both* of these episodes. He was one of the most respected and most active directors on the Paramount lot, and in less than one year, I'd be screen-testing for his newest directorial project, "The Brady Bunch."

4
The Story, from a Man Named Sherwood

While I was trying to figure out if I could bounce quarters off Marlo Thomas' hair, the idea for "The Brady Bunch" was being born. It didn't come from a Hollywood brain trust or a formal "power meeting." It came from the newspaper.

I didn't know much about the fetal stages of "The Brady Bunch" until I started researching this book and got the inside scoop from a man named Sherwood Schwartz.

Abundantly talented, and equally likable, Mr. Schwartz is a charter member of Hollywood's old school, and he's got a mile-long rap sheet to prove it. A few of the highlights include writing for Bob Hope, Ozzie and Harriet, and Red Skelton, then creating "Gilligan's Island" and "The Brady Bunch." Sherwood is also a master storyteller. His face lights up as he speaks; he adds his own sound effects; he sometimes rambles off onto (vaguely) related tangents, and in short, he's vastly entertaining. When I asked *him* about the birth of the Bradys, I got back more than I bargained for. Here then, straight from the Schwartz's mouth, is the story of a family named Brady:

"What sprung the whole idea was a tiny little item I had read in the paper in 1966. It said that at that time, almost 30 percent of marriages involved a spouse who had at least one child from a *previous* marriage. Now, in 1966, this was a new phenomenon, and I realized that there really was a whole new kind of family springing up. Y'know, television was loaded with happily married couples, and single widows and widowers, but there wasn't *any* show that revolved around the marital amalgamation of two preexisting families.

"A lightbulb clicked on in my head.

"But I had a problem when it came time to try and sell the 'Brady' idea. I had just finished doing 'Gilligan's Island,' which was full of broad comedy, and broad characters doing silly things. But there's a lot of underlying philosophy to the characters on 'Gilligan's Island.' They're *really* a metaphor for the nations of the world, and their purpose was to show how the nations of the world have to get along together or cease to exist. I made the mistake of bringing all of that up at a network meeting, and it almost cost me the show. I called 'Gilligan's Island' a 'social microcosm,' which was a bad choice of words because Bill Paley himself, who was president of CBS, and happened to be at the meeting, got this flushed look on his face. Then he stood up and said, with exasperation dripping from his voice and sweat dripping from his upper lip, 'Oh, my God, I *thought* we were talking about a sitcom!'

"But it *was* a microcosm. I mean, here's a show about a group of people who have absolutely nothing in common, forced to live together and work together toward a common goal of survival. That's the philosophy of the show. Of course we buried that message under a lot of pratfalls and bamboo and silly stuff, but I used to get a lot of mail from psychiatrists and philosophers who understood it.

"Anyway, when I finished with 'Gilligan,' I worked on the idea for 'The Brady Bunch,' and tried to sell it. Knowing that I'd just done 'Gilligan,' I felt uneasy about trusting the network to visualize this completely different kind of show. Y'know, they simply pigeonhole you by what you did last.

"I had never written a script in selling 'Gilligan.' I had

come up with thirty storylines and developed all the characters, but I never wrote a script until they said 'Hey, let's do a pilot.' But I was afraid to go in with just stories for 'The Brady Bunch,' because I thought people might perceive it as another big, broad, rollicking comedy, without the dramatic or sentimental aspects that were so important to the show. And there's no way to go into a meeting and explain that. I mean, I could have talked to these executives about it until I was blue in the face, and they *still* would have left the meeting believing that 'The Brady Bunch' would have the same basic feel to it as 'Gilligan's Island' did.

"So, to protect myself and 'The Brady Bunch,' I took a different approach. I wrote stories, maybe the first ten or so, but I *also* came in with the script for the pilot already written. That way they'd *have* to see that this was a much more subtle, more sentimental show. For example, there's a scene in the pilot where Mike Brady tells Bobby that he doesn't have to put his mother's picture away just because he's getting remarried, and there's no way in the world you could imagine that kind of a scene with the image of Gilligan falling out of a coconut tree still fresh in your head.

"Even with all that, the idea went no place for two years. I am, if nothing else, stubborn. So I'd keep going back, and fortunately for me, the personnel turnover rate in network television is phenomenally quick. So I'd keep going back to the same places with this idea for 'The Brady Bunch,' but I'd keep talking to different people.

"Now, all through those two years when the show was selling like coldcakes, *nobody* disliked it. All three networks liked 'The Brady Bunch,' but none of 'em bought it. NBC wanted me to change the ending of the pilot, because they felt it was absolutely ridiculous for people on their honeymoon to double back, go home, and get their kids. They felt like no two people alive would do that. They said, 'Put a new ending on your script, and we'll shoot the pilot, but don't you agree that the parents' behavior is ridiculous? And I said, 'If I thought it was ridiculous, I wouldn't have written it.' Y'know . . . dumb question.

"CBS liked the show too, but they thought I should develop it by having the first six or seven episodes revolve around the courtship between Mike and Carol—how they met, how they fell in love, the whole ball of wax—and we'd have the wedding take place in the seventh or eighth show. I said, 'In that case, how are people gonna know what the show is about?' The show isn't about a courtship, it's about two families having problems becoming one family. That's what the show is about, and I *have* to have the wedding take place in the first episode.' Well, that was it; CBS passed.

"Then I went to ABC, and it so happened that this was the first year of a new thing called the Movie of the Week. They said, 'This is a great idea, let's do the pilot as a ninety-minute movie.' I said, 'Okay, in that case I *can* start this whole thing with how Mike and Carol meet, and we can get into the problems they have in deciding to get married'; and they said, 'Wait—stop right there. We like your script as is. We just want you to stretch it out to ninety minutes.' I said, 'You like this half-hour—why not let me give you another hour that you'll like in front of it, and we'll use the wedding as a culmination of the ninety minutes?' They said, 'No, we like this half-hour, just make it longer.' I said, 'I *can* make this half-hour longer, but I will succeed only in making it duller. There's not enough plot here to carry ninety minutes.' They said, 'Oh, sure there is.' So now I'm slapping my forehead, trying to explain to these guys why their idea would be awful, but they just keep saying, 'That's the only way we want to do it.' Finally I just said, 'Thank you very much. . . . Goodbye,' and I walked out. No deal.

"And then a wondrous thing happened. A movie came out called *Yours, Mine and Ours* starring Henry Fonda and Lucille Ball, which had essentially the same plot as my 'Brady Bunch' script except with a few more kids. Anyway, the film became a pretty respectable-sized hit, and all of a sudden ABC, who'd wanted it as a ninety-minute movie, called me up and said, 'Hey, why don't we sit down and talk again about that great "Brady Bunch" idea of yours?' And I said, 'Fine.' I sold it in a half-hour.

"A funny footnote about this whole thing is that when 'The Brady Bunch' finally got on the air, the producer of *Yours, Mine and Ours* threatened to sue Paramount for stealing his idea. Now, I had written the script for 'The Brady Bunch' a good couple of years before the *Yours, Mine and Ours* script was done. So I called Paramount and said to them, 'Why don't you just have this gentleman go down to the Writers Guild office and check out the registration date on my "Brady" script? And when he gets a hold of my script, you should also ask him to be grateful that *I* didn't sue *him*.' I said that because my original title on the script that would later become 'The Brady Bunch' was 'Yours and Mine.'

"I never heard from him again."

And there you have it. After a long and painful pregnancy, "The Brady Bunch" had finally been born. Plans were made to film a pilot episode, the script was polished, and then Sherwood proceeded to do something that would forever change the lives of nine innocent human beings: he cast them as Bradys.

The casting process for "The Brady Bunch" followed standard Hollywood procedure: it was a *nightmare*. Casting *one* kid on a sitcom involves *months* of work, and every theatrical agency in Hollywood. Interviews are conducted, then call backs, and finally screen tests are shot. Experience, age, height, coloring, ability, and energy are all considered, and after all *that*, the actors are chosen.

Imagine the horror of trying to cast six kids in the same show. In researching this book, I found that *twelve hundred kids* auditioned, hoping to become a Brady. Of those twelve hundred, Sherwood Schwartz called back and personally interviewed *four hundred and fifty-four*. All that to cast just six roles.

My heart sank as I arrived to meet Mr. Schwartz for the first time. There were *hundreds* of kids in all sizes, shapes, and colors overflowing his reception area and spilling out into the halls. It was so crowded, I literally couldn't find his office. Finally, using my mom as a sort of an 'offensive lineman,' I made it into Sherwood's waiting room, where I added my name to a mile-long waiting list, sat down, and waited. After a couple of hours had passed, his secretary yelled out my name (somehow managing to mispronounce "Williams") and I went in.

Mr. Schwartz greeted me warmly (he greets *everybody* warmly), smiled (he *always* smiles), and invited me to sit down. We talked, hit it off, and the meeting went well. He asked me the usual questions—"How old are you?" "What are your hobbies?" "Do you have any experience?"—and somehow got a good feeling about me. I asked Sherwood what he was looking for in all those kid-actor interviews, and he once again came through with a truckload of information:

"It's interesting—with the little kids, I just put some toys on the table and talked with them. I was looking for attention span, because if you're talking to a kid and they're gradually paying less and less attention to you, and more and more attention to the toys laid out in front of them, you're in trouble. Attention span is about the most important quality to look for in a kid actor. Also, you're looking for attractive, and since these kids were supposed to be playing brothers and sisters, you're also looking for similar facial features and similar hair."

Actually, since two separate families were involved, and since Sherwood cast the Brady kids before the Brady parents, he had to find four sets of kids with similar features and hair. Sets one and two would match up with the possibility of a dark-haired Mike Brady and a blond Carol (that was us), while sets three and four would be ready to go should Mike turn out to be the blond and Carol the brunette.

It sounds confusing, and it was, because even after surviving the interviews, the callbacks, and the screen tests, my big break still hinged upon a fictional character's hair color.

Still, I felt good about getting *this* far. I was up for a pretty regular part in a network series; and I felt as though my interviews with Sherwood had gone so well that I was a lock, probably the first one cast.

Wrong.

Yet again Sherwood Schwartz set me straight. Turns out Greg *wasn't* a lock or the first Brady cast. The shoo-in was Cindy.

"Susan Olsen was the only one I had no doubt about. In fact, she was so absolutely perfect that once I saw her, I asked not to see any more Cindys.

"She came in, and I asked, 'Have you ever been on television before?'

"'Yeth, Mr. Thwartz,' she said. 'I wath on "Gunthmoke."'"

"So I swallowed a laugh and asked her, 'What did you *do* on "Gunsmoke"?'

"'Well, I rode a horth,' she continued. 'But y'know what, Mr. Thwartz? The horth came near a thnake! And hortheth are thcared of *thnakes.*'

"By now I've given up trying to maintain my composure. I'm laughing out loud, but she just keeps telling her story.

"'Tho the horth wath thenthitive, and nervouth about the thnake, but don't worry, Mr. Thwartz, it wath okay, becauth what he thaw wathn't a *real* thnake, it was jutht a fake thnake. In TV, that'th called propth. Get it?'

"So this five-and-a-half-year-old has me on the floor, with tears coming out of my eyes, telling me how television works. And that was it—I *had* to hire her.

The cast ... at last.
(©Paramount Pictures)

"But that's the only one. Everyone else had to fight for their jobs."

And that's just what we did. Time and again, the remaining five of us (plus a coupla hundred other hopefuls) came back to the Paramount Studios and competed through interviews, callbacks, and screen tests. Finally, when Sherwood had cast his brunette Mike and his blond Carol, we each got a phone call that made us official Bradys.

5
Bob and Carol and Mike and Florence

It was a well-known fact in Hollywood that Sherwood Schwartz was absolutely the worst writer working in television. But that all changed one day when suddenly there showed up one writer who was even worse. It was Lloyd, Sherwood's son. And of course our problem was that we had both of them on "The Brady Bunch."

—Robert Reed

Robert Reed is the kind of actor who could perform Hamlet, get booed off the stage, and say, "Hey, don't blame me—I didn't write this shit."

—Lloyd Schwartz

"What?" you gasp. "Dissension in the comfy, cozy, suburban-tract Brady house?" The answer, quite bluntly, is uh-huh. From the very beginning, two distinct and exclusively opposite camps were set up. In one corner were Sherwood Schwartz and his son, Lloyd. In the other was Dad Brady himself, Robert Reed. Their battles became legendary at the Paramount complex, and a lot of the stories that will pop up in the pages to come won't make much sense unless you've been briefed on the very

44

real animosity that existed between the camps almost from day one.

Actually, the seeds of war were sown even *before* day one.

Y'see, Robert Reed is an extremely accomplished actor. He studied at Northwestern University and at London's Royal Academy of Dramatic Art, and he takes his work *very* seriously. Knowing the man, you'd come to the conclusion that the last television project in the world he'd get involved with would be "The Brady Bunch."

So how did it happen?

Robert had spent the better portion of 1967 appearing on Broadway in *Barefoot in the Park.* When Paramount decided to try and turn it into a TV series, he was invited to come to Hollywood and play the lead. Smash cut forward. It's now six weeks later, and Paramount has decided to dump the idea of turning *Barefoot* into a sitcom. At that point, Robert Reed's inescapable life as a Brady began.

I asked him to tell me how he became the legendary "man named Brady," and his story went like this:

"Shortly after Paramount decided to kill *Barefoot,* Doug Cramer"—then the vice-president of Paramount—"came to me and asked if I'd like to speak with a producer named Sherwood Schwartz about 'The Bradley Brood' "—we still hadn't become "The Brady Bunch"—"and I said 'Sure.' So Sherwood and I met over dinner in his office, and basically, he fooled me. You see, Sherwood has this remarkable facility for attaching a sociological concept to a movie or episodic project, but he hasn't the *least* capability of being able to realize it. And once he *hasn't* realized that sociological concept, he has even less capability for being able to realize that he *hasn't.*

"When he discussed 'The Brady Bunch' with me, it was all in sociological terms. You know, there was 'a need to discover these figures in American life,' and all about 'families put asunder,' and blah blah blah, and how he'd gotten the idea for doing a show about putting two of these families together, and that it would be in a general comic context, but that it would also 'represent American life to American people.' So I thought, 'Well, gee, that sounds pretty good to me,' and said, 'Okay, get me a script and I'll be glad to take a look.'

"And then the script came out, and I was absolutely *horrified!* I couldn't believe what I was reading! I mean, it's 'Gilligan' all over again, with just as much inanity, and I quickly said 'NO!'

"Anyway, the powers that be at the studio and Sherwood and I finally came to a meeting of the minds wherein I did an about-face and accepted the show, basically because there wasn't anything else for me to do. And honestly, my private feeling was that it'll never get off the ground—take the money and go.

"So we did the pilot, and of course it was terrible, so I was absolutely stunned when it got picked up. And even then, I thought, 'It can't last more than thirteen weeks.' And it went on forever, which shows you what *I* know."

Wanting to present both sides fairly, I asked Sherwood Schwartz for *his* spin on the same story. Here goes:

"The only reason Bob got a screen test in the *first* place was that my *personal* choice to play Mike Brady was rejected by the network, because they'd never heard of him. His name was Gene Hackman. This was a couple of years before *The French Connection* hit it so big. They said, 'Who the hell is Gene Hackman?' and I said, 'He's a terrific actor who's got a nice rough edge to him, and I think he could handle the part really well.' They said, 'Forget it—we never heard of him.'

"So we started scouting around and tried out a couple of actors, Robert Reed included. We did a screen test, and Bob was good, but he was absolutely dead set against going into a show where he'd play the dad to six kids, because it would *ruin* him as a young-leading-man type. And on top of that, he hated the pilot script, basically because he doesn't do comedy well and has no sense of humor. So when we got picked up, he went into the series kicking and screaming all the way.

"That's why throughout the series he always seemed to have a black cloud over him. He just plain didn't want to do it. And as the life of the series got longer, he wanted to be there even *less.* In fact, there were several episodes that we had to write Bob out of *completely,* because he was being such an enormous pain in the ass."

We'll get into all of that later, but for now you've got the basics. Robert Reed was signed to play Mike Brady, Sherwood Schwartz had found his leading man, and even before we'd started production on our first episode, a feud was brewing.

With Mike Brady in place, Sherwood Schwartz set out looking for the perfect Carol, and he found her almost immediately. Her name was Joyce Bulifant. With that task accomplished, it was time to cast the role of Alice, and Sherwood's obvious choice was . . . Monte Margetts. His *second* pick however, was . . . Kathleen Freeman.

Huh?

Kathleen "could'a been 'Alice' " Freeman.
(Courtesy Kathleen Freeman)

It's true; and though today it seems impossible to imagine *anybody* besides Florence Henderson and Ann B. Davis in those roles, neither one was a first choice.

Couch potatoes everywhere will immediately recognize Joyce Bulifant from "The Mary Tyler Moore Show," where she played the ever-perky Marie Slaughter, wife to Murray. She was also the longtime bottom-left celebrity on the world's worst-ever game show, "Match Game."

Monte Margetts had roles in a couple of obscure 1950s sitcoms, and has since retired from the acting world. Kathleen Freeman, on the other hand is an absolutely brilliant comedic character actress who spent most of the 1960s yelling at Jerry Lewis in films like *The Disorderly Orderly.* One look at her picture and you'll know *exactly* who I'm talking about.

So the real question to be answered here is: How did Joyce and Kathleen become Florence and Ann?

The answer: It wasn't easy.

Florence was always *supposed* to audition for the role of Carol, but when it came time to actually shoot the screen tests, she was performing her nightclub act. Up until she became Carol Brady, Florence was primarily known as a singer, and was working at a club in Texas. Unable to get herself to L.A. in time, Florence was forced to politely decline Sherwood Schwartz's request that she audition for the role of Carol. The part was offered to Joyce Bulifant, and that was that.

Once Joyce was in place, Sherwood was able to cast his Alice. He felt that Joyce had a naturally funny personality and that she'd play *very* well against a strong "straight man" type. Kathleen Freeman fit that bill perfectly and became Alice.

Meanwhile, Florence was rehearsing her act in Texas when an idea came to her: she could jet into L.A., get a cab to speed over to the Paramount lot, screen-test for "The Brady Bunch," speed back to LAX, and jet back to Texas, all in time for her nine o'clock nightclub performance. She called Sherwood back, explained her brainstorm, and asked if she could still squeeze in a screen test. Sherwood said sure, and twenty-four hours later she would have her chance to play Carol. Simple, right?

Wrong!, Florence's plane was delayed, she got stuck in traffic, and she didn't even get to the Paramount studios until she was almost two hours late. Desperate to make up some time, Florence ran in a mad rush toward the nearest available makeup man. Running from set to set, she finally found one on the set of—"Star Trek"! He agreed to do her makeup, but Florence's troubles weren't over yet.

"I was sitting in a makeup chair between William Shatner, Leonard Nimoy, and like six or eight space monsters. None of them had any idea who I was or made any attempt to be friendly, which really bugged me. Anyway, this makeup guy proceeded to put a makeup on me that was absolutely unbelievable. Put it this way: *Mr. Spock* ended up looking more attractive than I did. It was awful! I wound up with eyelashes that were like three inches long!

"Mortified, I went back to the Brady soundstage and I said to Sherwood, 'Look, I just want you to know that I think this makeup is all wrong for Carol Brady, or any other living human creature. So remember, when you see these eyelashes flapping around in the breeze, *I* think they look stupid too.' And Sherwood laughed. Maybe I should thank that terrible makeup man, because in a way, his botch job helped me get the part."

Despite the Mary Kay nightmare, Florence's screen test was a smash, and Sherwood had a new Carol. However, he also had a new *problem*: namely, two "straight men" in the same kitchen.

Sherwood knew that Carol and Alice would be sharing a lot of scenes together in the Brady kitchen, but he felt that Florence wasn't as naturally funny as Joyce. So Sherwood said maybe we should let Alice be the funny one and remembered Ann B. Davis, whom he calls "genuinely, immediately, and automatically funny." The chips started falling into place.

Incidentally, Florence *did* make it back to Texas in time for her nine o'clock show, and it went smoothly. But the very next morning she had to once again pack up and fly out to L.A.—this time, to start shooting the pilot for "The Brady Bunch."

Lastly, rather than simply blow off the rest of her nightclub engagement, Florence made a deal with the hotel's owner. He agreed to let her go to Hollywood and shoot her pilot and she agreed to return at a later date. They shook on it, and a year later, Florence Henderson—now a genuine TV star—went back and completed her run. She was a smash.

6
A Day at the Bradys'

We started shooting the pilot episode of "The Brady Bunch" on my fourteenth birthday, and six months later, much to my delight (and Robert Reed's horror), ABC bought it! Then we got *really* busy. The show was set to premiere in September of 1969, and by mid-

One of our first cast photos.
(© Paramount Pictures)

summer we were filming at an absolutely *furious* pace. It was hot, grueling work, and all I can say is that I was in heaven.

For me, there was always an air of excitement about going to the studio. Despite the long hours and hard work, I looked forward to each day on the Paramount Stage 5 with a real sense of anticipation. To me, it was even more exciting than

Stage 5, today. (Barry Williams)

Disneyland. Who needs Frontierland or Adventureland when you have the "Star Trek," "Mission Impossible," "Bonanza," "Odd Couple," "Love, American Style," and "Happy Days" sets to play on?

I loved it so much that I'd usually have my mom get us there early. I'd hang out, bother the assistant directors, say hi to Mrs. Whitfield, our welfare worker/teacher, ask the tech guys about nine hundred questions, and then sneak out for my all-important first cigarette. After I'd sufficiently blackened my lungs and stimulated my brain, I'd head back to the set, check in with wardrobe and makeup, and be in place, ready to go, all before my official eight a.m. call time. Such was my morning routine, day after day, season after season.

Scripts were handed out, and each Brady would take time to go over the script, and offer (generally) constructive input. Mostly we'd ask for minor line changes—things like avoiding a scriptwriter's "neat-o" where a "groovy" or "far out" belonged. Pretty funny in retrospect, but I can remember taking that duty *very* seriously. To our producers' credit, our suggestions almost always met with a positive response.

Then it was time to bring the script to life as we began to rehearse and shoot. That sounds like two separate processes, but in our case the two were always mixed together. Ours was a one-camera, filmed sitcom, as opposed to the three-camera, live-on-tape shows that are popular today. It's a more difficult and time-consuming shooting process because we couldn't simply run through the show in front of a studio audience. Instead, it had to be pieced together, one scene at a time.

It's a tedious method, but Lloyd Schwartz tells me that we endured it for a very definite reason. "Three-camera shows suffer in terms of kids, because it's very hard for them to sustain their concentration level for a full thirty minutes. From day one we knew that there were gonna be kids all over our set, and that the *best* way to shoot 'The Brady Bunch' would be to take our time with it, shoot it with just one camera, mostly in close-ups that we'd knock off a couple of lines at a time.

"Nowadays they throw these kids in front of a live studio audience and expect them to perform. Watch any kid on a three-camera sitcom and you'll find that it almost *never* works. In a best-case scenario they seem plastic and artificial, and at their worst they can be just plain unwatchable. So what we did was proper, I think, and really made the Brady kids much more believable *as* kids."

Studio time is ridiculously expensive. Even in 1972, it cost over $100,000 to produce each "Brady Bunch" episode. With that in mind, our producers left *nothing* to chance. Each evening, a call sheet was posted listing in detail the scenes that we'd film the following day, the order in which they'd be shot, which characters would appear in each, and what time we were expected to report. For the cast and crew of "The Brady Bunch," this was a very important piece of paper. We followed its instructions religiously, and to the letter.

Throughout the day, we Brady kids spent most of our time either in the studio schoolroom or on the set. Whenever one of our scenes was being readied, an assistant director would find us and herd us over to the set for rehearsal. This began the creative part of the "Brady Bunch" process.

For each scene, the participating actors would get together with the episode's director and give it a workout. We'd experiment, try things out, play with blocking, line readings, camera angles, and also work through the logistics of the scene. This was the niche in the creative process wherein we'd answer questions like "Where should I enter from?" and "How perky should I be?" and "How do we smack Marcia in the nose with a football and not bust it in the process?" It was fun, and we'd work on the scene until it had shaped up to the point where everyone was satisfied that it was ready to shoot.

Mike lectures the Bunch. (Courtesy Sherwood Schwartz)

At this point, we actors would dash off the set, and into wardrobe (we didn't generally don our bell-bottoms until the very last minute). Simultaneously, the crew would be lugging lights, loading cameras, and making sure every last prop detail had been readied.

Once the lights and camera were set, all that was missing was the action, and that's where we came in. We'd assemble on the set, lines firmly implanted in our cerebellums, and we'd shoot each scene.

First, we'd knock off a wide-angle master shot, with all of the actors in the scene pretty much visible throughout. It serves as a sort of overview for the scene and is used as the starting point later on in the editing process. Once we'd knocked off a decent take, the director would move in for closer coverage. On most shows this would entail shooting a couple of close-ups, but when you're producing a sitcom *overflowing* with main characters, you'd sometimes have to combine actors and shoot tight two-shots, three-shots, or even our most unique creation, the very intimate "tight nine." You've really gotta *love* your fellow actors to squish up to them that tightly.

Look closely at almost any "Brady" episode and you'll notice that whenever you happen across one of those tight nines, I'm generally pressed quite tightly up against Maureen McCormick. I was no dope.

Anyway, between each camera angle, the lights have to be changed, the camera has to be moved, cables have to be pulled, and chaos reigns supreme. Consequently, we kids would be expected to stay out of the way and inside the schoolroom. Fun, huh? Once, however, you had built up the daily school-time minimum of three hours, it was okay to hang out on the "Brady" set, or sneak into the sets of other shows (I used to *love* watching Jack Klugman and Tony Randall tape "The Odd Couple"). Sometimes, we'd just find a way to cause trouble. That's because Lloyd Schwartz went out of his way to guarantee that at any given time, any one of us Brady kids could break an arm.

Close-up in the kitchen. (Michael Ochs Archives/Venice Beach, CA)

That sounds like a joke, but it's not. Lloyd explains it: "One time the kids were running around like lunatics, as kids do, and I was ordered to put a stop to it. I was ordered to keep 'em off the overhead catwalks and off the backyard swings on the set, and basically to put 'em in glass cases and pull 'em out for their close-ups. So I went to the president of the studio and said, 'I'm *not* gonna do that, because what's coming across on-screen is that these are real kids, and the minute we start imposing these restrictions on them, we'll remove them from *being* real kids, and on-screen, they won't *react* as real kids. I hope it never happens, but every one of those kids needs a chance to break an arm.' And they said okay."

So thanks to Lloyd Schwartz, we Brady kids spent a blissful five years running amok throughout the Paramount lot, having fun, driving people crazy, and generally, just being kids.

7
Cindy the Geek

Most of us Brady kids didn't have to stretch too far in bringing life to our Brady alter-egos. That's because Sherwood Schwartz thought it would be more natural to have us more or less "be ourselves" on-screen rather than superficial, stereotypical, or one-dimensional characters. There was, however, one glaring exception: Cindy.

The Geek. (Courtesy Sherwood Schwartz)

Susan Olsen is almost *nothing* like Cindy. In fact, she is more her opposite, the "anti-Cindy"—perhaps even an evil twin. I asked Susan about it:

"I thought Cindy was the single biggest geek in the world!" she said. "She was an idiot! I mean, I didn't like Cindy, but I really *hated* the fact that she was so stupid. Even as a kid in the first season, I can remember running up to my Mom and asking her, 'Why is it funny and cute to be stupid? Why is Cindy stupid? And why is that a good thing?' If you ever stop and listen to some of the lines that come out of Cindy's mouth, you come away with the idea that she's retarded.

"I remember the worst one came during the first season in that episode where we all had the measles. Carol comes into Cindy's room and gives her a peanut butter and jelly sandwich, and Cindy asks, 'How come you alwayth gimme peanut butter and jelly?' And Carol says, 'Because they're your faaaaaavorite.' To which moron Cindy replies, 'Oh yeah, I keep forgetting.' I can remember even *then* being really distressed about it and asking my mother, 'Why? Why do I have to say this stuff?'

"And what made it worse is that I'd have to go back to school after this, and try to live down what Cindy did . . . you know, with *my* body. Lets face it, kids are horrible psychotic maniacs, and just plain cruel a lot of the time, so it could be really tough. I remember going to school the Monday after the tattletale episode aired, and *no one* would talk to me. I'd be like 'C'mon, you know that wasn't me. You know I don't squeal. You *know* that I can keep a secret.' But, in the world of schoolyard justice, being a tattletale is about as low as you can possibly sink, and I hated catching shit for what Cindy the geek did."

It's funny how a coupla pigtails, a coupla piñafores, and a few dumb lines could so thoroughly hide the real kid underneath the Cindy character. Even Sherwood Schwartz, who created the role of Cindy for Susan, was blinded by her feminine exterior. "It's funny," Susan says, "because I'm sure if you asked him, Sherwood would tell you that he tailored the role of Cindy around me. But I don't know that Sherwood's ever really met *me*.

"But Lloyd knew that I was a little different. Once he came over to my Mom and said, 'Your kid is an imposter.' And my Mom said, 'What?' And he said, 'She's an imposter. She looks one way, but she's *not* that way. She's not Cindy.'

"Actually, if the character of Darlene on the 'Roseanne' show had existed then, I would have killed for it. It really used to bug me that every single tomboy role on television used to go to Jodie Foster. But I just sorta looked like this little lady and those are the parts I always ended up getting. It's funny, because that same incongruity used to really annoy my schoolteachers. One telling my mother, 'It's so strange, she comes in here with her hair all perfect, and looking like a little angel, and then she goes outside, beats the crap out of the boys, comes back in, and her hair is *still* perfect.'"

Speaking of hair, let me finally squash an ugly rumor by saying that as phony as Cindy's personality may have been, her hair was real. For years now the only Brady hair rumor more heinous than the one about bad perms on the guys has been the one about Cindy's hair being clipped on before each episode. Even today that rumor drives Susan Olsen nuts, and as you might have guessed by now, she's got something to say about it.

"The whole thing with my hair started long before I got the part of Cindy. I used to love watching 'Family Affair,' and I'd say to my Mom, 'Oh, please fix my hair like Buffy's.' So I was a knock-off really. I wasn't the first one with those spaghetti-looking appendages hanging off my head, but *mine* were real. Buffy's were prosthetic.*

"And I asked my mom to fix my hair up in those pigtail-

---

*Just a note. I was curious about prosthetic pigtails. I checked with Johnny "Jody" Whitaker and Kathy "Sissy" Garver who busted the rumor. They said Anissa Jones, who played Buffy, did a little bleaching but never resorted to wiglets.

curl things for my first interview with Sherwood for 'The Brady Bunch.' Biggest mistake I ever made, because it *stayed* like that for five years!

"In the beginning, if you look closely you'll notice that they were changing my hair color literally every week. Me and Florence both. They would dye us at the same time and give us the exact same color, so there are some episodes where it's basically white, and a couple where we're even sorta reddish brunettes—very dark. By the middle of the first season, my hair just started coming out in clumps, and I had a terrible rash all down my neck from the hair dye. It finally got so bad that I started to cry and said, 'Mom, if I have to keep doing this, tell Sherwood he has to get another Cindy.' And she said, 'I want *you* to go up and tell him that, because he should know that it's coming directly from you.' So I went up to his office and told him. He looked at me, and being the wonderful man that he is, actually got a little teary-eyed, and said, 'We won't color your hair *ever* again.' And he gave me a big hug and kiss, and that was that. I really loved him.

"But those damn pigtails were tough to live with, especially since I constantly had to have those rubber-band things strapped into my hair, and they were *tight!* I still cringe whenever I think of them yanking my hair back tight and wrapping those little dingle-ball things at the ends. Every now and then they'd drop an end and *whack*—hard little plastic ball snaps onto kid star's skull."

Susan's worst hair trauma of all came when our hairdresser showed her pigtail damage to Howard Leeds, Susan's least favorite producer. He looked at her head, put his big, meaty hands on her hair, and said, "Look, if it gets worse, we'll just cut it all off and slap a wig on your head."

At that point, "the youngest one in curls" quickly became the youngest one in tears.

8
Cindy and Bobby, Sittin' in a Tree

I know, I know, this is the stuff you've been waiting for. In fact, there's a pretty good chance that you skimmed through the book and decided to start *here* instead of at chapter 1. If that's the case, all I can say is I'm not surprised. Over the years, I can safely say, fans' questions about inter-Brady dating have outnumbered all other subjects by at least a hundred-to-one margin. *Why* you people are so interested in the gory little details of six teenagers' libidos is beyond me, but since you definitely are, I'll do my best to spill my guts.

At some point throughout the five years of filming, *every* Brady paired up romantically with their opposite-sex counterpart. (The *only* exceptions were Alice and Tiger. Hmm . . . you don't suppose . . .) The pairings varied in intensity, but no one was spared an attack of the adolescent hormones, not even little Cindy and Bobby.

My memories of the romance between Susan Olsen and Michael Lookinland were hazy, so once again, wanting to get the *whole* story for this book, I called up Susan, invited her over, plied her with Jack Daniel's, and interrogated her mercilessly until she fessed up. She hung tough for a while

The Newlyweds.
(Courtesy Sherwood
Schwartz)

but finally cracked, exposing for the first time, the dirt behind the romance between the youngest Bradys.

"It was funny," Susan said, taking a long drag on her cigarette and a long sip of Jack, "because I was very strange as a little girl. A couple of times boys had tried to kiss me and I reacted almost as though I had been assaulted. But during our first season, Michael got the notion that he had a major crush on me. And he'd put his arm around me, and he'd kiss me, and . . . uh . . . I kinda liked it. I remember he would drag me into his dressing room, and Maureen [McCormick] and Eve [Plumb] would try to be funny by locking the door. And I'd be going, 'Michael, Michael, get off me—Hee-Hee-Hee-Hee-Hee,' and here's Michael, this eight-year-old mini-stud going, 'I love you, I love you,' and trying to put his lips and his tongue on me. So I said what *any* reasonable nine-year-old would say in a situation like that, I said 'Let'th get married.'

"So Maureen made like a minister, and we held a ceremony. She asked Michael if he wanted to take me as his 'awfully wedded wife' and did like six other bad wedding jokes, but when it was over, me and Mikey were married. We were filming that camping episode at the time, and *that* became our honeymoon. So we're on location, walking along hand in hand like a coupla geeks, and I remember Michael gushing to Ann B., 'We're maaaaarried now,' and Annie of course just said something like 'Oh, that's nice, I'm very happy for you.'

"But it didn't end there. For most of that first season, we used to sneak off into Tiger's doghouse and make out. This will probably *really* embarrass Michael, but a couple of years later, he became *maniacally* horny. He'd see a woman with big boobs—he seemed to have a kinda 'boob thing'— and he'd be fascinated. This is like at age ten or eleven. And right about that time Maureen had 'em, and Eve was acquiring a pretty respectable set. I of course had none, so he decided it was time to get rid of me and chase after Eve for a while.

"So we got a divorce. And the way that our twisted little brains worked we decided that to really be divorced, we'd have to do the entire wedding ceremony over again, only *this* time we'd have to do it backwards. I remember instead of kissing, we kinda spit on each other, and we walked *backwards* down the aisle, and that did it. We were official-ly divorced."

If only real life were that simple!

9
Reed vs. Schwartz: On the Set

I think America looks at "The Brady Bunch," sees Bob, and thinks, "Wow, what a great guy!" I don't think that they have a clue about how impossible he really is.
—Lloyd Schwartz

Sherwood and his cohorts—Lloyd, and whoever else he had writing—had no sense of reality whatsoever. I mean, they'd write this beyond-farce "Gilligan's Island"-level shit, look at it, and say, "Yeah, that's great. That's wonderful. We've done it." And try as you might, you couldn't talk them out of it.
—Robert Reed

Robert and the Schwartzes had their horns firmly locked. Their feud rattled throughout the lifetime of "The Brady Bunch" and beyond. Their battles were always heated, usually bitter, and so ongoing that page space alone prevents me from hacking through them all. What I *can* do, however, is delve into some of the really good stuff.

I'm also going to spend the next several pages absolutely refusing to take sides. Sherwood Schwartz, Lloyd Schwartz, and Robert Reed are three men whom I truly respect, so throughout this book their fight will remain just that—*their* fight.

With that disclaimer out of the way, we'll pick up the story where we left off. Bob had appeared in the pilot episode for "The Brady Bunch," *hated* the results, and was (to put it mildly) less than enthusiastic about being a part of the series. With that in mind, I asked Bob the obvious question: "If you were so unhappy with the show, why not quit?" He answered like this:

"First of all, I couldn't get out of my contract. If I tried, what would I say? 'I'm unhappy with the show'? With a signed, sealed contract, I'd simply have been sued. And the other thing was, once we got at it, the problems seemed easy to fix. We had a good cast, and frankly I thought you kids were wonderful, certainly the best thing in it. So in watching John Rich direct you"—he directed the first seven episodes—"I couldn't help but think, 'Get a *good* director in here and we might really have something good.'

"Once having taken the first bite out of the show, I wanted to stay around and watch it become something that we might not be ashamed of. And another reason was that my business manager said that my tail would be in crap if I didn't!"

So Robert Reed became Mike Brady, and Sherwood Schwartz became a severe migraine sufferer. Even before our first thirteen weeks had gone by, they were at odds over the direction of the show. Sherwood was trying to make "The Brady Bunch" as funny as possible, and Bob was working *against* that cause, toward a more realistic, less jokey focus. That's important, because from here on, almost *every* fight between Robert and the Schwartzes can be traced back to this basic conceptual conflict.

This is Bob's description: "My theory was—and Sherwood and I argued about this dozens of times—that either you have a show like 'Gilligan's Island,' where kids can just sit back and laugh at what they see, like a cartoon, or you do a show that's grounded in reality, wherein you deal with real kids, and present their characters as identifiable peers for your audience. That's what I'd always hoped for 'The Brady Bunch.'" And the adult characters? "There are dozens of other shows where the father figures run around telling jokes, stepping on relationships, and acting stupid. But I thought, 'God damn it, the father's supposed to be an authority figure here, and we'd better keep him that way.' I mean, he can make mistakes, and do dumb things, but at all times he's got to be a *father,* and Florence has to be a *mother.*"

And therein lies the heart of the argument that kept the Alka-Seltzer flowing on the Brady set for years. I asked both Sherwood and Lloyd Schwartz for their take on Bob's strict code of ethics regarding "The Brady Bunch." Sherwood blamed Bob's aversion to all things slapstick on the fact that "he came into the series with a kind of a black cloud over him, and just plain didn't want to do it. He doesn't do comedy, and has no sense of humor . . . at least on a commercial level." But Lloyd went a step further.

"Bob is *not* a comedian. Listen to the theme song and you'll hear it's 'the story of a man named Brady,' but in reality 'The Brady Bunch' is *not* the story of a man named Brady, it's instead the story of a man named Brady's kids. And personally, I think that's because due to Bob's reluctance, or inability to step forward and be funny, he let the show get taken away from him. Even today, people remember the names of all six kids, but nobody remembers 'Mike.'

"The show really *should* have been centered around Bob's comedic reactions to his kids' goings-on around him, but we could never *depend* upon Bob for that. As a result we started centering our stories around the kids and became very successful that way. So I think Bob did himself a real disservice. I think he let the show get taken."

With both parties unwavering in their quest to model "The Brady Bunch" after their own personal vision, the Battle over the Bunch began in earnest, with both sides tolerant but leery. At face value, it would seem that Sherwood, as creator *and* producer of "The Brady Bunch," would certainly have had *much* more authority over its direction than Robert. However, the cagey Mr. Reed could sometimes overcome his subordinate political position by employing the age-old piece of strategy known as the "end run."

"Sherwood and I tried talking about the problems with the show," he told me, "but we were *constantly* at loggerheads. In fact, I gave him his very first migraine. But then I found a method of working around him. I went to the head of Paramount, Doug Cramer, and told him about what was going on, and he said, 'You *can't* get what you want by arguing with Sherwood.' So we came up with an alternate plan.

"Even before my first meeting with Doug, I'd taken my 'Brady Bunch' scripts, rewritten them, and sent them off to his office with a note saying, 'This is what the arguing is about. Here's my revised script. Is this an improvement or not?' His reply was 'Yes, it is,' and together we devised a plan wherein I would work with another writer, or on my own, rewrite each week's 'Brady Bunch,' and turn in the revisions to Paramount's front office. Paramount, in turn, would send the rewrites down to Sherwood as if the changes came from *them*. And because Paramount owned one-third of 'The Brady Bunch,' they had clout. There would still be discussion about the changes, but they certainly had more bargaining power than *I* did.

"That's the way we operated for as long as Doug was there. But after some personnel changes in Paramount's front office, I started sending my changes straight to Sherwood. And sometimes there'd be periods wherein we'd try our best to be nice to each other and to be polite, and considerate of each other's feelings, but the problem was that when this happened, Sherwood would take my changes, rewrite them himself, and they'd end up very watered down. The system always seemed to me to work better when I'd say, 'You fucker! What the fuck is blah blah blah . . . ?' you know?

"Anyway, rather than go through all this, the studio finally decided to bring in a script editor that I liked, and so they hired my friend Tam Spiva. That worked better, but still, we were constantly at odds over scripts, and I guess I wasn't very flexible either.

"I remember every once in a while I'd lose perspective and issue critiques of the show and, geez, I'd get really vitriolic about this. It's no wonder Sherwood took issue with me. I mean, they were basically written from the point of view of 'You stupid asshole, how could you possibly write anything this dumb?' So there was crap on both sides of the fence, but certainly on mine."

Now, by the time we got around to actually shooting each episode, the fighting over its script was usually finished. But there were exceptions. Lloyd Schwartz remembers it this way:

"It was constant gamesmanship with Bob, and he's a very difficult man. For example, stage time, when you've got a full crew working, and the lights on, is *incredibly* expensive. I remember one time we were filming an episode, and all we had left to shoot was its tag"—that's the short little piece of schtick you see on sitcoms in between their last commercial break and the credits. "Bob decides, on set, that he hates this tag. So I go back up to the production office and I say, 'We need a new tag,' and we discuss the situation, which goes like this.

"Bob is one of those actors who says, 'I don't think this material is very good. I'm gonna play it for what it's worth.' And so, of course, he was doing the original tag *very* badly. Ann B. Davis, on the other hand, would do the exact opposite. She'd say, 'A lot of people worked very hard on this, and maybe it isn't great, but if that's the case, they really need me to make it work.' Opposite attitudes.

"Anyway, Bob is out there playing the original tag right into the ground, and because of that, it's dying. And now he's saying, 'Y'see, see how bad it is?' So now I come down from the office to give them a new tag, but when I get there I find they're already *doing* a new tag that *Bob* wrote. And *now* Bob's playing the hell out of the thing, and the crew is laughing, but to be honest, it wasn't anywhere *near* as good as the original. I get to the set, where Bob glares at me and says, 'Well, what have *you* got?' Now I *know* whatever I have, he'll play it into the ground and ruin it. So I just said, 'Uh . . . we couldn't come up with anything,' because I know I'd much rather have him do his mediocre tag with a lot of energy and spark than do a good one badly. That's how you deal with Bob."

Bickering was common between Robert and the Schwartzes; but every once in a while, when things got uncommonly heated between the two camps, the infighting would escalate a notch. Bob Reed remembers:

"Oh, God, sometimes I'd get so furious at Sherwood that I'd go over to O'Blath's"—a bar just outside the Paramount lot—"and have a belt or two, and I remember one time, com-

Maureen McCormick on the Braless Bradys

Nowadays if I'm changing channels and I happen across an episode of "The Brady Bunch," the first thing I notice is how ugly our clothes are. I mean, that polyester stuff is just *awful.*

There *were* clothes that I liked at the time, but for the most part I felt they were always dressing Marcia too young. And when a style was "out," we just kept wearing it, I guess the studio's wardrobe people were on a budget, and with six kids to dress, they had to use everything more than once. Actually, being the oldest, I was pretty lucky, and so I was able to avoid hand-me-downs. Still, I think Florence's stuff was the worst of all.

I remember when I was trying to get my hemlines a lot shorter. Lloyd Schwartz and the crew guys *loved* the idea, so that was pretty easy to change. On the other hand, there were other times on "The Brady Bunch" where Eve and I kept trying to sneak onto the set without bras—You know, it was the seventies, and that was the look, everyone was going without bras. It got to the point where every time we'd go out onto the set, Lloyd Schwartz would have to come up behind us and feel our backs to see if we had our bras on. If we didn't it was back out to the trailer.

I was successful more than Eve. She had ... uh ... more to hide. But I could slide by ... unless it was a particularly cold set.

---

ing back *loaded* . . . okay, maybe a couple of times, always after big blowups with Sherwood. And I'd come back to the set drunk, thinking, 'I don't give a fuck—shoot *this.*' And of course I made a complete asshole of myself."

When I asked Bob if he could remember a specific episode where that took place, he didn't come up with one. But Lloyd Schwartz did:

"One time where we had Bob doing a scene with a mouse"—Episode 34, "The Impractical Joker"—"and this just drove him *nuts*, absolutely nuts. I mean, here's a guy who thinks of himself as a great Shakespearean actor, and he's trading lines with a mouse. And I remember he was smashed. At the same time, because of our shooting schedule, this was gonna have to be the last shot of the day, and if we finished the sequence, the episode would be complete. So I'm on the stage watching, and Bob's just plain drunk. And I found that an insult to the company, an insult to the show, and an insult to himself.

"I didn't want a tainted scene like this going to dailies, because the higher-up network types all paid close attention to dailies. Basically, I have to prevent the scene from being finished, so that we'll have to shut down for the day and pick it up the next day. So now I'm watching this scene and I say, 'Okay, this is it. We've got to get it in this take.' Of course I'm lying because I knew that if we printed this take, it'd go to dailies, and there Bob would be, on display, drunk. I wasn't particularly interested in protecting Bob, because I'm not necessarily a fan of him as a person, but I did want to protect the show.

"So I wait until about halfway through the scene, when all eyes are on Bob, and I take a big metal lighting scrim and toss it *way* up into the rafters. A half-second later, the thing goes CLASH, CLATTER, BOOM, SMASH!!! The place falls dead silent, and I go, 'Ohhhhhhh, noooooooooo! Okay, we'll have to wrap now.'"

Before I go even a half-sentence further, I want to make it crystal clear that this sort of tension was not commonplace on the set of "The Brady Bunch," and was *not* exhibited in front of us kids—it almost always took place late in the shooting day, long after the Brady kids had gone home. Under normal everyday circumstances, our working conditions were friendly, comfortable, relaxed, and enjoyable; on-set friction was an exception, not the rule.

Still, the battling between Robert and the Schwartzes was well known around the Paramount lot. Both sides were locked into their own unbending, uncompromising, and diametrically opposed vision of what "The Brady Bunch" should be, and a satisfactory compromise was an absolute impossibility. The fighting would continue throughout the lifetime of "The Brady Bunch," and right on through every reincarnation.

10
On the Make for "Mo"

For the better part of five years, the shooting schedule on "The Brady Bunch" pretty much clobbered the social lives of us Brady kids. The long hours we'd spend together on the Paramount lot pretty much *demanded* that the six of us do one of two things: become good friends or beat the crap out of each other.

Actually, we did both. But for the most part, we became great friends. We worked with each other, laughed with each other, leaned on each other, and over the course of time, as our adolescent hormones ran amok, became attracted to each other.

When sparks began to fly between Maureen and me, it took us both by surprise. Friends off-screen as well as on, Maureen and I were often asked to attend various Tinseltown events and benefits together. I would generally drive, and sometimes on the way home we'd stop off for dinner or a soda. (Geez, even my *real* dates sound like they belong to Greg.) Anyway, these weren't exactly "dates," but I knew, at least on my part, *something* was cooking, and that my attraction for Mo (we almost never called her Maureen) was rapidly becoming more than just brotherly.

Still, it wasn't until "The Brady Bunch" got to Hawaii

that I was able to work up the guts to actually *do* anything about my feelings.

It's funny: things like the warmth of the sun, the sand, and romantic tropical breezes sound completely corny in print, but in reality, I think, they had an effect on both of us.

On one particularly perfect, particularly balmy island evening, after a full day of filming, all of us Bradys had dinner together at the Royal Hawaiian Hotel. We had a terrific time together, but by eight o'clock it was over. Lloyd Schwartz told us kids that we should head back to our rooms and rest up for tomorrow's long shoot day, but of course, like *any* kids in that situation, we ignored him. Everyone ran off in different directions, and I took the unsupervised opportunity to nervously make my move.

"Hey . . . uh . . . Mo . . . you . . . uh . . . wanna go down to the beach?" I stammered.

"Uh . . . um . . . okay," she stammered back.

Three minutes later we were strolling along the unbelievably beautiful beach at Waikiki. Under tropical skies, we took off our shoes and walked on the water's edge, enjoying our good fortune at being in the islands. The moon was enormous, and as the surf rolled in, I realized that what had been friendship was rapidly turning into attraction, at least for me.

I *had* to kiss her, but at the same time I was terrified that she might reject my advances. My stomach churned as I made small talk and thought about kissing my "sister."

"Why not?" I rationalized. "I mean, if millions of young guys all over America find Mo attractive, why can't I? After all, we're not *really* related." We continued walking, came upon a secluded point, stopped, looked out at the sea, and then only at each other. I wanted desperately to ask her if this was okay, but her eyes looked up into mine and answered my question wordlessly.

I kissed her, and the floodgates opened: warm and hard and packed with the kind of osculatory excitement that only teenagers can transmit. It was fantastic, and with the breeze and the trees and the water, the world seemed absolutely perfect. In fact, I remember regretting not making my move *long* ago. Years later, I'd find out that *this* had been Mo's first kiss.

At the same time, however, I had a rush of "What in hell are you doing? This is dangerous" come over me. I think it was mutual, because immediately we both became quiet, perhaps afraid of verbally expressing exactly what it was that we felt for each other. We didn't stay out on the beach for long, but for the rest of my life I'll be glad we went.

The remainder of the trip went smoothly, but something changed that night. From then on, Maureen and I would struggle to forget about what happened that night in Hawaii.

We'd often fail miserably.

11
Wiped Out in Hawaii

I magine this. You're a snow skier with one of the world's greatest slopes all to yourself. No crowds, no lines . . . nothing between you and a mountain of powder.

Or imagine you're seven years old, running amok in Disney World. No crowds, no lines, just rides, food, and fun.

Or imagine you're a really *fat* guy with a buffet at The Sizzler steaming solely for you. No crowds, no lines . . . you get the picture.

That's how I felt on the beach in Hawaii.

When I first heard that the Bradys were gonna pack up and ship off to Hawaii for the filming of a three-part episode, I was excited. When I found out that the episodes called for Greg to hang ten at Oahu's world-famous surf spot, Queen's Beach, I was ecstatic. Hawaii, of course, is home to some of the hottest waves on the planet. Now I, a longtime beach bum, and dude-in-training, would get a chance to show off my skills, complete with camera crew in primo surf that I'd have all to myself.

I was up to my ears in adrenaline.

You remember the story. Greg spends most of his time

in Hawaii surfing, until he's cursed by that evil tiki and wipes out into the treacherous island foam. Is he dead? Tune in next week and find out. It was the "Brady" cliffhanger to end all cliffhangers.

Actually, I didn't give a rat's ass *what* the story was about. All I cared about was hitting the beach. This trip was gonna be a dream come true.

But there *was* a catch. Turns out there was a lot of concern among Paramount's necktie-bedecked higher-ups about me doing my own stunts. The bean counters didn't fully fathom my status as "surf God" and were worried that I might do something silly like . . . oh, I don't know . . . drown.

Anyway, right around the time I was "sex-waxing" my "stick," word trickled downstream that I would be allowed to enter the water and paddle around, but some *other* guy would be hired as my stunt double, and *he'd* do all the actual surfing.

Major bummer!

Hmmm . . . there was no way in hell that I was gonna go along with this nauseating turn of events quietly. Bob Reed may have had his script problems, but I had my pride. However, I had no idea how to battle this obvious case of corporate psychosis. After a great deal of thought, I decided to fall back on the course of action that had served me so well in my youth: I'd simply look the authority figures squarely in the eye and lie like a cheap toupee.

I appealed to the producers shamelessly, inventing stories about how I was legendary in southern California as the recognized leader of the Cowabunga Surf Movement (I made it up). I told them that I was globally ranked in competitive surfing events, and that I could surf Oahu's six-foot surf with a sandwich in one hand and a Marlboro in the other. Basically, I said whatever I thought might actually change their minds.

The producers looked at me as if I were something they'd like to scrape off the bottom of their shoes, but they had no way to disprove my outlandish claims, and because I just plain wouldn't shut up, they eventually caved in, took me at my word, and pointed me toward the beach.

The surf was definitely looking up!

Once again, my budding acting skills and bold-faced lies had served me well. I may not have been able to live up to my self-appointed world-class status, but I *was* a good surfer, and very safe in the water.

Or so I thought. Two weeks later, Oahu's pounding surf would come close to prematurely ending my career—and my life!

Shortly after I'd convinced the powers brokers at Paramount that it would be in the company's best interest to let me surf for myself on screen, I also convinced them that in order to ensure a good-looking on-camera ride, a seven-day Hawaiian test-surf (at their expense) was vitally necessary.

They bought it.

My real-life brothers and I whooped over this bit of good fortune and caught the next plane.

We touched down, checked in, and spent the next week riding every wave and soaking up every bit of sunshine that the Oahu shore could throw at us. Seven days later, the rest of the Bradys arrived and found us sunburnt, waterlogged, shriveled, and happy.

Almost immediately, we got to work, settling in with a meeting that outlined our entire Hawaiian production schedule. It was a typically dull, typically businesslike function, but it *did* get exciting when they told me about how the city of Honolulu was actually going to let us lease Queen's Beach (and all of its waves) for two whole days.

Why is that exciting? Simple. Our "lease" meant that the beach, the ocean, and all of the people in both places would be part of our company. It also guaranteed that "Greg" would spend forty-eight hours as the surf area's "Big Kahuna."

You see, in any halfway-decent surfing spot (and especially in Hawaii), there are *always* more good surfers than good waves. Needless to say, the competition for curls can be cutthroat, and the overcrowding generally assures that most of the best waves pass you by. But now, for two glorious days, *everybody* on a surfboard except for me would be an extra, paid to paddle around and make sure that Greg got the *big* ones. I was thrilled.

Our first day of filming dawned warm, clear, and full of excitement. We all assembled on the beach, ate breakfast, worked on our tans, and went over the breakdown of the day. Our schedule called for some shots of the Bradys on the beach, some swimming, and finally my long-awaited surfathon—not exactly the proverbial day in the salt mines. But before it was over, the salt mines would seem a cinch by comparison.

The grips set up an enormous raft, complete with cameraman, camera, and elaborate braces that held 'em both in place. They set sail. At the same time, I paddled out about a quarter-mile, found the surf line (the spot where the waves break), and started to rehearse.

The conditions were picture-postcard perfect: warm water, blue skies, and surf that was consistent, happening, and breaking at about five feet. With a heightened heartbeat, I took my place among the sea gulls, seaweed, and local surfing extras, waiting anxiously for that all-important first wave. It was heaven—except for one thing.

Our shooting schedule forced us to shoot at low tide. Now, that's normally no big deal, but in Hawaii it can be a nightmare. Oahu's ocean floor is made up not of soft sand but of hard, solid, and often jagged coral. Wipe out at high tide, and there's about six feet between you and the ocean floor; wipe out at *low* tide, and you have as little as eighteen *inches!* You also have big, *big* trouble. The only way you can avoid getting sliced and diced is to fall absolutely flat and skim the water's surface, using your body as a sort of human boogie board. For the first hour, things went great. I was riding waves, cranking bottom turns, pulling off "roller coasters," and finishing with flyaway kickouts. Then it happened.

Guess who wiped out at low tide.

Yep, with cameras rolling, I managed to catch an overhead wave with good shape and started jamming across its wall. Things were getting hot, and I was picking up speed when—

WHAM!!!

A section of the wave closed out, and I flew through the air, careening toward an exposed coral head that was sticking up out of the water by a good two feet, and drooling over its chance to chew me to shreds. A sickening feeling of total helplessness washed over me, and with a heartfelt cry of "SHIIIIIIIIIIT!!!" I sailed toward my doom.

Greg's wipeout was a lot more spontaneous than planned.

Back on the beach, they'd seen the fall, noticed my head tearing toward the jagged coral, and seen me disappear under the wave's white-water. They panicked, and at once my dad (who was watching from the beach), the camera guys, the lifeguards, and a handful of gawkers were barreling into the surf, determined (I suppose) to scoop up whatever was left of me and see that it got a proper burial. The cameraman continued to film.

Fortunately, I *hadn't* become fish food. As I fell, the top half of the wave broke over me, and I tucked, using its force to turn myself completely around. I was *still* on a coral collision course, but now, thanks to luck, reflexes, and the forces of nature, my *head* was spared.

My *feet,* however got turned into hamburger meat.

Once I realized that I wasn't dead, I meekly bobbed up to the surface and waved my arms to signal the beach that I was okay.

Relieved, everyone calmed down, and it wasn't long before the multitudinous cries of happiness turned into taunts of "I told you so!"

In short, things were back to normal, and the *worst* part

of the whole thing was that it cut short my fantasy day in the surf.

Coulda been a *lot* worse.

A postscript: When we got back to L.A., the network took one look at Greg's wipeout and got nervous about the footage being "too frightening for the nature of the show." However, after some debate, the shot was indeed included.

Twenty years later, I figure I've wiped out on syndicated worldwide reruns about thirty-seven hundred times, and the scene *still* scares the hell out of me every time I see it.

You don't think there was anything to that Curse of the Tiki, do you?

12
A-Sailing
We Won't Go

$\mathbb{S}$ hortly after fishing Greg out of the Pacific, the Bradys were up, working, and back on schedule once more. We were shooting a three part episode, and Paramount wanted to make sure that our viewers knew we were actually in Hawaii not just faking it on a soundstage somewhere. Therefore, the Brady Bunch spent almost all of their time in Hawaii engaging in outdoor activities and wandering through the lush tropical scenery of Oahu.

One particular run-in with the local seascape left us soggy, shaken, and just plain scared.

It started when the Bradys, eager to enjoy the gorgeous Hawaiian waters, loaded themselves into an outrigger (it's a sort of extra-long seafaring canoe) and paddled out into the Hawaiian surf. The script called for us to row out, catch a wave, and ride it toward shore. The locals do it all the time and make it look easy, but of course we Bradys lacked their experience and coordination—and in the case of Susan Olsen, the ability to swim.

The floating camera crew. (Courtesy Sherwood Schwartz)

We boarded our craft shakily, but after several moments we actually seemed to have it almost under control. At about this time, a second outrigger, full of cameramen, grips, and professional paddlers floated up next to us and began filming our pathetic first cracks at group seamanship. Little did they know, the most exciting scene they'd film that day wouldn't be scripted, or expected. Instead, carelessness, poor judgment, and lack of sea savvy would combine to ambush us all.

First of all, *none* of us were wearing life jackets. We had discussed donning them, but our director decided that they were big, bulky, and an ugly shade of orange. Worst of all, they'd hide the girls' pretty Hawaiian shirts. We quickly forsook safety in favor of a "beauty shot."

Next, it was time for both outriggers (camera guys in one, nine Bradys in the other) to paddle out where the waves were breaking, turn around, catch a big one, and film the Bradys riding toward shore, smiling broad Brady smiles and having the time of their lives.

Yeah, sure. If you've ever gone canoeing, you know that trying to get *two* novice sailors to row a boat with some degree of coordination is tough. Try and imagine getting *nine* novice oars in sync. Does the word "nightmare" come to mind?

The better part of an hour passed as we Bradys flailed about spastically at sea. We drifted, missed waves, and even with the Hawaiian paddlers in the next boat yelling instructions at us, we managed to always remain pointed in the wrong direction. Basically, we Bradys were sweaty, exhausted, and proved ourselves to be bona fide landlubbers.

Finally, somewhere above Hawaii, the spirit of King Kamehameha must have looked down upon us and decided to end our misery. I say that because all of a sudden, from out of nowhere, a wave began to crest and pick up speed, and as it swelled toward our outrigger, all nine of us got excited. We had managed to get ourselves pointed in the *right* direction, with oars at the ready, in perfect position.

We were actually going to catch a wave!

The wave loomed over us. We paddled. We caught it. We smiled for the camera. We were rammed by the camera

In real life, we weren't *nearly* this coordinated.
(© Paramount Pictures)

Robert Reed on The Golf Cart Races

While we were shooting "The Brady Bunch," I was also working on "Mannix" a lot, and so I'd have to tool around the Paramount lot in a golf cart, back and forth, from set to set, and to the gym every once in a while, and I'd meet a lot of people doing that. Somehow, it came to pass that I threw a weekly party in my dressing room. So I brought in booze and stuff, and whoever wanted to drop by would drop by. Sometimes twenty, thirty, forty people would show up. It was *great* fun, and we always seemed to end up boffing secretaries ... and the worst ones too.

Anyway, we'd carry on, and the guards all knew us and were very indulgent, until one night we took the studios' golf carts and raced around the lot. And I remember we drove down under one of the sets and into an area that was used for prop storage. I mean, you could just *drive* down there and—well, I *still*, to this day, have things up in my storeroom that I stole from there. In fact, there was a memo that came out the next day about stealing on the lot. I think they knew who did it.

So we were flooring these little golf carts, and racing around the lot, and we hit the western street of the "Bonanza" set, and we hit that dirt road, screaming and hollering, and singing and laughing. There were six of us in each golf cart, and we all lost traction and flipped the damn things over. And one of the girls got hurt—nothing too serious, abrasions and stuff, but it was enough to sober us up.

We were stupid and silly, but it *was* fun. Anyway, next day there came another memo that said "From now on, all golf carts will be locked up," and that edict exists to this day. That kinda put a pall on the parties for a while.

---

guys' boat. Our stern started sinking, and we capsized.

Susan Olsen remembered it like this.

"You'll notice when you see the episode that there are all these smiling faces in the outrigger, except for Florence and I, who are scowling. After we got rammed, the wave washed over us, and our part of the boat ended up underwater. I was hanging on to the side, and Florence was hanging on by her ankles. Then just at the point where I thought to myself 'I can't hang on anymore' Florence grabbed me."

Florence kicked in "all I could think of was 'Hang on to Susie,' and the next thing I knew I was hanging upside down under the boat, and my eyelashes fell off.

"And then they made us do it again!"

So we did, this time smiling plastic smiles and grumbling all the way to shore.

13
Dating Your Mom

Robert Reed was a lot less comfortable doing the bedroom scenes than I was, so I'd slide up next to him and use "Carol" to make him comfortable. And I think it worked, because afterward he'd always come up with a racy comment intimating that I'd gotten him really horny. I liked that. I liked that a lot.

—Florence Henderson

Most everybody thinks of Florence Henderson as the quintessential television mom, and that vaguely oedipal association seems to have successfully inhibited the American public from ever realizing what a totally white-hot babe she really is. I mean, just once put the apron and the six kids out of your mind and take a good long look at her in *that way*. You'll see what I mean.

On top of all that, Florence is sharp, sassy, and energetic, with a very adult sense of humor that seems to fall somewhere between Benny Hill and Andrew Dice Clay.

To put a woman like that in close daily proximity to a normally sex-obsessed teenage guy is to drive that poor young man wild. At least that's what happened to me. Almost from day one, my feelings toward Florence were more carnal than maternal. I can remember that even as we Bradys did our very first photo shoot together, her somewhat sweaty sense of humor took me by surprise, then held me entranced.

85

Posing in the park.
(© Paramount Pictures)

Under a huge shade tree in a Santa Monica park, all nine of us were posing for hokey, overly cute group shots and being choreographed into all sorts of saccharine poses. One of the worst featured the Brady girls and some enormous prop lollipops. Florence remarked that they were so big it would take about four hours to finish them. At which point I, neglecting to bite my tongue, and with some energetic mincing about, said, "Yeah, and four hours is a long time to suck on *anything*."

My joke was met with dead silence and uncomfortable stares by almost everyone—everyone, that is, except Florence. She simply rolled her eyes, laughed heartily, and said, "Not for me it isn't." From then on we just somehow seemed to click.

From that point on Florence never wavered in her friendship, and I did what any young guy might: I got a case of the hots for my "mom." It finally got so intense that one day I just couldn't control myself anymore and wound up asking her out.

Amazingly, she accepted.

Yeah, I know it struck me as completely weird too. I was thrilled to have successfully hit on Florence Henderson, but absolutely terrified about having to look cool on a grown-up date.

Basically, I had no concept of what grown-ups actually *did* when they went out on dates, and preparing for it presented me with all sorts of problems. First, I was still three months shy of my sixteenth birthday, which meant that I was also three months shy of having a driver's license, which in Los Angeles, meant that I had about as much freedom as a chained-up dog.

I did, however, have a learner's permit, which allowed me to drive legally as long as a licensed driver, over the age of twenty-five came along with me. "Oh, great," I thought, "when I pick up my TV mom for our date, I'll just be sure and have my *real* mom riding shotgun in the backseat."

Then a stroke of brilliance hit me, and I bounced it off my brother Craig. We made a deal that if he let me illegally drive his car solo on my date, I'd wash and wax the monster twice a week for a month. I got the idea from a Brady script. We haggled a little and spit-shook on it. Seemed fair.

With my wheels finally figured out, it was time to decide where to take the fair maiden Florence. I asked around on the Paramount lot, and after collecting a *lot* of advice, most of it awful, settled on L.A.'s most extra-double-swanky nightclub, the legendary Coconut Grove. I found out that a Mediterranean Crooner named Rouvan (the name would better suit a Japanese monster than a singer) would be performing there soon, ran the idea past Florence, and we had ourselves a date.

In the ensuing days, I had what seemed like an endless parade of details to take care of. There were tickets to buy, a new sport coat and tie to purchase (I was going all out), cash to dig up (I had no credit cards), colognes to try out, and a *hundred* other odds and ends to attend to. I wanted to leave *nothing* to chance. The goal was to stay calm and never let Florence know that I had absolutely *no* idea what I was doing.

I ran through my things-to-do list one item at a time, and it wasn't long before I was almost ready to go. I say "almost" because I still had to learn how to drive my brother's car: a humongous, smoke-belching, gas-guzzling, rubber-burning, modified Formula 400 Pontiac Firebird.

I learned to drive a stick shift while working on a ranch. However on the street I had only ever driven our boxy, boring family Buick, which bore almost *no* resemblance to my brother's cruise missile. His was one of those mid-sixties American sports cars on a muscle trip, the kind of car that teenage guys love and insurance companies hate. The car came out of the factory begging for speeding tickets, but my brother had seen to it that whatever power GM had installed in his baby was *doubled* with some nifty (albeit insane) engine modifications.

The car was difficult to operate for the noninitiated, and difficult to understand for the nonpsychotic. Its *huge* engine had been further souped up at the hands of my grease-monkey brother; its *factory* clutch had been ripped out and replaced with a custom shift-lever, that operated a two-thousand-pound *racing* clutch. Needless to say, this made changing gears a *major* task, especially for a kinda skinny 15-year-old kid. Just to get the thing out of reverse, I'd have to press my back against the seat, stiffen my arms against the steering wheel, and push down on the clutch pedal like holy hell. Still, I was determined, and after a half-hour lesson, and a half-hour warning that if I scratched his car, my brother would disembowel me, I was all set to go.

On the night of my date it came time for me to get cleaned up, dressed up, look my folks squarely in the eye, and lie. My brother and I both knew there was no way in the *world* my parents would let me drive his metal beast, so we came up with a story: we told my overly trusting parents that Craig would drive me to Florence's apartment, Florence would drive from there, and that Craig would pick me up later in the evening. Of course in reality, our plans were completely different. I just dropped my brother off at a friend's house, leaving him to find his own way home, then sped toward Florence's place with adrenaline coursing mightily through every single one of my veins.

Luckily, the drive to her apartment went smoothly. I got to the gate, rang for my date, waited nervously in the lobby for her to come down, made small talk with the doorman, heard my name, looked up, and was stunned.

Florence had arrived in the lobby and looked absolutely beautiful—sexy, sophisticated, and not at all like Carol Brady. As she stood shimmering in chiffon, I stood stammering in the doorway, dumbstruck by the fact that this amazing creature had actually consented to a date with me. Still, as my teenager's sense of cockiness overrode my genuine astonishment, I came to the conclusion that for me to land a babe like *this*, I must be pretty hot stuff too! I convinced myself that Florence had gotten all dolled up just to impress me, and we headed toward my brother's car.

"Oh, this is . . . uh . . . nice," Florence said, half-smiling at my brother Craig's creation. "I've never . . . uh . . . seen anything quite like it."

"Why, thank you, Florence!" I beamed, still too naive to accurately read between the lines.

I suavely opened her door, helped her in, ran around to the other side, got in, turned the ignition, stiffly shifted into reverse, and promptly backed the car into a wall. It was the rear retaining wall of Florence's building. Still trying to keep cool, I sputtered out, "It's . . . uh . . . no problem. I'll just take a quick look-see."

Happily, while I *had* put a small hole in the building's cinderblock wall, I hadn't damaged my brother's roadhog in the least, thus sparing my entrails. I jumped back into the car, reassured Florence that there was nothing to worry about (I don't think she believed me), and sped off. I was still feeling pretty good . . . except I noticed that I had started to sweat, profusely.

We drove to the Grove, watched a valet wrestle with the

car, and went inside. Since I'd never before been any place as ornate as the Coconut Grove, my immediate thought was "Wow!"; my second, "Good choice"; and my third, "Oh my God, this is gonna be expensive!" Still, I had the prettiest date in the place, and cast aside my monetary concerns in favor of just plain having a great time.

At the door we were immediately met by a slick-haired, nose-in-the-air, tuxedo-clad "captain." Having no experience in frequenting swanky supper clubs, I had the mistaken impression that since I had bought our tickets in advance, we would simply pick them up at the door, find our assigned seats, eat, drink, and be merry. Now, however, we were faced with this frowning guy who asked for my reservation. I still didn't understand what was going on, and I knew that the room was sold out, but felt confident that we'd get a nice table. I mean, I *had* phoned in my reservation over a week ago. So I smiled, gave the guy my name, and Florence and I were promptly and courteously escorted to the back corner of the room . . . behind a pole.

I wanted to die, and wasn't even sure what had just transpired. In my mind, I couldn't understand how. We'd arrived early, with plenty of good tables still unoccupied, but were seated in these awful nosebleed/binocular seats (that even Bob Uecker would've turned down). My disappointment must have showed, because Florence suggested, quite sweetly, that if I wanted better seats, I might try talking to the captain again, perhaps even offering him a little gratuity.

"Good idea," I replied, kicking myself for not knowing enough to think of that *myself*. It made perfect sense. "Of course," I thought. "Tip the man—grease his palm." I'd seen James Bond do it a hundred times, and now it was my turn. But . . . oh, *shit* . . . how much? The biggest tip I had *ever* given *anyone* up until now was a buck, and I couldn't ask Florence, because that might tip her off to the fact that I was completely clueless.

Not wanting to take *any* chances, I dug into my wallet, pulled out *three* one-dollar bills, folded them up, clutched them between thumb and forefinger "Bond style," and slipped them to the captain, while politely asking if there might not be an available table somewhat closer to the stage. To this day I don't know if he just didn't bother to count his cash or if he just somehow understood my predicament; but he smiled, nodded, and promptly moved us to a *much* better location.

I was thrilled, so thrilled that I barely noticed that the crowd was now staring at the two of us, and quite obviously wondering why in the world Carol Brady would date Greg. As we started crisscrossing through the club toward our new, improved seats, the stares seemed to intensify; but for her part, Florence just smiled and calmly went along with the program.

Of our evening on the town, Florence told me that "I could tell you were *very* nervous, and trying to make sure that every last detail was absolutely perfect, but at the same time I didn't want to take over. It was more fun just watching you try and take charge of the evening."

The rest of the evening went pretty well. Dinner was good, and the show was . . . well, strange. Rouvan turned out to be a sort of poor man's Enrico Caruso, with a huge, pompous voice that belted out songs like "Laugh, Clown, Laugh" with a vocal ferocity that would make even Robert Goulet cringe. Anyway, we talked about singers (good ones *and* Rouvan), songs, and traveling, and I confided to her that I wanted someday to sing and do my *own* shows. She was very encouraging.

Afterward, we piled back into Craig's Formula Firebird and tore out toward home. I ground a few gears, and stalled once at a red light while fighting with its musclebound clutch; but no matter, because back at Florence's place, she told me that she'd had a wonderful time.

I'm forever grateful to Florence, because even though she was on to my secret that evening, she never let me know. In my mind, I had taken on all the potential disasters of our date and kicked 'em in the ass.

We said goodbye, Florence let me give her a kiss good-night (no tongue, but nice), and I drew my first deep breath in what seemed like hours.

I went home feeling like a *major* stud.

Twenty years later, Florence and I talked about our escapade over a long, long, long lunch, where she spilled this quote: "We went from liking each other to having a crush on each other and you were *always* on the make with me. I had to worry about that. You were really cute, and I was tempted a few times. I think we're lucky Carol never slept with Greg, but . . . uh . . . it coulda been, coulda been."

I went home feeling like a *major* stud . . . again.

14
Guess Who's Guesting

It's funny, but when I think of "The Brady Bunch," I never think of guest stars, I just think of us.
                                        —Florence Henderson

While most people would probably agree with Florence's point of view, there's no way this book could be considered complete without giving a once-over to the "Brady Bunch" guest list. Guest stars show up on a *lot* of the "Brady" episodes that have attained fan-favorite status, and I'm asked about them constantly. People just naturally seem to assume that any time a guest star showed up in our "Brady Bunch" living room, we'd become fast friends, bosom buddies, and pals for life. That, I'm sorry to say, was *never* the case. Hectic shooting schedules and lack of free time made socializing with our guests nearly impossible.

Knight meets Jones.
(© Capital Cities/ABC, Inc.)

That's not to say we didn't give it our best shot. *Whenever* a sports star would appear on the show, Chris, Mike, and I would make a beeline toward them and start hounding them until they'd consent to playing ball with us or at least offer up a coupla training tips. Wes Parker, Don Drysdale, and Deacon Jones *all* went home exhausted from our triple-teaming. But the biggest sporting thrill we ever had on set, was to meet and work with NY Jets' quarterback Joe Namath.

In 1973 "Broadway Joe" was something much larger than just a football hero. With his awards, personal mystique, mountains of press, and high-profile luxury life-style, he had become a bona fide superstar. The anticipation of his visit to our set had all of us *really* excited. We *expected* an entourage; we expected babes draped on each arm with spares following behind; we expected cheerleaders to do cartwheels over his every move. But none of that happened.

What we *did* get was a genuinely nice, genuinely down-to-earth guy, who wasn't at all flashy, wasn't *nearly* as slick as we'd assumed, and wasn't nearly the invincible superjock we'd envisioned. Clobbered through season after season of abuse and injury, Joe's legendarily wobbly knees were obviously causing him an incredible amount of pain. Ann B. Davis remembers that she was "crazy about the guy and had a bit of

Lookinland meets Namath.
(© Capital Cities/ABC, Inc.)

(© 1991 Capital Cities/ABC, Inc.)

a crush on him too" but that when he actually showed up, she just "felt sorry for the man, because he could barely walk."

Florence, on the other hand, made no bones about her infatuation with the handsome Number 12. She was simply nuts about the guy, and her behavior on the set during his visit made that fact crystal clear. All week long she flirted with Joe, hugged him, teased him, and finally—Well, maybe I should let *her* tell it.

"All right, I was crazy about Joe Namath," Florence confessed. "And I remember his last scene took place in the fake driveway, where Joe was supposed to say goodbye to all the Bradys. So with the cameras rolling, he said goodbye to the kids, and to Mike, and to Alice, but when he got to me, I jumped up on him, wrapped my thighs around his waist, and said, 'Take me. Take me with you, Joe. I can't stand this family anymore.' And he just said, 'Sure, Mrs. Brady,' and carried me off the set."

Turns out, Flo wasn't the only Brady woman to fall for a guest star. While Marcia Brady's dream of dreams was to someday become *Mrs*. Desi Arnaz, Jr., Maureen McCormick may have had similar aspirations. She remembers that even as they met, she felt sparks; and while their age difference loomed large enough to effectively keep them apart in 1970 (Maureen was only thirteen at the time), it proved a much less formidable obstacle several years later, when she and Desi would meet again, rekindle those sparks, and begin dating.

I should probably add that Davy Jones, Marcia's only other celebrity flame, didn't quite have the same effect on Maureen. "He was veeeeeery nice," Mo told me, "but there were no sparks . . . no sparks." That's got to come as a shock to the "Brady" fans who *still*, even to this day, ask me whether or not anything romantic ever blossomed between the blondest Brady and the shortest Monkee.

However, the vast majority of "Brady" guest-star stories aren't romantic in nature. For example, when Imogene Coca showed up to play Carol's eccentric aunt Jenny, we were amazed to find that she was *extremely* shy. I'm not talking demure-introspective shy, I'm talking more along the lines of hide-under-the-table shy. I mean, here was this *legendary* comedienne, who made her living with her hundreds of bigger-than-life, over-the-top comic characterizations; yet every moment that she's not on camera, she's in a corner or behind a set, sitting all alone, terrified that some-

"Nice, but no sparks."
(© 1991 Capital Cities/ABC, Inc.)

Imogene Coca and Florence Henderson.
(© 1991 Capital Cities/ABC, Inc.)

one might actually want to speak with her.

Of course, whenever the lights came up and the cameras rolled, she'd burst forward, full of the broad bravado that breathes such incredible comic energy into whatever role she plays. That week, I learned a lot about physical comedy and pacing simply by watching her work.

On the flip side of the coin, Jim Backus was sociable, talkative, and spent his visits with us Bradys sounding an awful lot like his previous television incarnation Thurston Howell III. Mr. Backus prided himself on his business acumen, and he'd dispense financial advice to anyone who'd listen, even us kids. "Barry," he'd say, "mark my words. Before long, the price of gas is going to skyrocket, right up past [a then *unheard*-of] one dollar a gallon. Get into it now, and you could do very well for yourself." That was in 1974. And I, employing my own keen sense of business savvy, ignored his advice completely.

I get a headache every time I think about that.

Anyway, to change the subject and spare myself a

Schwartz, Williams, and "Who *is* that asshole?"

migraine, I want to mention that not *all* of the celebrities who hung around the "Brady Bunch" set actually appeared in an episode. For example, right around the time when Nelson Rockefeller was becoming (for better or worse) a major political figure in the United States, he attempted to soften up his image by having some publicity pictures taken, right in the middle of the "Brady Bunch" set. To be honest with you, the chance to meet a New York politician didn't mean much to this California Kid (I was a lot more impressed with Wes Parker), so I asked Lloyd Schwartz to recap Nelson's visit:

"Rockefeller was governor of New York at the time, and when he came to the set, he had no idea of what anybody actually *did*. And so, in an attempt to make sure he didn't offend anyone 'important,' he was glad-handing *everybody*. And finally he went over to one of our grips, who was just sort of standing near a reflector drinking coffee, and he says to the guy, '*You* are doing a real good job, a helluva job—keep it up, keep it up.' So then the grip comes over to me and says, 'Who the fuck *is* that asshole?'"

Rockefeller was a big man politically, but he was by no

Brady Bunch meets Kissinger Klan. (Barry Williams)

means the most powerful politician to visit the synthetic grass and orange Formica of the Brady homestead. That honor goes to Henry Kissinger. This time I *was* impressed, but I wasn't sure why. Lloyd Schwartz once again tells the story:

"He was secretary of state, and just beginning to hit his stride as this sort of huge celebrity, so when he hit the stage, the place went nuts, absolutely nuts. The place was crawling with Secret Service types. And I remember one of them was trying his best to hit on our makeup girl. And so I went over to Dr. Kissinger and I said, 'Uh, sir, your Secret Service guy is putting the moves on our makeup girl, and I think he's succeeding.' With which Dr. Kissinger turned to me, smiled, and said, 'He's been taking lessons from the master—I taught him everything he knows.'"

By now you *must* have asked yourself, "Why on earth would Henry Kissinger go out of his way to visit 'The Brady Bunch'?" The answer, quite simply, is that he was trying to impress his daughter. She was a big "Brady" fan, and when she asked her father if he might arrange for her to meet us, he simply made a phone call, blew off an afternoon full of globally significant meetings, and arranged for the visit. I still find it nothing short of amazing that a man who was arguably the single most powerful politician in the world needed "The Brady Bunch" to impress his kid—sort of an eerie commentary on the power of the tube and its signifi-

Me and "Hank."
(Barry Williams)

cance in the lives of American children.

An even more blatant example of the egregiously potent power of "The Bunch" came when astronaut James McDivitt appeared on the show in a cameo role. McDivitt had piloted both NASA's Gemini 4 and Apollo 9 missions, and had been to the *moon*, for chrissake; but when he got to our set, the first words out of his mouth were "Boy, being on 'The Brady Bunch' is gonna make me a *hero* at my house."

Scary, very scary.

15
Chlorine and Candlelight

After our Hawaiian interlude, I got *really* nuts about Maureen. Of course that's not unique (millions of pubescent American boys shared my same burning yearning), but I had an advantage: *I* knew her; I liked her; and I was at all times within groping distance. Best of all, for a while, *she* was nuts about *me* too!

So nuts that we'd habitually sneak off the "Brady" set and spend camera breaks lip-locked in my dressing room.

So nuts that much to the chagrin of the producers, you can often see Greg and Marcia making eyes at one another in episodes of "The Brady Bunch."

So nuts that our overheated behavior would at times actually cause shooting delays on the set.

I asked Lloyd Schwartz for an example, and he jumped at the chance to rat me out.

"Oh, this is great. Early on, I was presented with the following problem: the libido among the six kids was showing

"... no, I'm just happy to see her."
(Michael Ochs Archives/Venice, CA)

signs that it might one day become . . . uh . . . a problem. So I made up, and Barry, you bought for a while, this whole sales pitch that went like, 'Yeah, Maureen sure is beautiful, but did you ever notice how many really attractive friends she has? And wouldn't it be better to have her introduce you to *all* of them instead of just being with her?' That kept you guys apart for a little while, but then of course the whole thing blew up in Hawaii.

"So now we're back in L.A., and I'm directing an episode called 'Room At The Top.' And there's this scene where you're supposed to come into the girls' room, sit on the bed with Maureen, and talk to her about moving into the attic. At at the end of it, Maureen was supposed to turn to you, hug you, and say something like, 'Oh, you're such a good brother.'

"Now at this point, you two were crazy about each other, and every time you came in and sat next to Maureen, the scene became *very* romantic. I mean, this was supposed to be Greg and Marcia, brother and sister, and you were panting all over each other. Anyway, finally, after the thirteenth take, I had you make a fist and put your hand in between you and

Maureen. Thankfully, that physical barrier let us get through the scene without melting the camera lens."

We got through that scene, but *I* was starting to get paranoid. That's because *everywhere*, it seemed, there was someone intent on keeping the youthful hormonal entanglement between Maureen and me from getting too friendly. Lloyd certainly did his part; and on one particularly frustrating occasion, so did my real-life dad.

It all started with a simple Friday-night visit. Maureen came over to my house for an innocent "dinner with my folks"—at least that's what I told her. I, on the other hand, being young, male, and nuts about the girl, had more exciting activities in mind.

7:00 P.M.: I sprang my plan into action at dinner. A little flirting, eye contact, hand contact, foot contact, and the groundwork was firmly in place.

7:58 P.M.: My mom was frantically clearing the dinner plates as Dad fiddled with the rabbit ears on the living room TV. "Two minutes to showtime!" he bellowed gleefully, alerting the world to the fact that it's nearly "Brady" time.

"Uh . . . Mo brought her swimsuit . . . I think we're gonna skip the show and take a dip in the pool instead," I said, smiling, hoping my virtuous look might mask my ulterior intentions and effectively snow both the folks *and* Maureen.

We changed into our bathing suits, hit poolside, jumped in, and my already overstimulated hormones ran amok. Maureen glistened in the moonlight, and as those huge blue eyes of hers locked onto mine, I stood transfixed, frozen breathlessly amid the chlorine and the inflatable toys. Steam was rising off my swimsuit.

It was now past 8:30, and while "The Brady Bunch" was over, I knew that my folks wouldn't budge from their La-Z-Boys until at *least* the end of "Love, American Style," and that was two and a half hours away. It was time to make my move.

Still wrapped in beach towels, I asked Maureen if she wanted to go to my room and see my new stereo. I'm not sure if she knew my real motives, but she said yes.

"I have a great new album I want Mo to hear," I told my mom, trying hard to keep my face straight.

"That's nice," she replied unsuspectingly. "Have fun."

I grinned, stifled a laugh, and led Mo to my bedroom.

I should mention that I really *did* have a new stereo system to show Mo. It was state of the art in 1973 (garbage today), and—aside from that *other* all-consuming pubescent preoccupation—my most cherished indulgence.

We entered my bedroom a bit uneasily, and Mo sat down, I cranked up the sound system *and* then joined her on the extremely groovy three-by-five-foot foam-filled throw pillows that I had scattered about my floor for lounging purposes. Soon, romantic hits like Elton John's "Your Song" and "Daniel" began blasting from my room at a volume easily capable of repelling parents and drowning out any noise that might begin emanating from within my thin plasterboard walls. I had stacked several romantic albums onto my automatic record changer—Jim Croce; Blood, Sweat and Tears; Bread (that one was a killer)—and as each one dropped onto the turntable, Maureen and I got closer . . . much closer . . . much, *much* closer.

Finally, it was time to haul out the big gun. No, I'm not speaking euphemistically about my anatomy, I simply mean that in the hope that Maureen and I might actually . . . uh . . . curl each other's toes, I peeled the shrinkwrap off the granddaddy of all seduction discs. Yes, *Stone Gon'* by Barry White dropped onto my turntable, and it served its purpose perfectly . . . almost.

Turns out that Barry White and his trademark narrative made his way from my turntable, out my speakers, through my bedroom walls, down the hallway, into the living room, over an easy chair, and into the ears of my dad. Nobody's fool, he caught onto my plot immediately and headed toward my room.

Meanwhile, back in the boudoir, Maureen and I were

blissfully (though not blissfully enough for *me*) unaware of our impending doom.

Then it hit. Actually, *he* hit—my door: three pounding resounding booms, followed by a terse statement about my mom wanting to see us right away. The force of his voice cut right through Mr. White's aural sex, and filled me first with surprise, then anger, then fear.

Immediately, we scrambled about the room, rebuttoned and rezipped what we'd undone, restraightened what we had loosened, and, glowing sweatily, made our way to the living room, trying our best to look *really* innocent.

My dad glared at us under a stern, knowing brow; but as it turned out, my mom really *did* want to see us. Dessert was ready.

It's not often that strawberry shortcake rates inferior on the sensory pleasure scale, but in this case it was definitely less than satisfying.

I was frustrated but undaunted. I had lost one opportunity, but more would follow.

Stay tuned.

16
Fear and Loathing at the Bradys'

ne of the toughest obstacles to overcome as a kid actor is getting the various and multitudinous adults that you work with every day to treat you like a human being. I guess it's simply easier for the producers, directors, and assistants to think of you as an object and speak to you condescendingly, as if you're some sort of miniature robot, awaiting their instructions on how to behave. Even amid the usually supportive, caring confines of the "Brady Bunch" set, this problem was not uncommon—and never more apparent than with our most frequent director, Oscar Rudolph.

Don't get me wrong—Oscar was a pleasant, truly likable older gentleman, with a round, ruddy face, a hearty laugh, and a history of credits that extended back to the DeMille days. Unfortunately, he *also* had an annoying habit of trying to maintain absolute control over everything in his path. While preparing to film a scene, he'd supervise the lighting guys, bother the cameramen, and when we were finally ready to shoot, he'd give in to his anal-retentive obsessive compulsion by trying to completely manipulate the performances of us kids.

"UP, UP, UP!!" he'd yell before each take, encouraging us to open our eyes wider, grin bigger, and exude manic amounts of energy. As a result, the Brady kids sometimes spend whole episodes bouncing around like they've had *way* too much coffee. "UP, UP, UP!" he'd yell again; and just when your energy level was soaring through the roof, he'd roll camera and spend the entire take getting even *more* involved in your performance.

Oscar Rudolph wasn't a man who could simply sit in his director's chair and observe your performance. In *his* mind, that would be leaving far too much to chance. Instead, this rotund gentleman would squat just underneath the camera lens, and proceed to "act" our scene along with us, throwing every bit of his "up-up-up" philosophy into his performance. His eyes would get buggy and wide, his wooly eyebrows would rise up until they'd nearly met with his receded hairline; but most memorable of all was his grin. Always, he'd slap this *huge* goofy grin across his face, and as he'd lip-synch the lines with us, his thick pink tongue always seemed to be protruding and retracting lizard-style.

We Brady kids did our best not to laugh.

What's less apparent, is the underlying message. Mr. Rudolph's misguided manipulations weren't so much based on his ideas of good television as they were based on his belief that we kids were simply incapable of understanding how to behave in any given scripted context. We were perceived as objects to be fed, watered, and told what to do.

The degree to which each of us kids was "objectified" ran in reverse order of age. I was the oldest, and I was patronized, but I never came close to experiencing what the younger kids had to put up with. Susan Olsen told me about it:

"I really resented being treated as an object, and *most* of the adults that worked with us respected us as people who were doing a job and being professional, and they were good with us. But some people refused to acknowledge the fact that kids could be communicated with. Y'know, they'd be surprised when other crew members would speak to us in the same manner they'd speak to an adult.

"But when I was at work I was a worker. I didn't want to be talked down to. I didn't want to be treated with less respect than anybody else, and what Oscar would do if he wanted me to move somewhere on the set, instead of saying, 'Okay, Susie, can you take three steps left?' or whatever, he'd just pick me up and move me. I can still remember his thumbs in my armpits. Even *then* I remember thinking, 'He doesn't do that to *Florence*.' One time, when he didn't like the shirt that wardrobe had put me in, he started taking my shirt off, just exactly like I was a little mannequin or something."

Mr. Rudolph's penchant for intrusive control came to a head when he attempted to give direction to . . . a mouse. We were filming an episode in our second year entitled "The Impractical Joker." The plot was loosely based around Jan, who tries to be funny by hiding Greg's school-science-project mouse, only to have the little white vermin get loose in the process.

It came time to shoot the rodent's big scene, and Mr. Rudolph had it all mapped out. The mouse was to enter the Brady living room, give a winsome look into camera, pause, turn left, and exit into the kitchen. The mouse had other ideas.

Wandering aimlessly about the set and completely ignoring Oscar's direction, the mouse soon had Mr. Rudolph's brow furrowed and the top of his head turning red. Still determined to get the shot *exactly* as he'd envisioned, Mr. Rudolph got personally involved, coaching the mouse with directions of "C'mon, mousey. . . . C'm'ere, mousey. . . . This way, mousey. . . . Up, *up,* UP. . . . Now pause. . . . Now go again." Robert Reed, who was watching the goings-on with raised eyebrows, commented, "My God, the man is giving acting lessons to a mouse!"

But Oscar Rudolph wasn't the only presence on the set

that drove the Brady kids crazy. For example, Susan Olsen also had a tough time with Howard Leeds, our show's producer. What you've got to understand is that Howard is a *wonderful* character, and the classic, stereotypical Hollywood producer. Handsome, funny, swank, silver-haired, and stylish, he could usually be found with a babe on each arm and his shirts unbuttoned to the navel, showing off six or eight gaudy gold chains. Essentially, he acted shallow, insincere, arrogant, and I admired him tremendously.

For all his flash and glitter, however, Howard Leeds could not for the life of him relate to the younger kids. On more than one occasion that drove Susan Olsen batty.

"Howard Leeds wanted to change things," she remembered. "He wasn't happy with my hair color. He wasn't happy with anything about me, and made my life kind of miserable for a while. I generally refer to him these days as 'Howard the Dick.'

"I remember he was always trying to tell me how to do my lines, and then I'd go on the set, do what he'd told me, and end up sounding like a cocktail waitress. And of course the director would look at me like I was crazy and say, 'No, Susan, don't do it like *that*.' So I was getting confused with the mixed messages.

"I also remember when I first realized that he didn't like me. I went running up to him with my little hair curl-things doinging away as I ran, and when I caught him I said, 'Hi, Mithter

**Sherwood Schwartz
and Howard Leeds,
April 1971.**
(© Karen Lipscomb)

Maureen McCormick on the Dressing-Room Make-Out Session

I remember toward the end of the series, Barry and I were in his dressing room, which was *really* just this tiny little trailer that they'd parked next to the "Brady Bunch" set. And we were on the floor, kissing, making out, and it was so funny. I mean, just think about it: there we were in this little trailer on stage 5, and right outside were all of our parents and our teachers, not to mention the cast and crew, and we were in there making out with the door *locked,* and our teacher, Frances Whitfield came and knocked on the door and said something like "Uh, hellooooo," and they were looking for one of us, and we actually said—with the door locked, mind you "Oh, Okay, we'll be right there, we're just ... uh ... talking."

Then I remember Karen Lookinland (Michael's mother) coming to the door and knocking for us too, harder, and it really struck me as strange, having to hide like that.

But good for *us.*

Leeds!!!' probably getting spit all over him. And then he said to me 'Uh, hi, pussycat. Listen, when you smile on camera, don't ever squish your eyes up because it makes you look *really* ugly.' And I was like crushed, and walked away thinking, 'Well, he sure doesn't like *me.*'"

Knowing Howard, I'm certain he had a much different intention behind his remarks, and thought, in his bull-in-a-china-shop way, that he was being supportive.

17
One Toke Over the Line

ctors who work in series television are rarely afforded the luxury of an official day off. Instead, the studio puts you "on hold." What that means is that even though your name is not on the day's shooting schedule, you *must* be available to come into the studio at a moment's notice, just in case. During the course of "The Brady Bunch," I was often put on hold. However, throughout all those "hold days," I was actually only called in to work twice. That was once too often.

The Bradys were in their fourth year of production, and at seventeen I had become physically adult, but remained emotionally immature and adolescent. One particularly gorgeous day in the summer of '72, I found myself on hold, and bored, until I was paid an unexpected visit by that same bunch of miscreants that had, in younger years, populated my brothers' "gang." You'll recall that these are the same wayward souls that had previously introduced me to girlie mags, cigarettes, bee stings, and the cumulative effects of chugalugged Kamchatka.

Times had changed, and the vice of the day was now cannabis.

At seventeen years old, I had long since become immune to the effects of peer pressure, and no longer felt it necessary to fit in with this motley assemblage. Thus, I've gotta take the rap for this particular fiasco myself. I had heard a lot about marijuana (who *hadn't* in 1972), and wanted to try it for myself.

There were four of us sitting scattered around my bedroom floor, comfortably lounging on my oversized, overstuffed, foam-filled floor pillows. It was late morning, around eleven; I had stacks of records piled onto my automatic turntable, and we were grooving to the strains of the Moody Blues, Chicago, Buffalo Springfield, and Fleetwood Mac. The door was locked. The windows were open.

At this point, I was introduced to a thin, hand-rolled, yellow joint. "Listen, man," said one of the buds, "toke slow—this is some really heavy shit."

"Cooool," I thought, having learned nothing from my projectile experience with alcohol. Determined to get the full effect of this curious smoke, we all took deep drags, and we then held our breath until our faces turned red. My immediate thoughts were that this stuff *really* burned my windpipe and that it tasted something like singed hair. I then put those logical thoughts to rest by reasoning that bad taste must equal potent effect.

Several drags later, the stuff had kicked in . . . hard. I didn't get high, so much as fuzzy, light-headed, and disoriented. Still, the experience wasn't at all unpleasant; and as our fingers gave way to a roach clip, and as the music blared from my sound system, I thought to myself that this might be a pretty cool way to spend my day off.

Then the phone rang.

"Huh? . . . Who? . . . Yeah? . . . Hello?" I inarticulately sputtered.

"Barry? This is Bill McGarry down at the set." Whoa . . . it was the assistant director from "The Brady Bunch." Then he said, "We had to change our shooting schedule, so we'll need you to come in and shoot the driveway scene at one o'clock, first thing after lunch."

"Uhhhhhhh, right, no problem, I'll be there in an hour."

"Jesus," I thought, "I'm gonna have to shoot a 'Brady'

scene *stoned!*" With my heart pounding, I checked my watch. It was eleven-thirty. Quickly, I grabbed hold of my script and checked out how many lines I'd have to say. Only six. "Okay, Okay," I thought, "I can handle that. In fact, this creative experiment might turn out to be fun."

I made my excuses, got dressed, headed for the studio, and found that the marijuana had, among other things, badly distorted my perception of time: the forty-five-minute trip to Paramount seemed literally three hours long. It was not a good omen.

Neither was the fact that once I got to the set, I found that the crew had spent their lunch hour setting up for my scene and were ready to film, *ahead* of schedule. Now there was no doubt: Greg was gonna be one stoned Brady.

I arrived at my dressing room, got into wardrobe, and headed over to see my pal Tom Miller, the makeup man. I was still feeling the strong effects of the smoke, but I did feel adequately in control to get through the scene.

"Hi, Tom. Fix me up, will ya?"

"Sure, Barry," he replied. "I'll . . . uh . . . do my best."

He proceeded to apply the thin layer of base makeup that we Bradys always used to soften the glare of the lights and give us that "eternally tan" look. Five minutes later, Tom was finished and, with a crooked smile, said, "Here, Barry, you'll need some of this." At which point he handed me a bottle of Visine eye drops.

"Oh, yeah," I lamely responded. "That pool chlorine is a killer." "My God!" I thought. "Does he *know?* Is it *obvious?* Can anyone *else* tell?"

Just then, Bill the AD appeared and told me that Robert Reed, Florence Henderson, and Hal Cooper (the episode's director) were on the set, ready for rehearsal and waiting for me. "Fine," I told myself. "Be cool."

Having taken a deep breath, and made sure that Tom's Visine took the red out, my mood began to swing, and I began strutting toward the set, feeling just *great* about life. It now was about ninety minutes since my last toke, but the after-effects were still evident. I started thinking to myself that my now-heightened sense of consciousness and intensity might give me a chance to completely recreate my role of Greg Brady, top to bottom.

Up till now, I told myself, Greg had been a bit of a bore—drippy, predictable, and *way* too goody-goody. This was my chance to make him come alive, give him depth and dimension.

Onto the set I strolled, slapping high-fives all around, feeling *very* cool, and acting . . . well, acting pretty weird. Some of the crew were starting to stare, but I wasn't paying any attention to unsupportive nonfollowers. I was a man on a mission.

Assistant director McGarry loudly yelled for quiet and rehearsal began. In his typical laid-back way, our director, Hal Cooper, gave us the bare-bones blocking, and I took this as my cue to begin a new ultimate creative process. "This is going to be *great*," I assured myself. "Now, for the very first time, I can fully explore the vast potential of a 'Brady Bunch' scene."

The scene had me in the Brady driveway pumping some air into my bicycle tire. In drove Dad with a small sailboat strapped to the roof of the family station wagon. I walked over and asked him about the boat, then Mom entered and we traded a few lines. Cindy came in next, a little too excited, and Dad explained what was happening.

Okay. Basic, straightforward, cut and dry stuff. However in my tingly headed condition, I saw it as crying out for innovation and improvisation.

First, this bit about pumping air into the bicycle tire, boring, too simple. So in my mind, I made up a history for the bike; why it needed air, what happened to the tire, where I had been riding it at the time. When rehearsal began, I proceeded to get involved with the spokes of the wheel . . . forming a relationship with each individual spoke, and trying to come up with a more aerodynamic design for them. Instead of merely crossing over to the car and standing there as expected, I invented a new saunter, like that of an imaginary ship's captain. Instead of going to my mark, I went directly over to the boat and tried to figure out how to get it down from the car. This I reasoned, gave me something to do when Mom entered the scene. So instead of just standing and listening to them while they were talking, I opened the car door and stood on its threshold to reach boat height and worked on loosening the straps. This line of thought spawned some more creativity on my part and I considered going into a silent little inner monologue pretending to be Captain Queeg, or Captain Bligh, or maybe even Douglas MacArthur . . . oops he was an Army General. "This is *good*," I told myself, "reeeeal good."

Of course I looked like an ass and was largely ignored, until I went further. When the dialogue began, I didn't just say my lines, I experimented with my speaking patterns, and inflections, giving each individual word undue weight and significance:

> *YOU* didn't *SAY* anything *ABOUT* getting a boat, Dad.
> You *DIDN'T* say *ANYTHING* about *GETTING* a boat, Dad.
> *YOU* didn't *SAY ANYTHING ABOUT* getting a *BOAT, DAD!*

It was horrible, but as far as I was concerned, I was really cooking.

In subsequent rehearsals, I changed my lines altogether, or simply made up new ones as we went along, and altogether gave up on hitting my marks. In short, I was a one man freak show.

The crew was no longer staring, but casting their eyes downward. Now, short on time, they made the final set preparations and Hal Cooper pulled me aside and said, "Pretty unusual work Barry, but for this one scene, please do me a favor." His grip upon my shoulder tightened considerably, and he continued, "After I call action, cross over to the car, hit your mark, stand there, don't move, and deliver your lines as written . . . OKAY?"

Was he nuts?! I couldn't believe what I was hearing. Why

was he trying to suppress my creativity? Screw that, I just wouldn't listen. I mumbled something to him and took my place beside my bike. It was time to shoot. I focused on the bicycle spokes and let my imagination go. Once again I was a scientist full of ideas. Just then the "long-bell" on our sound stage pierced the air, warning everyone within earshot to be quiet, as a filmed "take" was about to begin.

And then it happened. The camera operator shouted "Rolling!," the audio department yelled "Speed!," the camera assistant ran in front of the camera yelling "Scene 2, take 1," and the stage fell silent.

I took that moment to look around the assembly of professionals and somehow became very anxious to start the scene. But then, just as we were about ready to go, something inside me began changing. Whereas I'd spent the last hour feeling cocky, self-assured, and full of myself, I now began to feel all alone and horribly insecure. I started to imagine that the crew was looking at me strangely, with an almost evil intent, as if there was something terribly *wrong* with me.

Was something terribly wrong with me? I wondered, "Is my brain's perception out of whack? Am I making a fool out of myself? Are they laughing at me? Do they know I'm high? I am screwing up," I thought. "Now what?" At that precise moment, Hal Cooper yelled "Action!"

That was it. Suddenly my ideas disappeared, my imagination stopped and I noticed cold sweat beginning to break out on my forehead. Bob Reed started the car, and the scene began . . . for *real*. Inside my head I was now listening to an unshakable, nonstop, and highly critical inner dialogue. Far from being carefree and innovative, I was now second- and third-guessing my every move, my every word, my every action. Nothing felt natural or right. It was as though I was outside my body, watching myself from a distance. I didn't know it at the time, but I was about to discover that for me, the most prevalent side-effect of grass was raging paranoia. What a time to find that out!

Now I'm asking myself all kinds of questions: "How long

will this last? Will this mental distortion ever go away? How will I ever get through this scene?" My answer to that last one was to become the most conservative actor in the history of the world.

So I threw out all of the creative concepts that I'd been practicing in rehearsal. Faced with the tension of the moment, I delivered the safest, blandest, least noticeable take I could muster.

The first thing I did as the take began, was to trip on my bicycle pump while crossing over to the the car. This was not a part of the innovative approach I had been concentrating on earlier. Unfortunately, my ability to be spontaneous was nearly nonexistent. So I pretended not to notice my stumble. I didn't want to be the one responsible for blowing the take, so I continued on like nothing happened and hoped somebody else would mess up. Nobody did.

During the scene itself I tried to hide my unnaturalness by slapping on this kind of phony, cover-all smile in an attempt to bluff my way through. When Cindy came in I forgot to even *look* at her and just kept staring at Mike and Carol with this goofy grin.

I was overflowing with self-doubt, and simply did my best to get it over with and get the hell out of there. Far from being the pleasurable, freeing, mind-expanding experience that I'd expected, getting stoned instead left me inhibited, stifled, self-conscious, and feeling as phony as the turf in the Bradys' backyard. Maybe I should've just smoked *that*.

I *still* don't know for sure if anyone actually *knew* my secret. Some probably suspected, but *I* sure never asked. I just felt lucky to have gotten through it, and thankful that I had no more scenes that day.

18
The Fishbowl

e Bradys did almost all of our filming within the confines of the Paramount lot; but every once in a while we *did* manage to get out of the studio and go on location. The year 1971 found us at the bottom of the Grand Canyon, and '72 found us in Hawaii. However, etched even more vividly into my memory is our fifth season opener, shot on location in that fabulous exotic wonderland known as Cincinnati.

As weird as this may sound, we Brady kids were *very* enthused about our Cincinnati journey. That's because our entire Ohio episode was going to be filmed at the (then) brand-new King's Island amusement park! Visions of unlimited access to the attractions danced in heads and we became bound and determined to hit every thrill-ride in the place, time and again, until we were either satisfied or too busy puking to continue.

Come travel day, we were flown to Ohio, driven to the park, and given the full VIP treatment . . . at least by local standards. Y'see, the King's Island park wasn't actually *in*

The Bunch hits King's Island. It would soon hit back.
(© Paramount Pictures)

Cincinnati but off in a fairly remote suburb. And while everyone did their best to accommodate us, none of our well-intentioned hosts had *any* idea about how a television show was actually shot. Thus, they had no way to anticipate the tremendous havoc that a full cast, crew, and on-location production staff could wreak upon their fledgling resort.

By week's end, we'd nearly closed 'em down.

The first disaster would have to go under the heading of "accomodations." King's Island was an ambitious, blossoming amusement park in a *tiny* town, with only *one* motel, and that meant there wasn't much choice about where we would stay. Instead, the entire Bunch was assigned living quarters in the considerably less-than-swanky Island Resort Motel . . . which, due to its lack of privacy, and vaguely fishy smell, we redubbed "the aquarium."

The motif was early Motel 6. The plumbing worked, and the bed had sheets, but there weren't many extras. No little mints on the pillows, no shampoo, no soap . . . you get the picture. Still, I had no real aversion to roughing it—until the swarm began arriving.

While I did notice a *couple* of six-legged roommates in my bathtub, the swarm I'm referring to was of the two-legged variety. You see, the Island Resort Motel was within a stone's throw of the King's Island amusement park, and it didn't exactly take a genius to put two and two together, and figure out where we Bradys were staying at the end of each shooting day.

Now, take *that* fact and add to it the fact that park management went all out to advertise our filming in the local papers, and you'll understand how each night, like clockwork, our motel became infested with dozens of Instamatic-toting park patrons intent on creating a Kodak moment with a real live Brady. There were kids, a *lot* of teens, adults, and sometimes whole families wandering through the un-air-conditioned hallways, knocking on doors, and peeking through our windows. Eventually, the hotel called in some Barney Fife–ish security guards, but mostly they just created a minor obstacle for the more determined gawkers. All of this was incredibly flattering but terribly uncomfortable.

The girls had it even worse than the guys. Maureen and Eve often couldn't even use their bathrooms for fear of finding human faces pressed up against their windows. There was no place to run, no place to hide.

Then there was the filming. Trying to make up for the motel horror story, our King's Island hosts devised a plan to let us Bradys spend every free moment in the park riding the very *best* rides, all without the nuisance of waiting in line. They were gonna let us cut any line, any time, anywhere in the park. Our fantasy had come true.

It sounded brilliant to us kids, and soon, with our own

Shooting in the park.
(© Paramount Pictures)

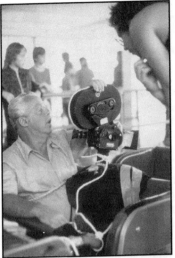

The ill-fated camera rig.
(© Paramount Pictures)

personal gun-toting park escort running interference for us, we were happily pushing and shoving our way to the front of all the longest lines in the park. A two-hour wait? Not for us Bradys. *We* were special. *We* were stars; *we* had been on TV for four years. *Millions* of people love us . . . right?

Not the people we'd pushed past. In fact, understandably enraged, *they* quickly learned to hate us. Our line-cutting scheme soon became so frighteningly ugly that by the end of our second day as VIP guests, our special ride treatment came to an abrupt and unceremonious halt.

So now, with the uncomfortable lodgings and angry mobs calling for our heads, the Bradys' trip to Ohio had become an absolute nightmare. Little did we know it was just beginning.

One of the most important scenes in this episode called for all of the Bradys to ride the park's biggest, fastest, meanest roller coaster. Finally, we were gonna pig out on adrenaline. Our first shot called for the camera to be mounted onto the front of the coaster and pointed backwards toward the family. After lengthy discussions among the crew about how to safely attach camera to coaster, the crew rigged together a sort of platform device, strapped on the camera, and we were set to go. The camera was loaded, and all of us Bradys got ready to take our places . . . all of us, that is, except Robert Reed, who flatly refused.

His refusal may have saved eight lives.

As Robert recalls: "I wouldn't ride on that thing, because they make me sick, and that made me the butt of a lot of jokes. But everyone else was going on, and the crew guys were mounting the camera on the front, facing back. So now I'm thinking to myself, When that thing gets going at sixty miles an hour, I'm not sure that whole rig's gonna clear all the overhead stuff on the tracks. So now I take a walk down the coaster tracks, checking things out, and I can plainly see *several* places where it would *never* get through. I couldn't *believe* no one had noticed this. So then I said, 'For chrissake, look at this!' So they grumbled at me, and measured the heights and clearances, and sure enough they had to lower it. If they hadn't, that camera would've come down and hit the kids straight in the face!"

And then Lloyd Schwartz got *his* chance to save eight lives. Y'see, once Robert had pointed out the near disaster of the roller coaster shoot, the entire crew seemed to get *really* spooked. They lowered the camera rig, secured it to the coaster as best they knew how, and got ready for the Bradys to ride. Time and light were getting tight, and we were already behind schedule, but Lloyd insisted that we send the rigged coaster through *without* Bradys, just to double-check the camera's security.

The crew guys thought it was just a waste of time, but when Lloyd pulled rank, they gave in, pulled the lever, and started the ride. They ran the coaster through one complete cycle, and then gasped in horror as it came back—without the camera!

Once again, fate had stepped in and (literally) saved our necks. No one ever figured out what exactly caused the camera to fall, but speculation has it that the coaster's vibrations had loosened its moorings.

Another camera was brought in, rigged, and run through a cycle by our now extraordinarily cautious director, Leslie Martinson. This time it came back unharmed, and the Bradys were called upon to climb aboard.

Obviously, we didn't get killed, and came through the harrowing experience without a scratch. All I can say is that I think eight guardian angels worked overtime that day.

Next time you happen across this episode, watch for the ill-fated coaster shot. You'll notice that all eight of us Bradys look genuinely horrified, and that's because . . . we *were!!!*

A coaster full of terrified Bradys.
(© Paramount Pictures)

19
The Follicle Follies

I don't know what it is about kid actors on sitcoms, but I keep seeing the same strange phenomenon over and over and over again: the irrational preoccupation with hair that runs rampant throughout the city of Hollywood. Take a look at the priority lists of most kid actors and you'll find that hair ranks just above eating, and slightly ahead of breathing.

I told you about how Marlo Thomas had absolutely no compunction about holding up her shooting schedule while her bangs were pinched, picked, sprayed, and resprayed. What I *didn't* explain is that the Brady set was often a lot like that . . . only times *nine!*

Actually, it was only times eight: Ann B. Davis always just pulled it back, glued it down, and went to work. For the rest of us, however, life was not nearly so easy.

Let's begin with Susan Olsen. To this day she regrets ever having asked her mother to make her hair "look like Buffy's," and that's because once Sherwood Schwartz got a look at those cute little dangly pigtails, he insisted that Cindy

124

wear her hair like that *forever*. In fact, Sherwood was *so* crazy about Susan's tails, he even gave them special mention in our theme song ("the youngest one in curls").

But Susan wasn't the only Brady with hair problems—not by a long shot. Michael Lookinland, for example, has naturally reddish blond hair—yep, that stringy black stuff that sits on Bobby Brady's little round head throughout the first couple of seasons of "The Brady Bunch" came out of a bottle. For a while the hair-and-makeup folks experimented with a temporary and washable black rinse, but the problems with *that* were double-edged. First, whenever Michael got under the intense illumination of our large studio lights, you could see right *through* the rinse and down into his natural reddish-blond hair (this is very evident in the pilot episode). And second, if we were working on a scene for any extended period of time, the heat of those same lights would cause Michael's scalp to perspire, and before you knew it, little Bobby Brady had big black streams rolling down his face and neck.

Finally, they just settled on a permanent color. Twenty-two years after his first dye job, Michael still remembers that the coloring was Miss Clairol #43, Jet Black, and that he hated it.

Florence Henderson and her hair suffered through multiple traumas as well, and for her they began right off the bat. As we began shooting "Brady Bunch" episodes, Flo had just finished production on a film called *Song of Norway*. In it she sported a very short, sort of combed-over hairdo, not unlike the one you see today on . . . uh . . . Pat Sajak.

Obviously, that kind of hairdo wasn't gonna work for Carol Brady. And so, with tight shooting schedules breathing down their necks, the producers decided to forget about waiting for Flo's hair to grow out and instead slapped a wig on her head. The only problem was that the wig they chose for Carol may have been the biggest, *ugliest* phony-hair mass in the history of prosthetic coifs.

Take a look at *any* of the first dozen episodes of "The

Brady Bunch" and you'll find that Florence Henderson's petite head is squashed under an absolute avalanche of stiff platinum-blond beehive-style hair. It was (and remains today) a hideous hairdo. Shaped like an astronaut's helmet, the wig came off as soon as Flo's real hair got even close to normal length.

Once the big bubble-do wig had met its maker and Flo's hair was once again allowed to see the light of day, the producers immediately began experimenting with it. For a while they tried out every shade of blond in the book, dyeing, dyeing, and redyeing the Henderson hair until it nearly fell out. After that, they settled in with the subtly frosted and highlighted look Flo maintained for the bulk of her "Brady" years.

Florence also is quick to take credit for popularizing the famous Carol Brady flip Do—you know, short in front, long in back. Even today you can spy Carol Brady wannabes wandering through any supermarket in the country, and Flo attests, "I *still* have women running up to me with that hairdo and telling me that after they saw it on Carol, they just *had* to have it too."

Of us all, Eve Plumb had the most natural, beautiful hair. Long, blond, full of bounce and shine, hers was one gorgeous head, and not for one moment did her mom let us forget it. Mrs. Plumb was an omnipresent figure on the "Brady" set and was *never* without brush in hand. I mean, I've heard of people who give their hair one hundred strokes per day, but this woman gave Eve's hair at least a hundred before each and every *take!* This behavior was politely tolerated, if never fully understood, throughout all five years of "The Bunch."

Maureen McCormick had that oh so California blond hair, and for the most part she was quite happy with it. Her face, on the other hand, drove her nuts. *Always* she was working on a plan to make her pretty round face appear more angular, and narrower, with pronounced cheekbones. With that in mind I should tell you that it wasn't at all unusual to find Mo walking around the set, and even shooting whole scenes, while sucking her cheeks together. Look closely at some of the later "Brady Bunch" episodes and you'll find her doing just that.

Chris Knight was the real exception in the group. He just plain didn't care *what* his hair looked like. He'd just kinda run his hands through it before each take and let his waves fall wherever they'd choose. Naturally, Chris's laissez-faire hair policy meant that Peter Brady is often found sporting truly heinous dos. I used to bust Chris about that a lot, but I think deep down I really envied his comfortable self-image.

Which brings us to my *own* hair. First of all, let me take this opportunity to say that I have never—*ever*—permed my hair.

Throughout my first two years on "The Bunch," I could get away with simply washing and blow-drying my hair. That way I could stretch it out a bit with my brush and let the blower's heat put an end to the unsightly natural curl that my parents had so callously bestowed upon me. I used no hair spray, no special spritzes, nothing. I'd just blow it, comb it, and go.

Then I turned sixteen, and my hair went insane. The first thing it did was to completely dry out until it was as coarse and wiry as a Brillo pad. Suddenly mere mortal shampoos and conditioners were unable to whip it back into a hairlike state, so I brought in the big guns—*super*-conditioning packs. You know the type: you heat 'em up, blob em all over your head, and sometimes even top off the concoction with a plastic-bag hat.

They didn't work, either; and then as my hair desperation deepened, the cures got more desperate. I started letting five days go by between each shampoo, hoping that the ensuing dirt/grease buildup might make my hair easier to manage. That didn't last long, thanks to Florence Henderson, who grimaced at me, asking, "What's that mess on your head?" I explained my dirty hair/nice hairdo theory, but she wasn't buying it. "It just looks dirty," she bluntly but honestly replied. Time for a new plan.

Then I began asking anyone and everyone for help. I thought that maybe the Paramount hairdressers could help, and they all had suggestions, with each one just slightly more demented than the next. However, as desperate as I was, I tried 'em all. Among them were:

1. *Hot* oil
2. Placenta (from goats, I think)
3. Mayonnaise (one-half jar: leave on for thirty minutes, rinse, repeat)
4. Beer shampoo
5. Curling irons

As I said, *nothing* really worked—until I desperately took a shot at having my curls chemically straightened. That was the biggest disaster of all, and for several full episodes (early in the fourth season) you'll find that my hair's not just its usual dry-and-brittle, but flat as a pancake as well.

I *did* learn something from all this ado about hair, and to sum it all up in one neat platitude, "Ya can't fool Mother Nature." Finally, when *everything* failed to fix my hair, I simply gave up, let it curl up—and *that's* what started those persistent "perm" rumors.

And speaking of perm rumors . . . that leaves us with Robert Reed. He too suffers from allegations of phony curls, but all I can say on the subject is "I don't know." You'll have to draw your own conclusions. I've asked Bob, on more than one occasion, for the real scoop on his hair, his answer is always terse, and is usually made up of just three statements. First, he tells me that his hair has *always* been naturally curly. Second, he tells me that when we started the show, he used a blow drier to stretch and straighten it out. And third, he says that when the Bradys got to Hawaii, the humidity was so intense that no matter *what* he did with his hair, it would just plain stay curly. He saw it in the dailies, liked it, and left it that way forever more . . . even to this day.

Now, I personally think that either Bob has the single

most perfect head of symmetrical curls God ever put onto a
human head, or he does indeed get chemical assistance. Okay,
perhaps I *am* jealous over the preponderance of big, bushy
locks on his head; but I've also seen the man arrive for work
at six a.m. with *every* hair in place, and I find it very hard to
believe that anyone has a head of hair *that* perfect. Still, only
his hairdresser knows for sure.

20
Frantic on the Atlantic

 *B*efore I can even begin this story, I have to explain a couple of things. First of all, up until now, every time Robert Reed has showed up in a reminiscence, he's been mad about something, causing trouble on the Paramount lot, or fighting with the Schwartzes. But that's not the whole picture.

Robert Reed may have detested "The Brady Bunch," but he *adored* the six of us Brady kids. From day one, he was warm, and very supportive. His affection for us kids was genuine, and at times *far* beyond the call of duty.

Christmas 1971: Bob's unhappy with the show, butting heads with the Schwartzes, and *still* he goes out of his way to present each of us kids with our own Super-8 movie cameras, the equivalent of today's camcorder. Come summertime, he chartered a yacht and treated all of us to a full-blown fishing excursion, wherein our cagey ship's captain zeroed in upon a huge school of mackerel, allowing Susan and Michael to spend the better part of the day yanking the scaly little buggers out of the sea.

But Bob's most extraordinary outpouring of generosity came when he took us Brady kids—*all* of us, lock, stock, and barrel—to London, on the *QE 2*. Sounds completely *crazy*,

On the *QE 2*. From left, me, Bob Reed's dad, Frances Whitfield (our teacher/ guardian), Susan, Bob Reed's mom, Mo, Mike, Chris, Robert, and Eve. (Barry Williams)

right? I thought so too, and so I asked Bob what possessed him to undertake such an ambitious, logistical, and supervisory nightmare.

"I think it came about because I was trying to think of something for all of us to do *together*," he said. "*I* was about to set sail for London, and I'd gone to school there, and loved it, so I thought, 'My God, why not take the kids, expose them to it, and see if it's as intriguing to them, or as sparking to them, as it was to me. And even if it isn't, it's *still* a pretty nice vacation.' Well, I stepped into that puddle without ever realizing how deep it was."

I must interrupt Bob's story here to bring up the *second* thing I need to explain. Y'see, while Robert's hopes for the trip were absolutely noble, we kids, knowing that we'd be away from home, and free at last from parental supervision, had a less virtuous agenda. Essentially, we made Bob's vacation a living, breathing hell.

"I remember finding Mo and Eve out on the fantail smoking," he continued. "But *far* worse than that, we had a system wherein each night, just before each kid would go to bed, they'd slip a note under my door saying that they were safe, sound, and sleeping. Once I had six notes, I could sack out myself.

"Well, on one particular night, we're docked in London, it's *four* A.M., and the only notes I've got are from Susan and Michael. So there's *four* of you out there somewhere, and I was *really* upset. I mean, it turns out that it was just a really late night with the kids running around the ship, but *still* I was frantic, and absolutely positive that you'd all gone out someplace and gotten into something over your heads."

Actually, Robert's worries about us four elder Bradys weren't so much unwarranted as misplaced. We were far less interested in making trouble than we were making out with each other. Ever since Hawaii, Maureen and I had been awkwardly toying with an on-again off-again kind of infatuation. It ran hot and cold and was hindered by innumerable interruptions, pressures, and conflicts. But out at sea, aboard this beautiful ship, I took the liberty of attempting to heat up an old flame. "I think Bob arranged the whole trip just so you and I could finally consummate our relationship," said Mo.

So we're out in the middle of the Atlantic, traveling in style on one of the biggest, most luxurious passenger ships in the world, and heading toward the cultural and educational treasure trove of London. Naturally, my thoughts were focused solely on getting laid.

I was positive, absolutely *positive*, that the warm sea breezes and lack of parents would combine to finally allow my relationship with Maureen to . . . uh . . . expand to its fullest potential. Yeah, that's it.

The only problem was that Maureen wasn't buying any of it. As we were preparing for our cruise to London, Mo and I happened to be suffering through one of our cold spells. She'd play hard to get, *I'd* play hard to get, and we'd ignore each other until one of us gave up and gave in. She saw no reason that a long romantic cruise should change *any* of that.

I, on the other hand, was *sure* that romance would be flying through the air, and that by the time we left the dock,

Maureen would be all over me like ketchup on scrambled eggs.

Was I wrong. Most of our overseas trip came and went without even so much as a friendly handshake passing between the two of us. But then, on our third night of cruising—my eighteenth birthday—as we chugged toward the U.K., I came up with the perfect plan. This time my dad couldn't come between us, Frances Whitfield couldn't come knocking; and if my plan worked, there was no way in hell that we'd be thrown off course on our journey toward . . . uh . . . our destiny.

My roommate on the ship was Chris Knight. Maureen's roommate was Eve Plumb. That may sound immaterial, but it was in actuality the cornerstone upon which my grand, high, exalted plan for finally bedding Maureen was based. Y'see, at about the same time Maureen had only a cold shoulder for me, Eve was overheating over Chris.

A light bulb flashed on in my head. "It's simple," I thought. "I'll wait till tonight and, using Chris as bait, I'll lure Eve out of *her* stateroom and into ours. At the same time I'll pay an unexpected visit to the now solitary Maureen, our eyes will meet, and she'll go gaga over me."

So with the plan set, it was time for action. First up, I had to find Chris Knight and ask him to keep Eve busy while I made moves on Maureen.

"Uh . . . I don't really wanna do that," Chris said through a grimace.

"C'mon, man . . . Ya *gotta!*" I replied, giving the situation a sense of life-or-death importance.

Chris finally gave in, and I got ready to pay an unannounced social call on the girls. Showered, shaved, and awash in Vitalis and Hai Karate, I worked the mirror hard, convinced (as only an eighteen-year-old can be) that my good grooming habits might just make me irresistible to Mo.

Now, with the moon dancing high above the waves, it was time to make my move, and with one last backward glance toward my mirror image, I was on my way, heading determinedly across the ship and over to the girls' stateroom. A bunch of butterflies were slam-dancing in my gut, but once I got to the door, I swallowed hard and knocked. Eve answered.

"Who is it?"

"It's . . . uh . . . me . . . uh . . . Barry."

"Awwww, what do *you* want?" Eve replied, less than cordially.

"I need to talk to you—right away," I spit out, trying to manufacture some measure of believability in my voice.

"Maureen's asleep," replied the remarkably perceptive Eve. She'd heard my sugar-coated bull and sliced right through it.

"C'mon," I replied, rather desperately. "Open the door."

"Nope."

"All right, then, just listen. I only came over here to deliver a message to you from Chris."

"Chris?!!!" Eve beamed back at me through the door.

"Yeah," I continued. "He wants to see you. He's waiting over in our room."

That did it. Eve threw on a robe, threw open the door, and practically sprinted through the hallway toward the port side of the ship, and Chris. I was left standing in the girls' open doorway. In the distance, sprawled upon one of the bunks, was Maureen. She may have been half asleep, but my heart started racing anyway.

"Hi," I said rather loudly as I entered the stateroom. "Nice place you have here."

"Hunhhhh . . . ?" said Maureen, still trying to jar her brain out of REM sleep.

Not exactly the chock-full-o'-romance greeting I'd hoped for, but still, with my sense of resolve unshakable, and my sense of ethics the opposite, I kept plugging away, yammering toward the semicomatose Maureen, because you never know, she might just wake up, take one look at me . . . and melt. It could happen.

Finally, as Maureen became unable to even *fake* consciousness, an evil, twisted, uniquely teenaged plan came rushing up from my groin to attack my brain. Somehow I came to the conclusion that if I were to snuggle up next to Maureen in bed, she might wake up, notice the intimacy of our situation, and be convinced that she should try and have her way with me.

There are truly some things that make sense *only* to a teenager.

Anyway, I climbed into bed next to Maureen, I smelled her hair for a while, then gingerly laid my head upon her pillow, and my hand upon her waist . . . which moved. Maureen was awake!

"Barry?" she asked.

"Yeeeesss?" I replied, trying my best to ooze studliness, and quite sure that bliss was just around the corner.

"What . . . the . . . *hell* . . . are you doing?"

"I . . . uh . . . oh . . . nothing."

"Look, I don't know what you've got in mind," Maureen hissed, "but *get outta here.*"

And that was it. I'd lost the battle, and this time I'd lost the war too. My desperate groping killed something between us that night; and in the weeks, months, and years to come, while Mo and I stayed friendly, we never managed to rekindle the fire between us.

Fifteen years later I was able to sit down with Maureen and finally, once and for all, ask her about how come we always *seemed* to be crazy about each other but always choked whenever we had a chance to actually *do* anything about it. "I *wanted* to really try and have something serious with you," she told me, "but I think I was just scared about what it meant. I wasn't an adult at the time, and it got weird with all the parents, and the teachers, and the producers, who were like another father figure. And y'know, our relationship was just sooo close, in so many ways, that it got scary.

"But you know, maybe it was *good* that way. I mean, who knows *what* would've happened if all those people hadn't been there for us? I mean, here we were, teenagers, cocky, growing up on a television show, and *feeling* like adults. Who *knows* how far we could've gone, in many ways, during that time period?"

But back to the *QE* 2. I'd now skulked out of Mo's room and made the long walk back toward my side of the ship with tail dragging. Halfway back, it hit me: "I *can't* go back to the room—Chris is still in there with Eve." (Who by the way, insist that *they* spent the evening talking, with some mild "ear nibbling" marking the night's raciest moment.) So, locked out and miserable, I spent the rest of my eighteenth birthday watching the ship's waiters set up the dining hall for breakfast.

I think I deserved it.

21
Calling the Kettle Black

O f all the multitudinous Reed/Schwartz battles, the biggest and most serious was the Orange Hair War. We were getting ready to begin production on the one hundred sixteenth (and, it turned out, the last) episode of "The Brady Bunch." It was entitled "The Hair-Brained Scheme" and revolved around Greg Brady buying some cheesy mail-order hair tonic from Bobby, only to have it turn his curly locks a bright, nearly Day-Glo shade of orange. Robert Reed read the script, hated it, came to the conclusion that it was "the single dumbest thing I'd ever read," and decided to take a stand.

Flash forward, and now it's early on the morning of the episode's first shoot day. Sherwood Schwartz is shaving, and his phone rings:

"I got a call from Bob's agent, saying that Bob had decided the script was stupid, and that he's refusing to appear in the episode. He's had the script for two weeks, and this gets me furious—not because he's got a problem with the script, but because he hasn't bothered to say *anything* until now, the day of the shoot. Now he's demanding story changes, and script changes, and line changes, and you just can't do that, especially with such short notice. And in the past I'd changed a lot of things to keep him happy. I didn't usually agree with the changes, but I'd make them nonetheless. Changing an entire story on a shoot day, however, is something that I *couldn't* do even if I *wanted* to.

"So I hang up with Bob's agent, call the studio, and say, 'Change the schedule, and start shooting all of the scenes Bob's not in. By the time I get in, I'll have this thing figured out.' And I did. Y'know, in my mind I changed things around, and by the time I got to the studio was able to dictate a new script. Basically, I just gave some of Bob's lines to the kids, and worked the story into shape minus Bob. It wasn't really that difficult."

End of story, right? Wrong. Because come high noon, Sherwood got another call from Bob's agent. " 'What are you going to do about my client's demands?' he asked me. So I told him the truth: 'Nothing.' And the agent says to me, 'Well, then, Bob refuses to appear in the episode.' And I said, 'Okay,' and the agent got all hot and bothered and said, 'What do you *mean*, "Okay?" '

"And I said, 'I mean, if he doesn't want to be in the episode, fine. We can do it without him.' And the agent says to me, 'Well, he's supposed to be in all the shows.' And I said, 'He's also supposed to do what he's asked as a performer, so if he wants out, he's out.'

"Then the agent asks me, 'What does that mean financially?' and I said, 'What do you *think* it means? A guy asks me to let him out of an episode, and you expect me to pay him for it? And set him up with residuals for an episode that he nearly ruined?' "

So the battle lines were drawn, the horns were locked, and neither side was about to back down. Instead, they just dug in a little deeper, pushed each other a little harder; and by the time Sherwood got to the set, things were ready to blow up:

"So I get down to the stage. There's Bob—standing on the set! So I said, 'Uh, Bob, you don't have to be here. I spoke to your agent, and you're not going to be in this episode.' And *he* said, 'Well, whether or not I'm *in* the episode, I'm *interested* in how it turns out.'

"I said, 'I think you're going to be a disturbance. If you're standing around watching the shooting, and everybody *knows* you don't want to be in it, I think that's gonna bother people, especially the kids. I think you should go.'

"At which point he stared me down and, very slowly, very deliberately, said, 'I'm not going anywhere, and I have every intention of staying through this thing.' So Bob stayed on the set, scowling.

"Anyway, Paramount found out about the situation and called me, asking if they should send over a couple of security guards to cart Bob away. 'Over my dead body!' I told 'em. 'There's absolutely no way I'm going to allow those kids to see their father yanked away bodily.'

"So then they asked me, 'What are you gonna do about him?' and I said, 'If he doesn't bother anybody, and stays out of everybody's way, nothing.' They still wanted to haul him away, but I wouldn't allow it. That would have been awful."

So that's how we shot the episode. Every day Bob would show up, stand off in a corner, and scowl. At the same time, Sherwood would show up, sit in his office, and do a slow burn. Bob was now officially on borrowed time. In fact, if "The Brady Bunch" had survived for a sixth season, we would have definitely been *fatherless.* Yep, while Robert Reed stood grumbling in a corner, Sherwood Schwartz was quietly sitting in his office, smiling, and plotting Mike Brady's murder. Sherwood told me that had we gone into another season, by the time we filmed our first episode, Mike would have died, off camera (probably in a car wreck)—or at the very least, he would have been sent away on an extended architectural project, never to return.

Robert Reed's Original Memo
Regarding Episode 116

"The Hair-Brained Scheme" Segment of "The Brady Bunch"

To Sherwood Schwartz et al.
  Notes: Robert Reed

There is a fundamental difference in the theatre between:

1. Melodrama
2. Drama
3. Comedy
4. Farce
5. Slapstick
6. Satire &
7. Fantasy

They require not only a difference in terms of construction, but also in presentation and, most explicitly, styles of acting. Their dramatis personae are noninterchangeable. For example, Hamlet, archtypical of the dramatic character, could not be written into *Midsummer Night's Dream* and still retain his identity. Ophelia could not play a scene

"... this is for you Sherwood!"
(Courtesy Sherwood Schwartz)

with Titania; Richard II could not be found in *Twelfth Night.* In other words, a character indigenous to one style of the theatre cannot function in any of the other styles. Obviously, the precept holds true for any period. Andy Hardy could not suddenly appear in *Citizen Kane,* or even closer in style, Andy Hardy could not appear in a Laurel and Hardy film. Andy Hardy is a "comedic" character, Laurel and Hardy are of the purest slapstick. The boundaries are rigid, and within the confines of one theatrical piece the style must remain constant.

Why? It is a long since proven theorem in the theatre that an audience will adjust its suspension of belief to the degree that the opening of the presentation leads them. When a curtain rises on two French maids in a farce set discussing the peccadilloes of their master, the audience is now set for an evening of theatre in a certain style, and are prepared to accept having excluded certain levels of reality. And that is the prime difference in the styles of theatre, both for the actor and the writer—the degree of reality inherent. Pure drama and comedy are closest to core realism, slapstick and fantasy the farthest removed. It is also part of that theorem that one cannot change styles midstream. How often do we read damning critical reviews of, let's say, a drama in which a character has "hammed" or in stricter terms become melodramatic. How often have we criticized the "mumble and scratch" approach to Shakespearean melodrama, because ultra-realism is out of place when another style is required. And yet, any of these attacks could draw plaudits when played in the appropriate genre.

Television falls under exactly the same principle. What the networks in their oversimplification call "sitcoms" actually are quite diverse styles except where bastardized by careless writing or performing. For instance:

"M*A*S*H" ... comedy
"The Paul Lynde Show" ... Farce

"Beverly Hillbillies" . . . Slapstick
"Batman" . . . Satire
"I Dream of Jeannie" . . . Fantasy

And the same rules hold just as true. Imagine a scene in "M*A*S*H" in which Arthur Hill appears playing his "Owen Marshall" role, or Archie Bunker suddenly landing on "Gilligan's Island," or Dom DeLuise and his mother in "Mannix." Of course, any of these actors could play in any of these series in *different* roles predicated on the appropriate style of acting. But the maxim implicit in all this is: when the first-act curtain rises on a comedy, the second-act curtain has to rise on the same thing, with the actors playing in commensurate styles.

If it isn't already clear, not only does the audience accept a certain level of belief, but so must the actor in order to function at all. His consciousness opens like an iris to allow the proper amount of reality into his acting subtext. And *all* the actors in the same piece must deal with the *same* level, or the audience will not know to whom to adjust and will most often empathize with the character with the most credibility—total reality eliciting the most complete empathic response. Example: We are in the operating room in "M*A*S*H," with the usual pan shot across a myriad of operating tables filled with surgical teams at work. The leads are sweating away at their work, and at the same time engaged in banter with the head nurse. Suddenly, the doors fly open and Batman appears! Now the scene cannot go on. The "M*A*S*H" characters, dealing with their own level of quasi-comic reality, having subtext pertinent to the scene, cannot accept as real in their *own* terms this other character. Oh yes, they could make fast adjustments. He is a deranged member of some battle-fatigued platoon and somehow came upon a Batman suit. But the Batman character cannot then play his intended character true to his *own* series. Even if it were possible to mix both styles, it would have to be *dealt with* by the characters, not just *abruptly accepted*. Meanwhile, the audience will stick with that level of reality to which they have been introduced, and unless the added character quickly adjusts, will reject him.

The most generic problem to date in "The Brady Bunch" has been this almost constant scripted inner transposition of styles.

1. A pie-throwing sequence tacked unceremoniously onto the end of a weak script.
2. The youngest daughter in a matter of a few unexplained hours managing to look and dance like Shirley Temple.
3. The middle boy happening to run into a look-alike in the halls of his school, with so exact a resemblance he fools his parents.

And the list goes on.

Once again, we are infused with the slapstick. The oldest boy's hair turns bright orange in a twinkling of the writer's eye, having been doused with a non-FDA-approved hair tonic. (Why any boy of Bobby's age, or any age, would be investing in something as outmoded and unidentifiable as "hair tonic" remains to be explained. As any kid on the show could tell the writer, the old hair-tonic routine is right out of "Our Gang." Let's face it, we're long since past the "little dab'll do ya" era.)

Without belaboring the inequities of the script, which are varied and numerous, the major point to all this is: Once an actor has geared himself to play a given style with its prescribed level of belief, he cannot react to or accept within the same confines of the piece, a different style.

When the kid's hair turns red, it is Batman in the operating room.

I can't play it.

THE BRADY BUNCH

The official mugshots, guys...and gals. (© 1990 Paramount Pictures)

THE BRADY BUNCH

Brady 6 meets Jackson 5. Michael Jackson is in the foreground shaking hands with Michael Lookinland. (© 1991 Capital Cities/ABC, Inc.)

Bradys meet Partridges.
(© Karen Lipscomb)

Posing for publicity shots. (Courtesy Sherwood Schwartz)

Posing for publicity shots. (Courtesy Sherwood Schwartz)

No cavities here. (Courtesy Sherwood Schwartz)

22
And Away We Go!

O nce "The Brady Bunch" became a solid and proven
success, people everywhere began encouraging us
kids to branch out, break out, cross mediums, and
become the true superstars we were so obviously destined to
become. You can't sing? No problem! Can't dance? We'll get

The Teen Scene.
(Barry Williams)

you lessons! Don't think you're ready? Hey, babe, nobody's perfect.

You're in a TV show? Good. You're making 1100 dollars per episode? Great! Now what's next? How can we make some *more* money? How can we exploit the exploited?—We can train you, teach you, open doors, and show you the way. We *love* ya! You're the *greatest*. You're going straight to the *top!* Trust me on this one. You're big, and you're gonna get bigger! . . . You could be the *biggest!!!*

When you're seventeen years old and you start hearing that kinda stuff all day, *every* day, you start swallowing it wholeheartedly. At least *I* did. I really thought superstardom was simply there for the taking, and toward that end, I jumped head-first into whatever project my persuaders dangled in front of my nose.

Among them was "The Brady Kids," a Saturday-morning cartoon show created by Filmation Associates. Then ABC started using the six of us to promote its new fall season. Teen magazines (*16*, *Tiger Beat*, etc.) hounded us constantly for pictures and interviews that more often than not ended up in articles that were completely fabricated. Famous Music, a subsidiary of Paramount, hoping to outdo the recording sensation of the Partridge Family, talked to us about record deals and albums. And most prevalent of all were the merchandisers who, licensed or not, would squeeze bucks from "The Bunch" by plastering our six likenesses on lunch boxes, comic books, Viewmaster sets, dolls, coloring books, and for all I know, their mothers' asses.

This first wave of teen idolatry hit me at just about the same time that puberty did, and I went from clueless adolescent to teen idol almost overnight.

I liked it—a lot.

We made the cartoons. It went like this. Having no idea of what the cartoon would look like—it hadn't been drawn yet—we'd go into a recording room, or sometimes they'd come to our "Brady Bunch" dressing rooms and one at a time we'd simply rattle off our character's lines into a microphone.

We didn't know the storylines or the context of each line. We'd just read from a random list on a legal pad. For example, you might say:

1. Wow!
2. That's cool!
3. Hey, look at that dog!
4. Mom's not gonna like it.

Et cetera, et cetera, ad infinitum. We never knew *what* we were referring to, and as a result, when the cartoons were put together, the dialogue was terribly disjointed. We were told, that didn't matter—the kids watching "couldn't tell the difference," and we had "earned a nice chunk of change."

Still, as inherently slipshod as it was, there's nothing like waking up on a Saturday morning and watching a two-dimensional animated version of yourself run around the screen for a half-hour. It *was* kinda fun.

Oddly enough, this dopey little cartoon presented one of

The Merchandise Machine.
(Photo by John McGary. Toys by Kirk and Joanne Holcomb)

The Brady Kids.
(© Paramount
Pictures)

the first of the situations that would eventually undo the unity of our little group and ultimately bust up the Bunch.

We'll get to that later, because *now* it was time for Famous Music to hitch a ride on the Brady gravy train. At about this time in American history, sound-track albums from TV shows, good, bad, and ugly, were splattered all over the pop charts. The Partridge Family was *huge,* as were the Monkees and Bobby Sherman—even Sonny and Cher. The Brady kids seemed like a sure thing, but somehow our appeal played better on the television than on the turntable. That *may* have been due to poor advertising or poor marketing . . . or maybe, just maybe, it had to do with the fact that our singing sucked.

The first recording we ever did was called *Merry Christmas from the Brady Bunch,* and from the beginning, we were discouraged from contributing ideas, and told, "Be quiet, except for when you're singing."

At our first meeting, the record's producer showed up with a piece of paper listing the songs he wanted to include. He then rattled off titles at random, assigning one to each Brady kid: " 'Away in a Manger'. . . Marcia. 'Rudolph the Red-Nosed Reindeer'. . . Peter. 'Frosty the Snowman' . . . Cindy." He never bothered to learn our real names, nor our vocal ranges.

When he got to "Greg," I was assigned the beautiful—though nearly impossible to sing—"O Holy Night." This is

(Kirk Holcomb. Photo provided by Jeff Kilian)

the kinda thing that you usually hear sung by people like Mahalia Jackson or Leontyne Price; and now I, this pubescent, crack-voiced novice, was supposed to belt it out . . . in public . . . in front of my pals . . . and on a record for the whole world to hear. I was scared out of my wits.

And with good reason. When it finally came time to warble my rangy little ditty, and I took my place at the mike with hands—and voice—trembling, I summoned up all the intestinal fortitude I could bear, grit my teeth, belted out the song as best I could . . . and embarrassed myself royally. I think I made the recording guy's ears bleed.

Finally, when the torture became more than I or the engineers could bear, they summoned in Maureen. She actually had a pretty good voice, and since the song was in her range, *she* tackled the more treacherous first half, and I simply chimed in halfway through. With the two of us singing, it was only half awful—*my* half.

Anyway, mortified and unceasingly ragged on by my fellow Bradys, I made it through the rest of the session, wherein we all huddled up around an open mike and sang to prelaid musical tracks of classic Christmas favorites like "Silver Bells," "Silent Night," and "We Wish You a Merry Christmas."

We finished our vocals in one afternoon, and then listened intently as the audio engineers used every gimmick, trick, and echo chamber in the book to get us at least up to "listenable" status. I'm not sure they succeeded, because even with all their gadgetry, the end result still wasn't, by any stretch of the imagination, "easy" listening. In fact, should you ever come across this particular album in a record store, I suggest you run screaming in the opposite direction.

Amazingly, the record sold reasonably well; and despite our potential for damaging eardrums, more albums were scheduled.

This time, it was decided that a new producer was in order, someone different, someone hip, someone who'd help the Bradys grab their rightful place atop the pop/contemporary charts. Soon, Bobby Sherman's producer, the man responsible for inflicting such hits as "Julie, Do Ya Love Me" and "Easy Come, Easy Go" upon the American public, was brought in and asked to make us shine. His name was Jackie Mills, and we were certain he was gonna be our ticket to stardom.

Then the problems hit.

Almost from day one, Mr. Mills openly bemoaned the fact that he was producing *our* new record instead of Rod Stewart's or the Rolling Stones'. He was publicly ambivalent about working with us, and throughout the project he expended very little energy.

Next, Mr. Mills and the higher-ups at Famous Music got together and decided that one sure way to sell albums would be to cram a lot of already popular song titles onto both sides of the record. They scanned the Top 40, and almost immediately our new album was saddled with such wildly inappropriate songs as "Baby I'm-a Want You" and "Me and You and a Dog Named Boo." (Susan Olsen's suggestion of "(I Can't Get No) Satisfaction" met with a red-faced rejection.) Worst of all, though, was our extraordinarily awful rendition of "American Pie." Ouch!

Anyway, the point here is that even though the "Brady Bunch" kids were fast becoming a bona fide (if cheesy) musical group, *nobody* had *any* concept about what this newly formed musical family should be. What direction? What songs? What signature? We needed a leader but were too young, naive, and excited to complain. We were sure that our ride toward superstardom had begun, and we weren't about to get off.

Meet the Brady Bunch was released, and while it never got any radio airplay, it did manage to sell reasonably well. My guess is that it was mainly because our pictures were on the cover; word of mouth would be too optimistic. Two more albums were scheduled; and so as not to relive my "O Holy Night"–mare, I immediately began spending *all* of my free time taking voice lessons.

The Kids from "The Brady Bunch" and *The Brady Bunch: A Phonographic Album* were recorded, released, and sold pretty well. Now, we were told, it was time to grab our tepid success by the balls and explode it into full-blown Bradymania!

The Bradys were going on the road.

23
Road Warblers

You guys are gonna go far—you are really, really, really fabulous!

—Tony Orlando, after seeing the live
Brady Kids concert tour

Okay, the records were selling, the TV show was bigger than ever; and come hiatus time, we "Brady Bunch Kids" sequestered ourselves in the Paramount dance studio for weeks, and concocted a live concert act that we were sure was gonna blow the roof off the pop music business. We hired a couple of Vegas veterans, Ray Reese and Joe Seiter, who, we were told, could make *anyone* look good onstage. They were set to direct us, choreograph us, and help us select appropriate songs.

Good idea. These were talented, compassionate guys with a nice sense of how to transpose us TV Bradys onto a live stage. Then we agreed to let our moms get together and make our costumes by hand.

Bad idea. Bad, *bad* idea! Guided by their own fashion taste, our moms managed to stitch together costumes that were ugly even by 1970s standards. *Everything* was created in stretch polyester, with beads, flowers, and fringe flying all over the place. On some numbers, we'd even add straw hats, canes, and white patent-leather boots. We looked like Up With People on crack.

Our first gig was in Las Vegas, at Caesars Palace, per-

Rehearsing the act. (© Karen Lipscomb)

Meeting Ed Sullivan. (Barry Williams)

forming on a TV awards show hosted by Ed Sullivan. We were invited to sing the closest thing we ever had to a hit, "Time to Change" (a song from the "Brady Bunch" episode where Peter's voice is changing). We took our place onstage alongside an incredible array of stars. Sonny and Cher performed, then Lily Tomlin, Danny Thomas, and of course the multitalented Edwina the Elephant.

We were next. Ed introduced us, we took the stage and proceeded to spend the next three and a half minutes doing our rudimentary sidesteps and kickball changes while carefully skirting the numerous piles of Edwina residue which now dotted the stage like land mines.

We got through our number, survived, and actually did okay. The crowd responded warmly, and for the first time we knew about the instant gratification of a live audience. It felt great. We were excited that we'd done well, *amazed* that we hadn't embarrassed ourselves among genuine big-name talent, and more excited than ever to get our show on the road.

And that's exactly what we did.

We played state fairs. We played twelve-thousand-seat arenas. We co-headlined with the Fifth Dimension. Tony Orlando and Dawn *opened* for *us*. But the biggest thrill of all was to come face-to-face with our fans.

That sounds like a corny show-business cliché, but what

you've gotta understand is that for years, from 1969 through 1973, we six Brady Kids had simply worked on the Paramount lot and gone home everyday. I mean, we knew that our show was a hit, and we *did* get hundreds of fan letters each week; but somehow none of that ever translated into giving us any sense at all of just how enormous the Brady Bunch had become.

But now, in front of us were *thousands* of screaming, hand-clapping, foot-stomping, singing, dancing fan-atics, and for the first time, all six of us were unavoidably smacked in the face with our heretofore unrealized stardom.

The crowds were extraordinarily receptive to our act. Their reaction was *extremely* gratifying, over the top, and at times more than just a little scary. Everywhere we went, people were excited by us. Everywhere we stayed, crowds tailed us unmercifully. Everywhere we hid, we were sought out.

I remember the six of us being rushed by an especially riled-up arena crowd in Oklahoma and escorted away by a

The show:
Before ... (© Karen Lipscomb)

during. . . and after. (© Karen Lipscomb)

The Bradys on "American Bandstand."
(© Karen Lipscomb)

big team of security guys, who formed a sort of flying V in front of us and basically steamrolled over any human who got in our way. Cowering behind them, we kids *still* got mauled, losing handfuls of our groovy fringe, our jackets, and even locks of hair to the hands of the admiring mob. Finally, we broke free, scooted down an interior hallway, and laid low inside a janitor's storage room.

Safe at last . . . or so we thought.

The security team split up and ditched us, believing that our janitorial hideaway would prove inconspicuous enough to remain unexplored by Brady-seeking fans.

They were wrong, and almost immediately we began hearing a group of fans headed down the hall toward us. Silently we held our breath, hoping they'd pass by, but when a knock at the door was followed by eyeballs peering under its crack, all was lost.

"Hey, Bradys," we heard cringingly, "come on out. We *know* you're in there—we can see your feet!"

Ugh . . . Our white patent-leather Beatle boots had given us away. We were doomed. But Susan Olsen wasn't ready to give up just yet. "It'th not uth!" she yelled out under the door. "It'th really not uth. . . . The Bradyth are behind the thtage!"

Needless to say, her ploy didn't work. Thankfully, a mob of thick-necked security types finally showed up and helped us out. Without them, I think, we all might still be in there.

On another occasion, we came backstage after a state fair concert and began heading toward our Winnebago (there were no real dressing rooms) to find it swarming with fans who had convinced themselves that we were hiding inside.

The vehicle, clearly, and dumbly, marked with a banner that read "The Brady Bunch Kids," was surrounded with frighteningly enthusiastic fans. As we watched the goings-on from the relative safety of a side-stage area, our fans, six deep on all sides, yelled our names at the motor home, hoping that one of us might be inside. Next, they rapped on the doors, then pounded on the windows, and finally just plain shook the shit out of that Winnebago until they'd actually tipped it over.

Terrifying, but I clearly remember thinking to myself, "Wow, this is reeeeeally coooool."

Many more cities would follow. So would dozens of shows, dozens of plane flights, dozens of autograph sessions,

On "American Bandstand."
(© Karen Lipscomb)

dozens of photo opportunities, and dozens of hotel rooms. We even played "American Bandstand." To this day, I marvel at how well behaved we all were in the midst of this chaotic environment. None of us ever trashed a hotel room; none of us ever bit the head off a bat; and in a day and age when even a New Kid on the Block can douse a hotel hallway with vodka and ignite his puddle, I'm absolutely *floored* that *our* worst indiscretion was probably a particularly rough-and-tumble round of pillow fighting.

But then again, we *were* Bradys.

24
Busting the Bunch

ll right, we're playing The Minnesota State Fair in front of like twelve thousand people, and they're *really* going crazy for the "Brady Bunch Kids." I can remember getting about halfway through our set and thinking to myself that maybe—just maybe—we really do

The flying fringe.
(Michael Ochs Archives/Venice, CA)

have the potential to blow the Partridge Family and the Osmonds out of the water. We sail through our first twenty minutes, and then we get to my solo. And as the spotlight hits me, and my sequins and fringe begin to take on a glitzy show-biz glow, I look down into the footlights and see—Tony Orlando.

He's ducked below the lip of the stage, and out of the crowd's view, but nevertheless, here's the guy with the number-one song in the country ("Tie a Yellow Ribbon" had just exploded), and he's down in the pit, rooting *me* on, yelling "Yeah! Go for it! Get down! Do it!" All this guy needed was pom-poms. He was amazing; and *his* support coupled with the extra-large extra-enthusiastic throng in attendance made a huge impact on all of us.

I left the stage that night feeling like superstardom was just around the corner.

I think we all did. Shortly thereafter we Brady Kids came to a group decision that what *we* needed was some high-powered management that could unite us and represent us collectively as we zoomed toward large-scale musical success. We scouted most of the bigger names in Hollywood and settled on a guy named Harvey Shotz, who seemed genuinely enthusiastic about our future and was a master spewer of ego-inflating, head-expanding, overly complimentary hype. In short, he was one of those guys who could size you up, effortlessly look you in the eye, and spit out exactly what you wanted to hear.

"Make a stand!" he'd cheerlead at us. "You're the talent! You're the power! You can become *huge* stars, make *tons* of money, *ensure* your future, and *raise* your standing in the business!"

Sounded great to us.

Actually, I should correct myself by saying it sounded great to *most* of us. We had all swallowed the Shotz shit, but with six kids and ten parents involved in every decision—I was the only kid allowed to make my own decisions—dissension became the rule and not the exception.

We did our best to remain united, but with so many cooks in the kitchen, *nothing* came easy. We debated what direction the Kids should take musically, in terms of image, and in terms of commitment. Finally, when all was said and done, we'd usually reach a compromise and agree to disagree, oftentimes with parents and their own kids at opposite ends of an argument. Chris Knight, for example, really wanted *no part* of the live act. He hated singing, hated dancing, hated touring, and would probably have preferred to stay home and hang out like a normal kid. His mom, however, was one of the group's most ambitious strategists. On the flip side, Susan Olsen's dad wanted his daughter out of show business altogether, only to find her thrilled with life on the road.

Still, Harvey Shotz was confident that he knew exactly how to propel us toward musical superstardom, and with all six kids in his stable, he was confident that he had the *power* to do so as well. His big, bold plan was to use our collective bargaining power in squeezing ABC, Paramount, and Sherwood Schwartz into letting us use the "Brady Bunch" TV show simply as a tool to promote our live Brady Kids musical act. This would be accomplished by having us kids present a united front and demanding that seven of every thirteen "Brady" episodes include songs.

He took his idea to the "suits" at ABC, and (buoyed by the success of "The Partridge Family") they were surprisingly amenable. Now, Shotz concluded (and we all came to agree) we were simply going to have to convince Sherwood, through whatever means necessary, that it would be in his best interest to allow us to change the direction of his show.

First step was to call a meeting of the kids, wherein we all sat down and made suggestions for the "improvement" of "The Brady Bunch." One by one we spouted ideas at Mr. Shotz. I remember that my personal agenda included seeing us deal with some "serious" themes (I recall asking to have Mike and Greg get into an argument which would ultimately lead to Greg getting slugged). Michael Lookinland argued that Bobby should have a steady girlfriend, and Susan's idea was that Cindy should get a horse.

Finally, with "more musical episodes" at the top of our list, and a notebook full of follow-up demands, Shotz set up a meeting between himself, all six kids, and Lloyd and Sherwood Schwartz. It was time for us to present our demands, and with our newfound resolve to collectively strong-arm negotiations, Shotz was sure we would simply steamroll the Schwartzes and any resistance they might muster.

Meeting day. We piled into Sherwood's office, he greeted us with one of his big, genuine "glad to see ya" smiles, and we quickly managed to wipe it right off his face. One after another we railed at the guy with our criticisms of him and his show. We voiced our predetermined demands and made absolutely sure that he understood our implied threat of "Cave in to our demands, or collectively we can make contract negotiations for season six very, *very* difficult."

Basically, we stabbed him in the back . . . six times.

I'll never forget the look of disappointment on Sherwood's face as the "perfect family" he'd created, loaded down with demands from parents, managers, and selves, tried its best to bite the hand that fed it. Here we were, six kids with the audacity to march into the office of a man who'd been highly successful in the television industry for decades, who'd created, produced, and written the very show that launched our careers in the first place, and tell him in short order that his show stunk and that we were *demanding* changes.

So what did Sherwood do? Amazingly, even after we'd laid our huge, steaming pile on his desk and proceeded to rub his nose in it, he was cordial, he was polite, and he told us that he'd be more than happy to consider everything we'd discussed. He was smiling, but it wasn't one of his usual big grins; *this* smile was being worn as a mask. The six of us had hurt Mr. Schwartz, and I've got to say that the image of his crooked, counterfeit, crestfallen smile *still* haunts me sometimes.

Nevertheless, we kids left the meeting feeling good about

ourselves. We'd had our showdown with Sherwood and came away convinced that (with the six of us united managerially, and with contract negotiations for season six just around the corner) there was nothing that could keep us from getting *everything* we'd demanded.

We had a lot to learn.

Filmation Associates—who had produced the "Brady Kids" cartoon show—called, trying to put together a simple deal that would allow them to use our voices in producing five more episodes of the cartoon show. This would bring their total number of shows to twenty-two and would make the cartoon much easier to syndicate since affiliates generally bought programming in twenty-two-episode cycles.

It had been about a year since we'd last dealt with Filmation, and in that time the six of us had changed. We'd grown cocky, grown egos, and grown a manager to boot. Thus, when we were asked to simply extend our original cartoon show contracts by five more episodes with the same deal as before we were "highly insulted"—at least that's what Harvey Shotz told us.

He yelled about how Filmation was taking advantage of us, how unfair it was that *they'd* reap all the cartoons' syndication profits, and about how we were now "too big" to be treated so poorly. So now, us kids, our parents, and our manager, with a seemingly united front, told Filmation that we couldn't *possibly* work with them again unless our contracts were retroactively renegotiated all the way back to episode number 1. This, we told them, was to reflect our newfound, large-scale celebrity status.

Filmation was furious, but with our manager leading the way, the six of us held fast in our demands . . . at least for a while.

Immediately, Filmation told us to shove our demands and threatened to produce the shows without us, our voices, *or* our approval. At this point a couple of parents began to sweat, but we were still pretty much united, and we countered Filmation's threat with a doozy of our own. "Drop the six kids from the show," Harvey Shotz expostulated, "and we'll slap a lawsuit on you so fast it'll make your head spin. *And*," he continued, "since the cartoon's characters bear my clients' likenesses, we can hit you with an injunction that'll keep you from making another dime off the show until this whole legal mess gets cleaned up—and you know how long *that* could take."

He was playing hardball all right, but *we* were the ones who ended up getting hardballed. It came time for another volley from the folks at Filmation, and they did a strange thing . . . nothing. Several days went by, a week, ten days, and still we heard nothing. Now *all* the parents were sweating, and when faced with the possible loss of income, the possibility of their kid being tagged "difficult," and the queasiness of impending litigation, one by one they began to crack.

First to cave were Eve's folks, then Maureen's, Susan's, and Michael's. This left just Chris Knight, his parents, and I to battle it out alone. Harvey Shotz's grand scheme of tough and united group representation hadn't even survived its first battle.

Chris and I continued our holdout, but the rest of the bunch went ahead and made the cartoons without us (*years* later, our ensuing lawsuit was stopped short of the courtroom when the two of us received modest cash settlements from Filmation), but a great deal of damage had been done. Once the Bunch had been divided, we were never the same.

We kids still pretty much got along, but our parents (now in divided camps) could barely conceal their hostilities toward one another, and somehow the six of us were no longer the idealistic, optimistic bunch of the past. I think that really hurt the remainder of the "Brady Bunch" episodes. All along, we had basically been a bunch of fairly ordinary kids who liked each other, and who interacted naturally together on camera. Now, with burnt business deals, lawsuits, angry parents, and a jaded mistrust of those in charge thrown into the mix, our chemistry went from spontaneous to stilted, and our united ensemble mentality burst into six-sided selfishness. Worst of all, our spirits were dampened, and that resulted in some noticeably low-energy episodes (check out our last dozen shows sometime). We'd listened to the hype, believed it, and screwed up big-time.

Still, when season five of "The Brady Bunch" was finished, none of us had any reason to believe that there wouldn't be a year six. "Sanford and Son" was our strongest competition, but we still had a very strong, very loyal audience. For those reasons, it came as a major shock when two months later, my phone rang and I found myself talking to an ABC programming executive.

"Barry," he slurred, "I'm sittin' here at my deshk with a bottla bourbon." The drunken executive belched out the fact that he'd been given the unenviable and unpleasant task of notifying all the Bradys that the show had been canceled.

Silence.

"That's it," I thought. "It's over." Without the show there wouldn't be a live act, the cartoon show was all but dead, and before long, five of us kids would be returning to public school, and I'd become an unemployed adult.

Funny thing, that news didn't make me sad . . . at all. "The Brady Bunch" was great fun while it lasted, but now, even as my livelihood was being unceremoniously yanked out from under me, I wasn't upset. Instead, I simply came to the conclusion that maybe it was time to put all this behind me and just let it die. I'd never have to deal with Greg Brady again.

Yeah right.

25
Bad Luck in a Truck

I'd finally given up on chasing Maureen, but that didn't mean all of the Bradys had finished working toward fictional incest. Chris Knight and Eve Plumb had wrestled with an awkward on-again/off-again romance throughout the run of "The Brady Bunch," and just after the show was canceled, they took a stab at making their relationship a bit more intimate.

Disaster followed.

To begin, we'll have to take a step backward in time and flash back across the Atlantic, where we kids are once again working our way through Bob Reed's supervised tour of London. Here's how Chris remembered it:

"All through the time we were on the QE 2, Eve had been hinting and working on trying to knock into my skull the fact that the two of us should be something more than friends. And finally, as she nibbled on my ear, something clicked, and I realized that she was probably right. I mean, up until this

172

point I'd just plain been sort of oblivious toward the opposite sex, but after she'd nibbled on my ear for the first time, this wave of feeling came over me, and I thought to myself, 'Oh, my God—now I understand what all the fuss is about!' I was fourteen.

"Anyway, it was terrific, Eve was incredible, and the two of us were very comfortable together, y'know? I mean, most of the time when a guy's just beginning to experiment with the opposite sex, he's stuffed into a backseat somewhere with somebody he doesn't even *know* all that well. But here *I* was, relaxed, and genuinely attracted to someone that I literally knew as well as a sister. *That,* I have to say, was extremely eye-opening, and extremely arousing, and it yanked me out of my opposite-sex ignorance and put me into this sort of frenzy for more. And I mean, here's how innocent I was. We were rolling around on that bed for I don't know *how* long, and I wasn't even thinking about sex yet. Just the experience of having my neck kissed and my ears kissed was simply . . . enough. Making out had suddenly started making sense.

"So then we get back from the trip, go back to work, and I behave like a normal teenage guy in that I start acting like a *complete* turd toward the one person in the world who'd shown any romantic interest in me at all. I don't know *why* that was; it just sorta *was.*

"So anyway, a year comes and goes, we get canceled, I go back to public school, and all of a sudden it hits me . . . I don't know *anybody.* I mean, I'm new in school, and the only people I'm really comfortable with are Bradys.

"Now here's where this whole thing gets truly embarrassing. At about the same time that I'm feeling lonely, puberty has kicked in to make my ability to be content with just kissing a girl a thing of the past. I mean, like all normal, healthy teenaged boys, I was simply in heat all the time.

"Now at this point my hormones take over, and when they realize how long it's gonna take for me to meet someone, befriend them, win their trust, build and consummate a relationship, they opt for what they belive might be a quicker route toward satisfaction. They make me pull out my address book and force me to call Eve.

"So I call Eve. I say, 'Let's go to a movie.' She says okay, and I proceed to pick her up, and take her . . . nowhere *near* a movie theater. All I did was to drive her up into the hills, hoping that we might finally get to finish what we'd started in Hyde Park.

"Eve knew exactly what I was up to. I mean, my clumsy attempts at romance couldn't have fooled *anybody*. But we talked for a while, and actually *did* manage to rekindle what we'd felt toward one another, and *this* time we quickly moved beyond the sensory pleasures of just making out.

"Now it's just starting to get physical, so we move into the back of my truck, and things start getting *really* great. And at about this same time, I open my eyes, look up, and find that the back of my truck is now lit up like a night game at Dodger Stadium. And there's two cops parading up to the back of the truck with their flashlights. I had no curtains on the thing, and we're scrambling around trying to stay out of the light as the cops yell at us to put our clothes on and get out of the car.

"And now I'm thinking, 'Oh my God, this is sooooo embarrassing,' and Eve's mortified and starts to cry, and I'm out there and the cop says, 'What would your parents say if they knew you were up here?'—and that's the weirdest part of all, because actually, our parents would probably have thought this was great, just great! I mean, Eve's folks really liked me, and forever my Mom had been just plain *nuts* about Eve.

"Still, we drove home in silence, mumbled through an awkward goodbye, and went our separate ways . . . for good. I mean, I had been a real dick, calling her from out of the blue with an attitude of 'service me,' we'd been traumatized by the surprise police visit, and somehow the sum total of all the embarrassment we'd suffered through that night managed to keep us apart permanently.

"That's sad."

It's funny how your perspective changes with the passage of time. I can fully understand how Chris and Eve's awkward adventure with the cops drove an embarrassed wedge between them, in looking back it seems to me that what they were doing was completely natural, completely understand-able, and exactly what normal teenagers should be doing. I mean, here were a couple of kids who knew each other well, who felt safe and comfortable with each other, and who were interested in something larger than a solely physical relation-ship. What's wrong with that?

I also love the fact that the cops came and busted 'em up. I mean, I know it sounds dumb, but I can't help thinking of the whole escapade as a sort of R-rated episode of "The Brady Bunch."

26
Reunions, Reruns, and Reincarnations

Nineteen seventy-seven. The Brady Bunch is dead but still alive, gone but not forgotten, canceled but still on the air. Almost immediately after the Bunch bit the dust, Sherwood Schwartz cashed in big and sold all 117 "Brady Bunch"es into syndication. Now, instead of seeing the Bunch for a half-hour each week, we could be found all over the dial, at all times of the day. Thus, even though we'd been canceled, "The Brady Bunch" continued to thrive as a living, breathing, somehow *current* entity in the minds of tens of millions of Americans.

That caused all kinds of repercussions. First of all, "The Brady Bunch" *ruled* (and in a lot of markets *still* rules) syndication, consistently clobbering whatever sacrificial competition was lain in its path. That caused ABC to take notice (industry gossip always maintained that our syndicated rebirth caused heads to roll off of numerous ABC executives). Sherwood Schwartz, raking in huge licensing fees, couldn't *help* noticing. And oh yeah . . . one more guy noticed what was happening, too. His name was Fred Silverman.

Fred Silverman was the network executive responsible for television megahits like "Three's Company" and megaflops like "Supertrain." He's also the man responsible for "The Brady Bunch Hour." In many states he could be hanged for that.

That's because "The Brady Bunch Hour" was perhaps the single worst television program in the history of the medium. The premise, in a malodorous nutshell, asserted that the Bradys (at Bobby's request) had given up their cozy suburban life-style, convinced their dad to quit the architectural rat race, and devoted their lives to putting on the best darn variety show ever!

They didn't even come close.

To begin with, try to remember ABC's mid-seventies variety spectacular "Donny and Marie": huge white teeth, badly sung pop hits, extra-cheesy comedy sketches, and the Ice Vanities, a

What's new pussycat?
(© 1977 American
Broadcasting Co./
Michael Ochs
Archives/Venice, CA)

troupe of big-busted skaters who'd glide around the Osmonds as they smiled, sang, and waved. What you probably *won't* remember is that "Donny and Marie" was a *big* hit for ABC at a time when the network was fairly desperate for ratings. It consistently pulled in *very* respectable Nielsen numbers, and week after week it served as the building block of the network's Sunday-night lineup. One particular Sunday night, the Brady Kids were hauled out of retirement to appear as guest stars on "Donny and Marie," and a funny thing happened: the Osmonds' Nielsens shot way up. So Fred Silverman, then president of ABC, came to the decision to showcase the Bradys in a variety hour of their very own. Sherwood Schwartz recalled: "Silverman calls Sid and Marty Krofft"—who produced "Donny and Marie"—"and asks, 'Can you do *another* family-style variety show that would star the Brady family?' Now, of course, when you're offered this kind of a deal you just say, 'Sure, no problem.' Doesn't matter if that's the truth or not— you just say, 'Sure, no problem. Where's my check?'

"So anyway, Fred Silverman says to them, 'Great, let's sit down and work out a deal,' and they did. Mind you, all of this went on without the consent, or even the knowledge, of Paramount and myself. But to do this new show, with characters that I had created and that I owned, and to use a copyright that was owned jointly by Paramount and myself, they couldn't get to square one without our approval.

"So Marty Krofft calls me and says, 'Let's make some kind of arrangement.' So now what am I gonna do, sue him? And I've always felt that you Brady people should make as much money as you can from the show, and from the Brady name, so I gave in and said, 'Go ahead.'"

So with Sherwood's blessing, the Kroffts set out to re-enlist every one of us original Bradys. In my case, I was living in New York, having just finished a Broadway run as "Pippin," when I got a call from Marty Krofft. "Barry baby," he hollered into the phone excitedly, "we want to do a Brady Bunch variety hour, and *you* can be the *star!*"

Usually, I know better than to believe *anything* a producer

Those disco Bradys.
(© Paramount Pictures)

says, but in this case I bought it! I took the bait hook, line, and sinker, and within two weeks' time I'd packed up my things, said my goodbyes, and flown myself back to Los Angeles.

Once I was there, however, my heart sank, my stomach churned, and a sense of impending doom attached itself firmly to my soul. *Our* show, even from day one, was being hastily thrown together so that it could reach the airwaves quickly. It was also shaping up to be nothing more than a *complete* rip-off of "Donny and Marie." There we were, back in the polyester jumpsuits, back in the fringe, back in the sequins, and back on stage muddling through the weirdest musical numbers imaginable.

Can you possibly comprehend what sort of twisted logic went into having us Bradys perform a medley of "The Hustle" and "Love to Love Ya Baby"? I couldn't, but that's exactly what we did in the grand finale of the show's pilot. And believe it or not, the show actually went downhill from there.

"The Brady Bunch Hour" was incredibly bad, but even *more* incredible was the fact that Robert Reed (who you'd expect would be foaming at the mouth about this mess) really *enjoyed* being on it. I still couldn't figure that one out, so I recently asked Bob the obvious question: why?

"I really *did* want to do it," he confessed. "I mean, I've studied voice and dancing. I'm terrible at both, and proved it to be true, but when Sid and Marty met with me, they described the whole thing in very positive terms, and I thought, 'What fun! This'll be a hoot.' I knew you kids could sing and dance, and Florence obviously could sing, and so while I knew I wouldn't be very good at it, I thought it might be fun to kind of go along for the ride. And that's exactly what I did. I mean, I really *was* lousy, and always the last to learn any new dance step, but to me it was *fun*."

Still, it was gonna take a *lot* more than Robert Reed's enthusiasm to save *this* turkey. I mean, we rehearsed *hard*, working night and day trying to pull this debacle into shape,

YIKES!
(© Paramount Pictures)

but it didn't help. Actually, the situation can best be described by employing the age-old Hollywood edict that "no matter how hard you try, you just can't polish a turd."

By the time we'd spent a mere seven weeks fouling the airwaves, and embarrassing guests like Tina Turner, Farrah Fawcett, Lee Majors, Tony Randall, Vincent Price, and Milton Berle, ABC had seen enough. Our plug was mercifully yanked, and the American viewing public was put out of its misery. The Bradys were once again dead—this time for good . . . maybe.

Flash forward to 1981. Disco's dead, Nancy Reagan has begun redoing the White House, and the Bradys are clawing at their casket, trying to once again rise from the grave. This time around, the call came while I was in Houston, performing in a really enjoyable stage production of *Grease*. I pick up the phone, my agent tells me that the Schwartzes have written a two-hour script called "The Brady Girls Get Married" and that Paramount is interested in shooting the thing. He also starts to tell me about how they'll be using the end result as the pilot for a potential new series. I don't think he'd even half-finished his sentence before I cut him off with a firm "Forget it!"

Why? Simple. Y'see, by now, all of us kids had spent *years* trying to move forward in our careers and live down the whole "Brady Bunch" stigma. It wasn't easy, and despite a few successes, work remained scarce for us Brady Kids. Eve had scored a couple of good breaks with *Dawn: Portrait of a Teenage Runaway,* and *Little Women.* Maureen appeared in a few teen movies like *Skatetown U.S.A.* and *Moonshine County Express,* and I had been touring on stage in musical theater productions, but that was *it.* The other three Bradys were now pretty much out of the business, and we all agreed that our only hope of surviving the unshakable typecasting was to keep ourselves *far* away from Bradyland. On top of all that, from about 1977 through '81, the Bradys' idyllic look at family life had become perceived as laughable, naive, and vaguely threatening to the cynical sensibilities of the seventies. It had been a long time since being a Brady was considered cool, it had now become downright embarrassing.

Casting directors refused to see any of us as anything but Bradys, and that had left us kids just about unemployable.

I think it was Bruce Willis who once said that "television devours actors at about the same rate whales devour plankton." I think he lowballed it.

Now every one of us Bradys was squashed between the same rock and the same hard place. Do you retain your integrity, refuse to re-up as a Brady, and face the future hoping that you can hang on long enough to exorcise the Brady demons from the soul of your career? Or do you take advantage of the opportunity laid at your feet, make a few bucks, and worry about the consequences later?

Almost unanimously, we chose to sever our ties with the Bunch. But when Paramount chose to get "persuasive" ($$$), every one of us caved in and re-enlisted.

The film would mark the one and only time all nine of us original Brady Bunchers would reunite in our entirety. Eve had wisely steered herself clear of the "Variety Hour"; Susan's honeymoon would keep her away from *Brady Christmas*; and Maureen would later bail out of "The Bradys," saying, "I simply felt it was time to move on."

But for now, all nine of us were ready to do the big-happy-family thing one more time. Sherwood Schwartz recollects that Robert Reed even went so far as to loudly proclaim during contract talks that "*nobody* is going to give my Brady girls away but *me!*"

So now a little older, a little wiser, and a little less enthusiastic, the Bradys were once again gathered together on a soundstage, ready to take a stab at reviving the Bunch. The lights came on, the cameras rolled, Bob Reed grumbled about the lousy script . . . it was just like old times.

Only now the girls were married. The story:

Jan is all set to marry a tight-assed college professor named Philip Covington III, and Marcia makes it a double when she decides to marry the fun-loving, irresponsible Wally Logan. All of the Bradys reunite for the wedding, wish the newlyweds well, and then blend into the wallpaper as the two couples spend the last half-hour buying a house . . . together. In the

"The Brady Brides."
(© Paramount Pictures)

end, this "odd quadruple" buys that dream house, finds that their old pal Alice lives just down the street, and they've got themselves a sitcom.

It was simple stuff, standard, formulaic, kinda funny, likable, and it would have made a great TV movie. But that never happened. Shortly before we began shooting, NBC in its infinite wisdom decided that they didn't want to marry off the Brady girls in a ninety-minute blowout, and that three thirty-minute "specials" would suit their needs much better.

So that's what they did. "The Brady Girls Get Married" aired on three consecutive Friday nights in 1981, scored *very* impressively in the overnights, and quickly became a series. Of course, with the double wedding behind them, the newlyweds needed a new title. Thus, "The Brady Brides" was born.

They'd live thirteen weeks before succumbing to bombitis.

So now, the Brady Bunch had gone under a third time, and the clean-cut clan was hovering in a vegetative (so what else is new?), brain-dead (so what else is new?), coma. The end seemed inevitable.

But a Christmas miracle would change all that.

27

A Very Brady Christmas

his was a monster.
This was HUGE!
This was the second-highest-rated TV movie of
1988.

A Very Brady Christmas was the biggest success in the history of the Brady Bunch, but it sure didn't start out that way. With the encouragement of Paramount, CBS, and the Schwartzes, we all screwed on our Brady faces once more and reassembled on the Paramount lot with the joy of seeing old pals, glowing all over the place (the lone exception was Susan Olsen, who was busy honeymooning at Jamaica's "Reggae Sunsplash"). We were laughing, hugging, joking about the film's extremely corny story line, and all over the set there was an air of pleasant camaraderie. Even Robert Reed and the Schwartzes had (at least temporarily) buried the hatchet, meeting before production ever began to hammer out any differences they might face in shooting the Christmas extravaganza.

First day of shooting, a smiling (even "beaming") Robert Reed showed up on set and, sure that he and Sherwood were now beyond their disagreements of the

A Very Brady Christmas cast photo. (Courtesy Sherwood Schwartz)

Robert and Sherwood, burying the hatchet (yet again) at the *Brady Christmas* wrap party. (Courtesy Sherwood Schwartz)

Eve Plumb and Richard Dean ("MacGyver") Anderson at the *Brady Christmas* wrap party. (Courtesy Sherwood Schwartz)

past, made his pleasant hellos. And then it happened. Here's how Bob remembered it:

"When I first saw the script, I had a discussion with Sherwood because I felt that some of the characters were just absolutely clichéd. Especially [Jan's] husband, Philip—I mean, his every line was just a single-thrust joke. There was no character there. In fact there was *nothing* there. It was predictable, it was unfunny; and so I went in to Sherwood's office and I said, 'We've got to change this.' And Sherwood and I sat down together and had some *very* nice discussions about it.

"So now I go to the set on the first day of shooting, and I was a little early, so I'm watching this scene with this woman who's supposed to be in labor, and she's doing farce comedy—not well!—and my mouth fell open, because nobody's doing anything about it, not even the director. He's letting it go and looking like he's happy with it. So I just slapped my forehead and yelled, 'Jesus Christ!' And Lloyd Schwartz comes running up, so I said something like, 'We *are* going to keep our feet in reality, aren't we?' And he tried to be positive, but by now I was really burning, and I made some scathing remark like, 'Look at that overacting dildo up there. She couldn't act her way out of a wet paper bag!' At that point Lloyd took a beat, looked at me, and said, 'Bob . . . that's my wife' Just like that. Like a wounded puppy.

"I was obviously shocked and mortified. But then, when I began to assimilate the information, the whole thing struck me as *hugely* funny. Looking into his eyes, I knew I'd probably hurt him, but at the same time I was biting the insides of my mouth, thinking, 'Please don't laugh, *please* don't laugh.' I mean, I *was* outraged that anyone would let that person up there do this, but I *did* feel terrible about it, and it was just a *gross* thing to say."

Remarkably, though, even with that opening-day disaster, we all managed to stay on pretty good terms as we muddled through our hokey two-hour Yuletide melodrama. We smiled as the Bradys reunited for the holidays, smiled through subplots that found Marcia's husband Wally out of work, Bobby dropping out of college to become a race-car driver, and Jan, Philip, Alice, and Sam the Butcher contemplating divorce. We even did our best to be convincing when our heartfelt rendition of "O Come All Ye Faithful" miraculously saved Mike Brady from a construction-site cave-in.

Of course, our *biggest* smiles came when the overnight ratings showed up and we realized that *A Very Brady Christmas* had been the recipient of its very own Christmas miracle: MASSIVE Nielsen numbers. In fact, even capitalizing the word "massive" doesn't do our ratings justice. We'd scored a 39 share, which (translated into English) means that 39 percent of all the televisions turned on in America were tuned in to the Bradys' holiday heartwarmer.

Paramount was stunned, and ecstatically shaking its head over the unshakable, unbreakable Brady following. Sherwood too was thrilled, and within weeks those two entities were meeting and hashing out a plan to once again make the Brady Bunch an ongoing commodity.

It was a joyous occasion, but it may have been the beginning of the end.

28
"The Bradys"

his will take some explaining.

You already know that *A Very Brady Christmas* ran amok through the Nielsens, pummeling the competition.

CBS knew it too, and with that knowledge, their desire for more Brady product probably seems not only understandable but logical as well.

That's important, because it marks perhaps the one "logical" thought in the entire lifespan of the atrocious unnatural disaster that would come to be known as "The Bradys."

Still basking in the afterglow of their TV movie megahit, Sherwood Schwartz and CBS became chummy and began toying with the idea of doing three more two-hour TV movies. A plan was hatched wherein the first film would deal with Bobby's auto racing career, his crash, his subsequent injuries, his rehabilitation, and his wedding. As an extra added ratings ploy, it was set to air in May during the week of the Indianapolis 500. The second film would deal with Mike Brady's budding political career and would air in November during election week.

"The Bradys."
(© 1990 Paramount
Pictures)

All sides agreed that they'd come up with a pretty rational plan; but when CBS got greedy, that rational plan got tossed out the window. Y'see, the brain trust at the network reasoned that if doing three Brady movies was a good idea, then doing a six-episode series would be *twice* as good.

It wasn't, and from here on in, the latest Brady reunion began a slow, painful process of self-destruction. Leading off the lineup of destruction was CBS's unshakable belief that "The Bradys," which was at least *intended* to be a dramatic and adult-oriented sequel series to "The Brady Bunch," could best serve the network's needs by manning our old comfortable Friday-night-at-eight time slot (traditionally dominated by kid-oriented shows with *very* young demographics).

Over time, "The Bradys" would spark a veritable avalanche of heated confrontations, but the time-slot issue would bear the dubious distinction of igniting the inaugural one. The opponents in this preliminary bout were

Sherwood Schwartz and the entire programming department at CBS. Sherwood remembers it this way:

"They insisted that we go on at eight o'clock, and I said, 'It's absolutely gonna *fail* at eight o'clock. It'll succeed at nine, but it can't possibly succeed at eight.' And that was simply because it's now 1990, and the people who love these characters and who grew up with these characters aren't out there at eight o'clock anymore. They're grown-ups—nine o'clock and even ten o'clock viewers now. I mean, I practically begged, 'Put us on at ten, I don't care, but just don't stick us with that eight o'clock slot.'"

But they did, reasoning with typically tunnel-visioned insight, "Our problems are not at nine and ten, our problems are at eight—'Full House' is *killing* us." That *really* aggravated the normally unflappable Mr. Sherwood Schwartz: "I yelled at them, 'We *can't* fight against "Full House," because that's exactly what *we* used to be.' They were dead wrong, but wouldn't budge. All you had to do was look at the ratings for that special two-hour premiere episode. From eight to nine it got beaten up in the ratings, but from nine to ten it clobbered everything! We were in the wrong time slot, and obviously so."

But I'm getting ahead of myself. For now, it will suffice to say that an egregiously inappropriate time slot would cause "The Bradys" to be born with one strike already against it.

Strike two followed almost immediately, but this time the problems had nothing to do with scheduling and everything to do with the creative quality of the show. Basically, the Schwartzes sold the show to CBS, and to all of *us*, as a "continuing adult drama." They'd even nicknamed the project "Bradysomething," hoping to drive home the fact that they'd be striving for solid, believable, real-life story lines that would propel the Brady characters into the 1990s and even smudge their squeaky-clean image a bit.

But somehow that just never happened, and it left all of us a bit bewildered, and more than a bit disappointed. The *most* vocally dissatisfied among us (not surprisingly) was Robert Reed. He was quite simply appalled by the scripts, story lines, and direction of "The Bradys" and makes no bones about expressing his dissatisfaction:

"They failed to recognize that time has passed, times have changed, tastes have changed, we're older, and you just can't write the same old show. But here again Sherwood talks a great sociological notion. 'We'll bring them up to date. We'll bring in modern problems. We'll deal with issues like paraplegia and alcoholism.' And again I made the mistake of thinking, 'Yeah, that sounds pretty good. Why not?' and I asked Sherwood, 'You're not gonna just make the issues episodic, and have somebody paraplegic or alcoholic in one episode, and cured in the next, right?' 'Oh, no,' he said. 'We're gonna carry it on.'

"Sure we did. Marcia became alcoholic in two or three days and was busy preaching the Twelve Steps in less than a week. Again it was horse shit. But Sherwood doesn't recognize that."

So, like Godzilla and Mothra, Robert Reed and the Schwartzes had spent years apart from one another only to rise up and battle it out once more. Their disdain for one another was unmistakable, and even the notion of keeping up appearances went out the window. This time around, there were no rules, no disqualifications, and no holds barred.

Reed threw the first punch by going over Sherwood's head and taking his gripes to the programming executives at Paramount. Robert explains:

"Look, nothing on God's green earth could have saved that show," he said. "I know that from the other side now, from the network and studio's point of view. In dollars and cents, Paramount took it up the ass in order to produce the series. They were losing five hundred thousand dollars an episode, so they were *really* pulling for this show to catch on. But then they discovered right away, and I was *bellowing* this to them, that they couldn't let Sherwood write this show or it would end up in the dirt. And when that finally dawned on them, they couldn't get anyone else to write it. Nobody would take the job. Nobody would go in there with Sherwood executive-producing and calling the shots—nobody that was *good*, anyway. And if you just go out and hire some lumber to do it,

Sherwood's gonna dominate them anyway. The whole point was to get somebody in there who had good credits, and a credible line on the show.

"And then the studio's theory became 'We'll go through the first six, and then, whether Sherwood likes it or not, he's out. Not out entirely, but there'll be somebody else in there executive-producing, and somebody else in there to write.' And I kept saying, 'You're gonna lose this show before we get there. It won't last that long—you've got to do it *now*.'

"But the network was all in transition at the time. They knew [Jeff] Sagansky was coming in [as CBS's new president], and you couldn't get a straight answer from anybody because they were all afraid for their jobs. I'd send notes over there, but nobody would *do* anything. I think that's what killed the show."

Maybe. But I personally feel that the *real* problem with "The Bradys" wasn't so much its clichéd scripts and story lines as it was a complete lack of focus. I mean, whereas "The Brady Bunch" was always a series about a mom, a dad, and their kids, "The Bradys" multiplied that cast of characters exponentially by saddling almost every original character with a spouse, kids, problems, and story lines exclusively their own. That made for a cast of characters so complicated and story lines so confusing that it became nearly impossible to keep track of the action without a scorecard. Each episode of "The Bradys" revolved around the trials and tribulations of Marcia, Wally and their kids, Jessica and Mickey; Greg, his wife, Nora, and nerdy son, Kevin; Jan, hubby Philip, and their adopted Korean daughter, Patty; Bobby and *his* extra-perky wife, Tracey (played by extra-perky MTV veejay Martha Quinn); Peter and his fiancee, Valerie; Cindy and her boyfriend, Gary; Mike and Carol; and, of course, Alice . . . Whew! That's *nineteen* major characters. Maybe numbered uniforms would have helped keep things straight.

"The Bradys," for all the good intentions and hard work, was shaping up to be a disaster. CBS knew it, Paramount knew it, and of course we Bradys knew it too.

Too many Bradys. (Courtesy Sherwood Schwartz)

Then an even bigger disappointment occurred. In the midst of all this turmoil, infighting, and dissatisfaction, the "Bradys" set became an unhappy place. I mean, lord knows we'd done our share of less-than-stellar television work, but through it all, the "Brady" soundstage was always one of the happiest in Hollywood. Now, though, we were embarrassed by the series and exhausted from shooting it, and the novelty of reuniting had worn thin. Our bodies were tired, our nerves were shot, and the mood of the day turned sour.

The Bradys even started to fight among themselves. I'm not talking about knock-down-drag-outs, but by Brady-set standards, even a verbal blowout was something simply unheard of . . . until now. Florence was first to crack, going head-to-head against a griping Robert Reed. I didn't witness the altercation, but Lloyd Schwartz told me about it: "We were shooting a scene wherein Alice was supposed to come into the room carrying a cake that's just *loaded* with lit candles. Now Bob, being of course the master of reality that he is, sighs disgustedly and says, 'Where would Alice light all these candles?' So I just say, 'I don't know—out *there*.' And Bob answers, 'Well, one person couldn't possibly light all those candles alone.' Now Florence is wonderful, but if you somehow manage to get her mad at you, she'll let you have it big-time. And by now Bob is ranting and raving like, 'I cannot allow myself to participate in this implausible shit. I have built my career as an actor upon drawing from reality.' That statement packs a double wallop for Florence, because it implies that *he's* a great actor and *she's* a hack. Anyway, Florence turns to him, and hisses, 'Well, maybe it's time you thought about getting a *new* career.' And this happened in front of *everybody*. Bob ended up storming off the set."

Strike three?

We were doomed. There isn't *any* argument about the fact that we Bradys were the closest TV family in the history of television; and now, thanks to our frustrating situation, we'd begun coming apart at the seams. Even Ann B. Davis, the sweetest woman on the face of the planet, wasn't immune—as Bob Reed found out one day on the set. Bob was loudly parodying Mike Brady's lines, and as Ann remembers it: "Alice was supposed to be doing a bit in Bobby's wheelchair, and Bob decided to make fun of the script by adjusting his originally scripted line to read, 'Gee, Alice, if this doesn't work we'll be in deep shit.'" Normally, Ann B. would've simply let Bob's remark pass, but not now. This time, she shot back, "Well, I don't know, Mr. Brady—how deep *is* your shit?"

As the weeks passed, the situation got worse. By now, *all* of us were aware of just how awful this series had become, but Bob Reed (who'd gone from appalled to disgusted) took action. This time he bypassed Sherwood, bypassed Paramount, and went straight to the top of the totem pole by taking his gripes to the head honchos at CBS.

Right now, I can combine clichés by saying that Robert's rebellion opened up a *huge* can of worms and might just have been the straw that broke the Bradys' back. Here's *his* side of the story.

"I kept notes on the show, and used 'em in writing critiques, the first of which was twelve pages long and basically said, '*This* sucks, *this* sucks, *this* sucks.' And I sent 'em off to the network, as well as to the front office and to Sherwood.

"Well, the lid blew off at Paramount, and they said, 'How

dare you send this to the network!' And I replied, 'They've got to know—maybe they can help.' And the studio got used to that after a while, but Sherwood never did. I had made a permanent enemy. And he'd say, 'Come to *me*. Come to *me* if you have a problem,' so I did on the first one.

"We'd go over my complaints item by item, and Sherwood would interrupt and talk about saving Red Skelton's career or something for forty-five minutes, and Lloyd would sit by his side, nodding, and saying things like 'Go with Dad. Just trust Dad.' So anyway, we'd talk very nicely about it, but the changes we'd get back the next day in the green pages [rewrites] were tiny, and about as useful as a Band-Aid at a train wreck. Apparently everything we'd talked about, someone else was hearing, because Sherwood certainly didn't hear any of it. And after doing that for a while I thought, '*Bullshit!* Time to go to the source, hammer at it, and see what we can do.' Well, that may have helped to destroy the show. I don't know."

With or without Robert's assistance, CBS decided (probably wisely) that six episodes of "The Bradys" were enough, and America's favorite family was laid to rest once more—perhaps *this* time for good.

Actually, given the history and track record of the Bunch, we'll probably resurrect ourselves again sooner or later, and show up in something like *Return from Beneath the Planet of the Bradys*, Part 8: "Sam the Butcher's Revenge." I asked Sherwood Schwartz what *he* thought the future might hold for us Bradys, and after one of his trademark ear-to-ear grins and a thoughtful pause, he told me this:

"I don't know what's in store for the Bradys, but I *do* believe that at some point in the future they may very well come back.

"I mean, I think there will always be a place for positive role models on TV, and there really aren't any to be found anymore. Everywhere you look on television, parents are insulting kids, kids are insulting parents, and they're all based in negativity. And I think that's created a longing in viewers, even if it's a sub-conscious longing, for characters who are nice to each other, and who get along with each other, and who help each other, and who genuinely love each other, instead of simply volleying insults back and forth for a cheap, easy laugh."

I completely agree.

29
Once a Brady . . .

eople continually ask me questions about "The Brady Bunch" that I just plain can't answer. For instance, not a week goes by when someone doesn't come up to me and ask if the Bradys are like a real family *offscreen*. The answer to a question like that depends entirely upon your own personal definition of "family."

Do I feel like a brother to Florence Henderson's four real-life kids? No. Do I send a Father's Day card to Robert Reed each year? No. Do we Bradys get together for Thanksgiving, or Christmas, or the Fourth of July? Not without a television crew.

Webster's biggest dictionary defines "family" in part as "a group of related people," but for me, that definition's got to be expanded to cover any group of people who share experiences in common, who enjoy constancy, like purposes, similar goals, and the love and support of one another. Your "family" is made up of the people in your life that are there for the long haul, whom you *can't* get rid of even if you want to. They're the people you count on, that come through for you, and who share in the important events of your life.

With that understanding, there is no doubt that we Bradys are indeed family.

Like most families, the Bunch was not always harmonious and smooth-sailing. Most of the time, doing the show was a job, full of demands, annoyances, and responsibilities. We didn't sit down to discuss how important we were to one another or how great it was having a second family. In fact, there were large periods of time when most of us kids just didn't want to be Bradys anymore.

In looking back on my real family, the similarities are obvious. While the Bradys never sat around talking about being a family, neither did my real family, and lord knows there were *some* adolescent times when I just didn't want to be a member of *that* bunch either. However, in *both* cases, there was always an abundance of caring, compassion, affection, and positive intention. We covered for each other, made each other smile, and made sure we were there when it counted.

So while it's tough for me to come up with an all-encompassing definition of "family," I *do* know that it's got to be based more on feeling, understanding, and appreciation than on genetics. This was *clearly* illustrated for me in July 1990.

I had gotten extraordinarily lucky and managed to find someone wonderful. Her name is Diane, and soon after we met I found myself bound and determined to spend the rest of my life with her. I proposed, told Diane how absolutely crazy I was about her, and discovered that (fortunately) the feeling was mutual.

Now we had a wedding to plan.

Neither one of us was a big fan of those oversized, gaudy weddings full of distant relatives and bridesmaids in sherbet-colored gowns that they'll never wear again, so we decided to keep it moderate, including only those people who were *very* close to us and had made a real difference in our lives.

The Bradys were at the top of my invite list.

After months of planning, planning, and more planning, the big day finally dawned, and it was perfect. The ceremony took place on a warm summer evening under a brilliant orange sunset, overlooking the beach at Santa Monica. We had designed our seating so that as we were exchanging vows, we would be facing our guests; and there were a *couple* of reasons for that. First, we wanted our guests to be able to see *and* hear the vows; and second, as an actor, I couldn't stand the thought of Diane and me standing "center stage" with our backs to the audience!

The ceremony went off without a hitch. But the one thing I wasn't prepared for, and will never forget, was standing upon that low platform and facing our friends, guests, and families. It's funny, but there is a way that doing something really momentous in your life forces you to stop and reflect. As the minister spoke, I took the time to look at our friends and felt a warm flood of memories wash over me. I saw Susan Olsen and immediately she was back in pigtails. I noted that Eve Plumb's smile is still crooked and warm, and took a moment to look into Maureen's pretty eyes and recall the best of our times together. On my left, Chris Knight was standing tall as best man.

Sherwood Schwartz gazed toward me, as did Lloyd, with proud, almost fatherly stares. Frances Whitfield, who had been such a positive influence upon the lives of all the Brady kids, took my mind's eye back once more to her always bustling, always creative classroom. Robert Reed was perhaps happier than I ever remembered seeing him, laughing, joking, and mingling with my real parents, my brothers, and yes, even the Schwartzes.

I also took a moment to reflect upon Michael Lookinland. He was unable to attend, as he was busy at home attending to his lovely and *very* pregnant wife. She would deliver a beautiful baby boy just three days later.

And then there was Florence, my "mother," my onetime date, my constant theatrical supporter, smiling and misty-eyed just like my real mom. Adding to the emotion of the moment, Florence got up from her chair, stepped up to a microphone, and began to sing in clear, beautiful tones the song "All I Ask

A family portrait.
(© Photography by Henry/ Northridge, CA)

of You" from *Phantom of the Opera*. When she finished, there wasn't a dry eye left on the lawn.

And so from time to time, as I count my blessings, always included among the things I'm most grateful for are the experiences, both good and tough, that I've had over the years with my family, the Bradys.

An Insider's Guide To "The Brady Bunch"

PILOT: "THE HONEYMOON"

Michael Albert Brady takes Carol Tyler Martin to be his lawfully wedded wife, and 116 chaotic half-hours ensue.

Actually, as the episode begins, we find Mike jittery about his impending nuptials, but too busy with his three boys/best men to pay it much attention. With only moments to spare, the "men named Brady" still have four tuxedos to press, four bow ties to knot, and four hairstyles to Brylcreem into submission.

Over at Carol's place, the Aqua-Net's flying as the girls (as

(© Paramount Pictures)

The official wedding photo. I look like I'm passing a kidney stone.
(©Paramount Pictures)

a committee) help Carol into her bright yellow wedding gown. They're even more nervous than the boys; but with a group hug and "I love yous" all around, they manage to pull through just fine.

Come ceremony time, Mike says "I do," Carol says "I do," we've got ourselves a sitcom, and everything is perfect . . . until:

Tiger, the boys' ever-faithful pet pooch, gets overheated while patiently viewing the wedding from inside Mike's car. He spies Fluffy, the girls' fiendish feline (in a one-episode cameo) watching the ceremony from a much better seat, and mocking him with her eyes. That's too much for the old mutt to bear. With a bark, he jumps, hits the automatic window button, and, as it descends, pounces out of the car, and through the ceremony, lunging toward his feline lunch.

As bride, groom, ushers, bridesmaids, preacher, guests, and Alice the housekeeper scramble after the unruly beasts, they just make things worse. The hairy sprinters jump up, over, and through the caterer's table, dash across the floral centerpiece, barrel under the cake table, and then . . .

The large, beautifully tiered wedding cake takes a direct doggie hit and begins sliding toward its doom. Mike makes a last-ditch dive to save the day, but ends up covered with frosting instead.

Carol frantically catches up with her new hubby, and together they survey the canine carnage—and find humor amid the disaster. Then, their eyes meet, the music swells, and . . . Kissville.

Time for the honeymoon.

Our newlyweds are checking into their honeymoon suite when Mike absentmindedly signs the register "Mr. and Mrs. Mike Brady and Family."

"Mr. and Mrs. Mike Brady and *Family?*" asks the persnickety, Charles Nelson Reilly–esque desk clerk. "You *did* request the honeymoon suite?"

Carol blushes and tries to explain the situation, but Mike's not having it.

"Forget it, honey," Mike commands. "It's obvious that *he*

"Okay, stairway fight scene, take 1. Ready?...
(© Paramount Pictures)

... and Action!"
(© Paramount Pictures)

doesn't understand the *mod* generation." (Like Mike *does*.)

They march upstairs, prepare to consummate their brains out, but . . . just can't do it. Turns out they *both* feel bad about yelling at their kids during the Fluffy vs. Tiger fracas. So, before they even get to second base, they're back running home (in their pajamas) to pick up the Bunch.

They round up the girls first, and then it's on to Mike's house for the boys.

"I've never been on a honeymoon," squeaks Bobby. "Whatya take?"

"A *girl*, dummy!" cracks that cosmopolitan wisenheimer Greg.

As it turns out, they don't have to pack at all. Surprise! Alice has already done it for them. "I figured you'd be back," she chortles at Mike.

So, we're off to the hotel together. The entire Brady brood arrives, and much to the consternation of the smarmy desk clerk, marches upstairs toward five seasons of sitcom bliss.

WRITER: Sherwood Schwartz
DIRECTOR: John Rich

•Sherwood and the network locked horns over the fate of

Carol's first husband. Sherwood wanted him alive, well, and happily divorced from Carol, but the network demanded his death. Sherwood met with the brass, smiled, nodded, and was extremely polite, but paid no attention to their suggestions: he left the fate of the girls' father uncertain. You may notice she *never* refers to the guy as being dead. In *Sherwood's* mind, Carol Brady was television's first divorcee!

•We shot this pilot almost a full *year* before our first real episode, and as a result you'll notice that most of us kids are genuinely *tiny*, especially Bobby and Cindy. Also, notice Bobby's reddish blond hair color. That's his natural shade; the black stuff you'd see on his head for the next few years came out of a bottle.

EPISODE 1: "DEAR LIBBY"

Marcia reads the "Dear Libby" column one morning and nearly gags on her Lucky Charms over what she's found. An unhappy newlywed has written to Libby saying that the new spouse's kids are making life unbearable. The kids become convinced that the letter was written by either Mike or Carol, and panic.

Things calm down only after Dear Libby herself shows up on the Brady doorstep to verify that her original letter came from somewhere in Oklahoma, hundreds of miles away from the nearest Brady.

WRITER: Lois Hire
DIRECTOR: John Rich

•Episodes 1 through 6 were all filmed simultaneously. As we began production on the series, Florence Henderson was busy shooting *Song of Norway* and not yet available to begin shooting her Brady scenes. To accommodate her, the production company took all of the first six episodes, assigned them to director John Rich, and shot them completely out of order. With Florence away, we spent our days shooting all the scenes that she *wasn't* in. That created a hopelessly jumbled shooting schedule, and a number of scenes that were filmed without us ever knowing what episode they belonged to.

EPISODE 2: "A CLUBHOUSE IS NOT A HOME"

This episode marks one of the very few story lines wherein the Brady siblings interacted like *real* siblings. They yelled at each other, fist-fought with each other, and generally, hated each other's guts. The battle of the sexes explodes when the girls decide to integrate the boys' males-only clubhouse and form a picket line outside its front door.

WRITER: Skip Webster
DIRECTOR: John Rich

•This also marks the first time that we Brady kids became prop guys. Lloyd Schwartz was a stickler for realism, so any time a script called for a kid-made prop, that kid, not a prop man, was expected to actually make it. In this show, we made the picket signs that the girls parade around the boys' clubhouse, and are they ugly!

EPISODE 3: "KITTY KARRYALL IS MISSING"

This is one of the Brady episodes that people seem to remember vividly. You know: Cindy's beloved (ugly) doll "Kitty Karryall" turns up missing shortly after Bobby has angrily wished out loud that he'd like to get rid of the plastic-headed baby once and for all. Cindy accuses Bobby of assassinating Kitty. Then, when Bobby's kazoo disappears, *he* accuses Cindy of thievery too. Finally, after a whole lot of misplaced finger-pointing, we discover that *Tiger* (who else?) was the real dollnapper/kazoo-klepto. Ms. Karryall is found in the doghouse covered with dog slobber, but otherwise okay, and tranquility reigns once more at the Brady place.

WRITERS: Al Schwartz and Bill Freedman
DIRECTOR: John Rich

•There were actually two Kitty Karryalls that existed on the "Brady" set. Today, one lives at Eve Plumb's house, and the other is kept safe and warm with Susan Olsen. Sorta heartwarming, huh?

•*Nepotism Alert!* Al Schwartz, who co-wrote this episode, is the older brother of "Brady" creator Sherwood Schwartz. He's also the guy who got Sherwood his first-ever comedy-writing job, as a "joke man" on Bob Hope's radio show.

EPISODE 4: "KATCHOO"

Jan's sneezing like crazy, and the Bradys come to the conclusion that their beloved middle girl is suffering from a severe allergy. They have no idea what's *causing* the problem, but all eyes (and noses) eventually turn toward Tiger. Jan then takes a test whiff of the mutt and the phlegm flies big-time. Things look mighty bad for the barking Brady until an eleventh-hour realization that Jan's not actually allergic to Tiger but to his new brand of *flea powder!* A quick change in doggie toiletries saves the poor old pup from homelessness.

Normally whenever I'm asked "Whatever happened to Tiger?" I'll hide the truth, fake a plastic smile, and spit out some insipid euphemism like "Well, Tiger's in doggie heaven now." That's because the *real* answer to "Whatever happened to Tiger?" has been *just too gruesome* to talk about—till now.

Tiger's last photo.
(Courtesy
Sherwood Schwartz)

It's July 1969, and we're sweating through filming on "Katchoo." It's been a long, *hot* day on the set, and we still have to shoot the episode's climactic scene. In it, Mike and Carol uneasily tell the kids that the Brady house just isn't big enough for both Jan's nasal cavities and good ol' Tiger. The dog has got to go.

So all six of us Brady kids prepare for the scene. We run lines, we crank our waiflike pouts into overdrive, and a couple of us get artificially teary-eyed by tweezing out a few nosehairs. That way, when the camera rolls and we hang onto Tiger with maudlin fervor, we'll be able to convincingly sob goodbye forever to our faithful pet. Forget about tugging on America's heartstrings; we wanted to *yank* 'em.

Fifteen minutes later, the camera's loaded and we're ready to roll. Our bogus Brady bawling is at its zenith, and there's Kleenex aplenty standing by. Our only problem is that Tiger, *very* uncharacteristically, won't sit still for the shot. He also seems unusually nervous and keeps trying to run off the set. Finally, after several dog-flubbed takes, Lloyd Schwartz snaps and yells at the trainer. "What the hell's wrong with the dog? We've got a scene to shoot here!" he erupts.

The trainer hems and haws, looks down, shuffles his feet, stalls, and finally, sensing that all is lost, fesses up. "Well, uh . . . y'see . . . uh . . . it's a different dog," he mumbles.

"*What?!!!!!!!*" yelps Lloyd.

Turns out that during the previous evening the *real* Tiger had gone out for a walk, and in scouting around for a suitable location in which to relieve himself, had managed to get run over by a loaded florist's truck.

TV superstar one day, road pizza the next. Like Mansfield and Dean before him, Tiger had prematurely terminated his skyrocketing career, and become another one of Hollywood's tragic auto statistics.

Now you're asking "Who's this imposter dog?" Well, shortly after the *real* Tiger got squashed, his trainer, afraid of losing his canine meal ticket, went scouring the dog pounds of Los Angeles in search of a Tiger look-alike. Miraculously, he got lucky, found a reasonable facsimile, and with fingers crossed he dragged his counterfeit canine onto the set.

The only problem was that *this* dog couldn't act, couldn't do tricks, couldn't follow directions, peed on the props, and absolutely, positively refused to sit still in front of the camera. He *hoped* no one would notice.

In fact, the next time you happen across this "Katchoo" episode, look very closely at the "Farewell, Tiger" scene. You'll notice that our pseudo-Tiger is actually *nailed to the floor!* No, we didn't *hurt* him (c'mon, that wouldn't be Bradylike), but the only way we could get him to hold still through the scene was to have the prop guys nail a dog collar to the floor of the set, and then strap the imposter into it.

Shortly thereafter, we Bradys wisely limited Tiger's appearances to the occasional cameo.

WRITER: William Cowley
DIRECTOR: John Rich

EPISODE 5: "EENIE MEENIE MOMMY DADDY"

This was the first story Sherwood Schwartz ever came up with for "The Brady Bunch." Actually, that's a lie. Sherwood's *daughter* Hope came up with this particular story line—or maybe I should say "came home" with it. One day in 1966 she came home from junior high with a dilemma. She was going to be in a school play, but because the school had a very small auditorium, they could only give each kid one ticket. This presented a problem for Hope, but then she told her dad about a classmate who was *really* upset about the whole thing.

Turns out there was a boy in Hope's class whose mother had just gotten remarried, and he didn't know whether to give the ticket to his new dad, to show him that he was okay, or to give it to his mom, and risk hurting the new father's feelings.

Bingo, a Brady episode was born.

Obviously, Sherwood took the story and ran with it, by giving the problem of Hope's classmate to Cindy.

WRITER: Joanna Lee
DIRECTOR: John Rich

•Look closely at the elf in Cindy's play and you'll recognize him as Brian Forster, the kid who played Chris on that show about America's second-favorite oversized sitcom bunch, "The Partridge Family."

•By now, Robert Reed was already disgusted with the show's scripts, was constantly at odds with John Rich, and had tried on at least two occasions to be released from his contract.

EPISODE 6: "ALICE DOESN'T LIVE HERE ANYMORE"

Why does a family with a full-time mom/housewife need a maid? Good question, and it's the one that got Alice into all sorts of trouble. In an attempt to make Carol feel more need-ed in the Brady household, Alice stops dispensing free advice, first aid, and menial help, and starts sending the kids and their problems to their mom. Pretty soon, Carol's a whiz with skinned knees and bruised egos, and Alice gets the idea that she's not needed anymore. She decides to move out, and only a "Brady Kid scheme" wherein we all act like helpless, com-pletely incompetent geeks in order to prove Alice's indispens-ability, convinces her to stay.

WRITER: Paul West
DIRECTOR: John Rich

•This was the last episode directed by John Rich. In addi-tion to directing our first seven episodes, John Rich was a profit participant in the show along with Sherwood Schwartz. Sherwood by this time already had one genuine hit with "Gilligan's Island." Reasoning that "lightning doesn't strike the same place twice," Mr. Rich sold his share to Paramount for $25,000 during our first year of production. I guess he felt it was highly unlikely that the "Bunch" would enjoy the same success as the "Island."

I asked Sherwood what that percentage would be worth

today had John kept it, and he assured me, "A hell of a lot more than twenty-five thousand dollars!"

EPISODE 7: "FATHER OF THE YEAR"

Marcia goes gaga for Mike, decides to enter him in the local newspaper's "Father of the Year" contest, and kooky hijinks ensue. Marcia tries to keep it a secret and ends up sneaking out of the house in the middle of the night (clad in her PJs and yellow fuzzy slippers) to mail the entry. Mike, of course, finds out about Marcia's midnight stroll, goes banshee, and when Marcia fails to tell him *why* she snuck out, he grounds the gal, forbidding her to go on the family's upcoming ski trip. Ouch!

Marcia's miserable; betrayed by the man she loves, she sadly watches Alice flop about the backyard in her first ever ski-lesson, and bawls her head off at the slightest mention of her grounding. But then, just when things seem blackest, in come the newspaper types to present Mike's award. The light dawns, all is forgiven, and the Bradys continue happily onward.

WRITER: Skip Webster
DIRECTOR: George Cahan

EPISODE 8: "THE GRASS IS ALWAYS GREENER"

This one plays up the old husband-versus-wife "Let's switch places and prove who's got the harder job" cliché. Variations on this theme predate the episode at least as far back as "I Love Lucy," but somehow it always seems to work. Our version had Carol, with bouffant firmly shellacked into place over a dingy gray sweat suit, clumsily take over coaching the boys' baseball practice, while Mike works with his daughters on Marcia's Girl Scout cooking project (he drops a dozen eggs, falls down no less than three times, and ultimately ends up with his head in a sudsy mop bucket). It's a 1970s victory for women's lib.

WRITER: David P. Harmon
DIRECTOR: George Cahan

•Watch Bob Reed's first fall in the Brady kitchen. You'll notice that it looks a little slow and overly cautious. The reason, as Ann B. Davis tells it, is that in rehearsing the fall, Bob took a genuine header and nearly brained himself:

"The script called for Bob to drop an egg on the floor, step on it, and fall, which he asserted was ridiculous, asinine, totally unbelievable, and the *worst* kind of hack slapstick—the usual tirade. But he *did* consent to rehearse it once, and when he did, he really did slip on the egg, and I swear he hit the floor so hard that the walls shook.

"Then, after I'd ascertained that he hadn't killed himself, I asked him, 'Do you think you can play the scene realistically now?' At which point he looked up at me, smiled, and said, 'You know, Annie, the whole way down, I was thinking to myself, 'I deserve this.' "

EPISODE 9: "SORRY, RIGHT NUMBER"

Six kids, one phone: HUGE problem. This week, we kids are fighting over phone calls, the bills are astronomical (Mike says they're "over *thirty* dollars a month!"—wow!); so when Alice jokes that they oughta install a pay phone, Mike snaps, and gleefully does just that.

In the years since this episode first aired, I've met numerous real families who've tried the same thing.

WRITER: Ruth Brooks Flippen
DIRECTOR: George Cahan

•Alice gets a boyfriend—Hooray! This episode marks the birth of Sam Franklin (I bet you thought his last name was "Da Butcher"). Played by Allan Melvin, he'd show up in seven more "Brady Bunch" episodes, and come reunion time, he'd own the distinction of being married to our pal Alice Nelson (yep, *she* had a last name too).

EPISODE 10: "IS THERE A DOCTOR IN THE HOUSE?"

Yikes! Everybody's sick! Peter gets the measles, then Jan,

Reed, Henderson, Ross, and Anderson.
(© 1991 Capital Cities/ABC, Inc.)

and pretty soon those little red spots are *everywhere!* Problem is, whose doctor gets to heal the Bunch? The boys vote for *their* doctor, Dr. Cameron, a man; but the girls insist upon being treated by Dr. Porter, a woman. In the end, the Bradys solve the problem by employing *both* doctors, and that's that. Why we spent a half-hour reaching that obvious compromise, I have no idea.

WRITER: Ruth Brooks Flippen
DIRECTOR: Oscar Rudolph

•This episode is jam-packed with visiting TV parents. A guy named Herbert Anderson plays Dr. Cameron, but take one look at his face and you'll immediately recognize him as the father of Dennis the Menace. On the flip side of the doctor dilemma, you'll find Marion Ross. She plays Dr. Porter, but she's about to become Richie Cunningham's Mom, Mrs. C.

EPISODE 11: "54-40 AND FIGHT"

This episode is full of weird hobbies, weird activities, and *really* weird parenting. In it, you're asked to believe that all six Brady kids are fanatically into collecting trading stamps—like, the old "Green Stamps" that your mother might have saved. Once you've bought that, you discover that the trading stamp company is going out of business and that the kids have to cash in their booty soon, or lose it forever. The monkey wrench in all this is that the girls have fifty-four books of stamps, the boys have forty, and neither individual amount will get you anything that's even worth the trip to the store.

So, the kids decide to combine books for one *good* item, but then can't agree on what to get. They guys want a rowboat, and the girls (stereotypically) are just dying to get their hands on a sewing machine. Neither side gives in, so Mike and Carol have to make the decision.

Here's where the bizarre parenting comes in. Instead of preaching compromise, our normally sane parental units lose their minds and allow the kids to build a house of cards, with each kid adding a card in turn. Whoever knocks down the house loses their stamp booklets, disappoints their gender mates, and probably becomes scarred for life.

After a long, tense playing-card construction project, Tiger jumps on Greg, Greg *falls* into the table, and the girls win. However, once the gals actually get to the store (again stereotypically), they go soft and end up getting a present that everybody can share: a *color* (ooooooh!) TV.

WRITER: Burt Styler
DIRECTOR: Oscar Rudolph

•*Brady Mistake!* Watch this episode closely and you'll notice that during the climactic "house of cards" scene, Peter's shirt keeps changing colors. In the wide shots it's bright blue, but in all the close-ups it's magically turned red. Lloyd Schwartz was responsible for the error, and explains it with the credible alibi: "oops!"

EPISODE 12: "A-CAMPING WE WILL GO"

The Brady guys are sure that their camping trip is going to suck when Mike gives them the horrible news that (*gulp*) the *girls* are coming—even Alice. Depressed but (as always) obedient, the boys pack up and prepare to be miserable, but after suffering through a series of wacky mishaps (including piling into the girls' tent and causing it to collapse) and gobbling through Alice's emergency picnic basket, everybody realizes that co-ed togetherness might just work out after all.

WRITERS: Herbert Finn and Alan Dinehart
DIRECTOR: Oscar Rudolph

• Chris Knight's favorite episode, although he's quick to admit that being outdoors on location for a week probably made it a lot more fun to shoot than it is to watch.

• This episode came smack in the middle of the Olsen/Lookinland "marriage." Keep an eye open and you'll find they're kinda making eyes at each other in most of the episode's highly populated shots.

EPISODE 13: "VOTE FOR BRADY"

Classic "Brady Bunch"! Greg runs for student-body president . . . against Marcia!

"Greg Brady . . . this means war!" spews the angry but foxy Brady gal, and before long all six kids are duking it out, trying to get their biological sibling elected. Finally, after Mike and Carol's lengthy lecture on family unity, Marcia crumbles (Brady gals ain't big on guts) and lets Greg run unopposed.

WRITER: Elroy Schwartz
DIRECTOR: David Alexander

• *Nepotism Alert!* Elroy Schwartz is Sherwood's *younger* brother.

EPISODE 14: "EVERY BOY DOES IT ONCE"

Bobby watches a "Cinderella" on TV, then goes completely mental, drawing comparisons between *himself* and the fairy tale's poor, downtrodden little blond babe. *She's* got an evil stepmother—and so, Bobby convinces himself, does he.

Enter Carol, whose simple, but horrendously ill-timed

request that Bobby sweep out the fireplace sends the kid reeling. Things get worse, until finally, after he scuffles with his "evil stepsisters" and a new pile of hand-me-downs comes his way, Bobby decides he's had enough and prepares to run away.

At the same time, Carol begins sensing that Bobby feels unloved and she calls Mike at work to discuss it. Mike blows off a meeting, and the two senior Bradys come to the conclusion that Bobby's feelings can best be dealt with by . . . buying the kid a bike.

Huh? Flash forward and Mike and Carol are in the bike store (I guess Mike took the rest of the day off). They're kicking Schwinn tires when the basic impropriety of their impending purchase finally hits 'em. Buying Bobby a bike, they realize, would simply be buying his love.

They rush home bikeless and find Bobby all packed up and ready to bolt. Mike sits the little guy down on his bed, and we launch into another one of those now famous (albeit simplistic) Brady heart-to-hearts.

Mike asks Bobby what he's gonna do to make a living.

"I don't know—I never thought about it," replies Bobby. "But I'm pretty good at finger-painting and gluing."

With that assurance, Mike takes Bobby's suitcase in hand, assures him that he'll get along just fine in the real world, and they head toward the front door, where they find . . . Carol. She's packed a suitcase too, and tells Bobby that she loves him *much* too much to ever let him run away alone.

Now convinced that his stepmom isn't evil, and that he's loved like crazy, Bobby decides not to throw over the Brady plantation for the mean streets of Westdale after all.

WRITERS: Lois and Arnold Peyser
DIRECTOR: Oscar Rudolph

EPISODE 15: "THE VOICE OF CHRISTMAS"

Christmas is coming! There are presents to wrap, trees to decorate, holly to hang, and for Carol, choir practice to attend. *This* year Carol's been given the honor of singing "O Come, All Ye Faithful" at Christmas-morning services. She's absolutely thrilled, and the Bradys are coasting toward their "first united Christmas ever!" until—

Disaster! With only one day till Christmas, Carol loses her voice! She can't whisper, she can't talk, and worst of all, she won't be able to sing with the church choir!

Everybody bums, and it looks like this is gonna be a black Christmas.

Enter Cindy. She meets up with a department-store Santa (who's played by Hal Smith, who used to play Otis, Mayberry's town drunk, on "The Andy Griffith Show") and asks him not for a present, but for her Mom's voice to come back.

Santa takes one look at those blue eyes and blond pigtails, forgets everything he learned in Santa school, and guarantees delivery on her request. Sure that she's fixed *everything*, Cindy heads home and waits for the miracle.

Lo and behold, we wake up Christmas morning to find that it worked! Carol's carol is saved, and the Bradys have their best Christmas ever after all.

WRITER: John Fenton Murray
DIRECTOR: Oscar Rudolph

•The first of two "Christmas miracles" in the ratings. Up until this particular episode aired, "The Brady Bunch" was just sort of lamely dog-paddling in the Nielsen pool, trying (at times desperately) to stay afloat. This episode changed all that. It drew terrific numbers and started the show on the road to large-scale popular success.

•Brady Mistake: Listen very closely as Carol miraculously regains her voice on Christmas morning. Just before she bursts into her "O Come, All Ye Faithful," you can distinctly hear the sound of an off-camera pitch pipe giving her a musical cue. It should have been erased in the editing process but was over-looked.

EPISODE 16: "MIKE'S HORROR-SCOPE"

Carol gets edgy when Mike's newspaper horoscope makes it quite clear that a "strange and fascinating woman" is about to enter his life. Turns out she's Beebe Gallini, a red-headed

and bosomy sort of ersatz Coco Chanel. She's strange all right, fascinating too; and in her odd (and unplaceable) accent, she orders Mike to design her new cosmetics factory in "powder-poof peenk," with a "fluffy roof."
WRITER: Ruth Brooks Flippen
DIRECTOR: Oscar Rudolph

•Abbe Lane, who plays Beebe Gallini, enjoyed minor celebrity as an actress and singer but is probably best known as Charo's predecessor as wife/protégé of Latin bandleader Xavier Cugat.

EPISODE 17: "THE UNDERGRADUATE"

Greg goes into that goofy, catatonic sitcom-kid-in-love routine after falling *hard* for his teacher Linda O'Hara. He's moony, distracted, and completely nuts about the gal, until he finds out that she's going to first base with none other than L.A. Dodger Wes Parker! Oof!
WRITER: David P. Harmon
DIRECTOR: Oscar Rudolph

•Wes Parker played first base for the Dodgers and was a pretty big baseball star in 1970. (*Current* Mets first baseman Eddie Murray might make a good modern-day equivalent.) He knocked off his scenes in just one day; but Mike, Chris, and I made the *most* of that one day, whining at the poor guy incessantly until he finally cracked and agreed to play catch with us. We also stuck him up for batting tips, sliding techniques, and, of course, autographed balls. Perks of the trade.

EPISODE 18: "TO MOVE OR NOT TO MOVE"

How come a successful architect always lived in a house with a wife, six kids, and only three bedrooms? I get asked that question all the time, and about the *only* reason I can figure is that Sherwood Schwartz must've taken this episode *very* seriously. The six of us kids start bellyaching about how small the house is, living three to a bedroom and six to a bathroom. That prompts Mike to take note of the cramped quarters, and put up the For Sale sign.

At the same time, the six of us realize how dopey we've been, how much we really love our overcrowded digs, and how unhappy we'd be if we had to move. That triggers yet another Brady-kid scheme; and before you know it, Cindy and Bobby are running around the house clad in sheets, pretending to be ghosts and attempting to frighten off any prospective purchaser of Le Château Brady.

WRITER: Paul West
DIRECTOR: Oscar Rudolph

EPISODE 19: "TIGER! TIGER!"

By now, Tiger had long been terminally retired, but Sherwood Schwartz had an old script laying around that was all about the disappearance of the Brady dog. Sherwood realized that even though the story *revolved* around the dog, he wasn't actually seen on camera all that much. So, with a look-alike to the original Tiger, we pulled it off, and kept Sherwood from having to throw out a perfectly passable script.

The Bradys find Tiger missing, and immediately set out to bring him home. They run a newspaper ad, offer a reward ($42.76, chipped in by the kids), and finally spread out over the neighborhood on foot, on bikes, and in cars looking for the shaggy-haired vagabond.

No luck, and the Bradys become uncharacteristically depressed . . . until Peter hits pay dirt. He's found Tiger alive and well and busily fathering his newborn set of puppies.

WRITER: Elroy Schwartz
DIRECTOR: Herb Wallerstein

•Bobby has a couple of lines in the episode wherein he worries that Tiger's been run over . . . kinda creepy given the original Tiger's real-life demise.

EPISODE 20: "BRACE YOURSELF"

Marcia gets braces and gets depressed all in one afternoon. Convinced that her metal mouth has left her hideously deformed and horrendously ugly, Marcia doesn't listen to the common sense of her parents, and goes off the deep end when her school-dance date, Alan, dumps her at the last minute. He's got a legitimate excuse—parents going out of town and dragging him along too—but the now neurotic Brady babe won't even hear it. Instead, she runs up to the girls' room and bawls like crazy.

Flash forward, and Marcia's been fixed up with three different dates by three different well-meaning Bradys. All three show up, hoping to take Marcia to the school dance—and so does Alan. Seems he canceled his out-of-town trip shortly after he flipped over the handlebars of his bicycle, requiring a dentist's visit and—you guessed it—tinsel teeth.

He and Marcia share a metallic laugh and a dance; and judging from how nuts they seem about each other, we can assume that an aluminum-flavored make-out session was their nightcap.

WRITER: Brad Radnitz
DIRECTOR: Oscar Rudolph

•Fairly noticeable in this episode (and about one hundred others) is the fact that there was never any glass in the sliding doors that separated the Bradys' rec room and backyard. Also obvious is the fact that the backyard "grass" was actually a primitive form of Astroturf that had to be repainted regularly and was completely unforgiving if you had to slide on it. Band-Aids over the top of green-smudgy scabs became standard issue on the set.

EPISODE 21: "THE BIG SPRAIN"

Carol's crotchety old aunt Mary comes down sick, and the Brady mom shows her true saintly colors by packing up and leaving home to nurse the old bag back into shape. It's no problem, because Alice can take care of the family, right? Wrong! Alice's tennis shoe finds the Brady kids' Chinese checkers, and she ends up taking a major header, spraining her ankle in the process. Now what?

This. Mike puts all six kids to work. The boys (sort of) learn how to clean house. The girls (sort of) learn how to use the kitchen. Alice (sort of) learns to relax. And even Sam the Butcher proves himself slightly more sensitive than his sides of beef by skipping the Meatcutters' Ball (doesn't *that* conjure up images of light blue tuxedos and cocktail wienies?) just to cuddle up with his ailing main squeeze, Alice.

WRITER: Tam Spiva
DIRECTOR: Russ Mayberry

•Speaking of Sam the Butcher—Allan Melvin—did you know he was the voice of Magilla Gorilla?

EPISODE 22: "THE HERO"

Peter's hanging out in the local toy store when he sees a huge wall unit full of shelves getting ready to collapse onto a hapless little girl's head. With a heroic dive, our pal Pete saves the day—not to mention the toy shop owner's business—*and* the little girl's life.

Scan forward and you'll find that the girl's grateful mom has spread the word about Peter's heroism in the local newspaper. Scan forward *again* and you'll find that Peter's grown a *major* attitude, and that his overdeveloped ego is driving his siblings, parents, and housekeeper *nuts!* Things come to a head when Peter gets fifty bucks for winning the paper's weekly "Outstanding Citizen" award, throws a party in his own honor, and *nobody* comes. He's stunned into self-awareness, and it isn't long before Peter the Great once again becomes plain ol' lovable Pete.

WRITER: Elroy Schwartz
DIRECTOR: Oscar Rudolph

EPISODE 23: "LOST LOCKET, FOUND LOCKET"

The first of our many "Jan's depressed" episodes. This time it's about being an overlooked, underloved middle sibling. But just when things appear blackest for the gal, an

The *real* Brady house.
(©Paramount Pictures)

unknown admirer sends her a little gold locket on a little gold chain. He also sends her spirits soaring.

It isn't long, before Jan's in the dumps again (you don't think she was manic-depressive, do you?). *Now*, she's lost her new locket, and she's mad at the world. Anyway, with sleuth-like detective work she refinds the locket (it had fallen out the bedroom window as she stargazed). Her mood swings back toward happy again, and in the end she finds out that her secret admirer was *really* . . . Alice.

Alice explains she too grew up as a middle sister, knew exactly how bad Jan was feeling, and decided to give her the locket just so she could feel "special." Awwwwwwww.

WRITER: Charles Hoffman
DIRECTOR: Norman Abbott

•The Brady house that you see in every episode really does exist. It's in California's San Fernando Valley, but there's no upstairs window. That was just a prop, hammered onto the house, prior to shooting. When it came time to shoot "A Very Brady Christmas" the bogus window frame was nailed into place, and filmed once more.

EPISODE 24: "THE POSSIBLE DREAM"

This is it!—the grand high exalted corny ruler of Brady camp! If you're looking to bust Brady chops, you've come to the right episode.

Dopey little Cindy has accidentally given Marcia's treasured diary to the (*gulp!*) Salvation Army Book Drive! And even worse, inside of that diary, Marcia's just spilled the lurid truth that her "dream of dreams is to someday be *Mrs.* Desi Arnaz, Jr."—*gasp!* Needless to say, Marcia's just gonna *die* if they can't relocate her lost journal.

The Brady forces split up, scouring every single bookstore in town, and the results are futile, until . . . we return to the Brady living room, where Marcia gets a visit from—*Desi Arnaz Jr.!* Seems that Alice knows Lucy's housekeeper (oooh!), and *she* finagled the meeting to cheer Marcia up. Implausible, corny, goofy, and really, really funny. A true kitsch classic.

WRITERS: Al Schwartz and Bill Freedman
DIRECTOR: Oscar Rudolph

EPISODE 25: "GOING, GOING . . . STEADY"

The second Marcia-filled Brady classic in a row. This time, our most babe-ish Brady is out to capture the elusive Harvey Klinger, 4-eyed collector of bugs. Her strategy? Learn all about the disgusting little six-legged (but protein-rich) invertebrates, dazzle him with her knowledge, then pounce. Harvey arrives, takes the bait, and Marcia's plan works like a charm. Soon the two pubescent bug hunters are going steady.

WRITER: David P. Harmon
DIRECTOR: Oscar Rudolph

EPISODE 26: "THE DROPOUT"

We swung into our second season with an episode, which featured the Bradys' second Los Angeles Dodger houseguest. This time around, Mike is designing a new house for Dodger pitching great Don Drysdale, and casually mentions to the all-star hurler that his son Greg would really be thrilled to meet him. Immediately (as happens only in the reality of sitcoms), Drysdale pays a visit to the Brady house, gets a look at Greg's nasty curve ball, and makes the well-intentioned, but *large* mistake of telling the kid that with a

Me and Don Drysdale.
(© 1991 Capital
Cities/ABC, Inc.)

little practice, he just might be a Dodger himself someday.

That does it. Greg tells Mike and Carol that he's going to drop out of school and become a hugely successful major leaguer. Near-coronaries ensue, but the Brady parents can't get Greg to change his mind.

Re-enter Don Drysdale. He and Greg toss around the ol' apple while Don gives Greg the inside scoop on the extra-tough life of a pro baseball player—a plot twist that would be impossible nowadays. He yammers endlessly about the minor leagues, their broken-down buses, bad food, and bad hotels (leaving out the part about the poker, the booze, and the readily available bimbos). Anyway, after the speech, and a twelve-run Little League shellacking to boot, stubborn Greg finally decides to ease up on the baseball practice and stay in school.

Judging from Roger Clemens's wallet size, that was probably a *real* bad decision!

WRITERS: Bill Freedman and Ben Gershman
DIRECTOR: Peter Baldwin

EPISODE 27: "THE BABYSITTERS"

When Mike and Carol can't find a sitter, Greg and Marcia

volunteer to baby-sit the younger, punier, weaker Bradys. Mike and Carol give the plan a less than enthusiastic okay and head out for an evening at the theater.

However, once the parents are out of the house, the littlest Bradys rebel against the authority of their peers, launch a mini-revolution, and end up hating Greg and Marcia's guts. Meanwhile, over at the theater, Mike and Carol are so worried about the kids that they can't enjoy the play, and end up coming home early.

WRITER: Bruce Howard
DIRECTOR: Oscar Rudolph

•With all the running around in this episode, you get a pretty good look at how the Brady set was physically laid out. Basically, all the "downstairs" rooms, garage, driveway, front door, and backyard were indeed connected, and laid out together just as they appeared on TV, while the upstairs rooms (and later the attic) were housed in another area of the soundstage.

EPISODE 28: "THE TREASURE OF SIERRA AVENUE"

The boys pick up a football and head out of the Brady backyard (probably to avoid playing on Astroturf) to play ball in the street. The pigskin flies, but when Bobby muffs a long fly pattern, he drops the ball but picks up something *much* more exciting. It's a wallet, crammed full of money—eleven hundred dollars.

Bobby's rich . . . at least until all the other Brady kids start sticking their hands into his pockets. One by one, *everybody* wants a cut and Bobby goes from rich to a little better off. Still, he's thrilled with his newfound (yet dwindling) fortune.

Enter a fossilish old geezer named Mr. Stoner. He's the guy who lost the money, and when he launches into a melodramatic song-and-dance sob story about how the wallet contained his life savings and an "I thank God for honest people like you" schtick, Bobby reluctantly returns the wrinkled coot's cash.

But ya know, he's *still* "a little better off" just for helping another human being.

WRITERS: Gwen Bagni and Paul Dubov
DIRECTOR: Oscar Rudolph

EPISODE 29: "THE UN-UNDERGROUND MOVIE"

The Pilgrim episode! I love this one! We had a great time shooting the thing, and it's actually kind of funny, too.

Greg's thrown himself into directing that super-8 super-cinematic masterpiece *Our Pilgrim Fathers*, and every Brady gets a part. Mike and Carol play John Smith and Priscilla Alden, and Alice makes a nifty (but effeminate) Governor John Carver.

The kids fight like—kids, over everything; the shooting is chaotic; but when the dust settles, the movie's a smash (watch for the capsizing *Mayflower* in the Brady bathbub), and smiles abound once more.

This is definitely among my favorite "Brady Bunch"es.

WRITER: Albert E. Lewin
DIRECTOR: Jack Arnold

•As an aside: you'll notice that the Brady kids' bathroom has a sink, a tub, mirrors, but no toilet. I guess we kids really were supposed to be "immaculate."

EPISODE 30: "THE SLUMBER CAPER"

Now here's an episode that seems to be tattooed onto the brains of most Brady fanatics.

1. Marcia wants to throw her first-ever slumber party.
2. The boys hate the idea.
3. Mike and Carol okay the party, but then . . .
4. Marcia gets into trouble at school when her teacher, Mrs. Denton, takes one look at Marcia's art project and sees the words "Mrs. Denton . . . a Hippopotamus" scrawled under a picture of what looks like a hippo.
5. Marcia says that she never wrote *any* caption on her drawing, and that it wasn't a hippo at all. She claims

that she was simply trying to sketch George Washington, and that a classmate must've seen her inept work and written the caption as a gag.

6. Marcia's principal's not laughing, and he doesn't buy her story. She gets after-school detention for a week!
7. Party's canceled.
8. Marcia *swears* she's innocent, tells her sob story to Mike, and he believes that as farfetched as it may sound, Marcia's telling the truth.
9. Party's back on!
10. See number 2.
11. Marcia comes to the conclusion that her pal Jenny was the twisted caption creator and quickly yanks her name off the invite list.
12. The boys decide not to take this slumber business lying down.
13. Later that night, they start the chaos rolling by dressing like ghouls and terrorizing the gals.
14. Next, they haul out the coup de grace . . . itching powder in the sleeping bags. The stuff works, and the house is soon buzzing with itchy/screamy/wiggly girls (sorta like a "G" rated Hef's place)!
15. The boys crack up big-time.
16. Marcia's pal Paula chooses this particularly raucous occasion to make small talk and fesses up about writing that caption.
17. Red-faced, and having learned a lesson about jumping to conclusions, Marcia quickly reinvites her blackballed pal, Jenny.
18. Everybody smiles and hugs . . . again.
WRITER: Tam Spiva
DIRECTOR: Oscar Rudolph

•*Nepotism Alert 1!* Robert Reed's daughter, Carolyn, appears in this episode as Marcia's pal Karen.
•*Nepotism Alert 2!* Florence Henderson's daughter Barbara Bernstein plays Ruthie.

From left, Carolyn Reed, Robert Reed, Maureen McCormick, Eve Plumb, Susan Olsen, Florence Henderson, Barbara Henderson (a.k.a. Bernstein).
(© Paramount Pictures)

•*Nepotism Alert 3!* Sherwood Schwartz's daughter Hope makes her first of several appearances on the show. This time she's playing Jenny, but she'd later spend three episodes appearing as Greg's girlfriend Rachel.

•E. G. Marshall and Robert Reed, who starred together in "The Defenders," are reunited in this episode. Marshall shows up in the small, rather inconsequential part of Marcia's principal, crabby old Mr. Stoner.

EPISODE 31: "CONFESSIONS, CONFESSIONS"

Peter is tossing a basketball around the Brady living room (ignoring Mike and Carol and Alice's warnings) and ends up busting his mother's favorite vase into about three bazillion little pieces.

Peter freaks, convinced that he's in *big* trouble and that the old folks will punish him by cancelling his weekend camping trip.

Desperately looking for a way out, Peter tries gluing the vase back together, but when Carol fills it with water, the floodgates open, and it looks like Peter's proverbial goose is cooked.

Or is it? One by one, all five *innocent* Brady kids start trying to save Pete's ass *and* camping trip by confessing to the dastardly pottery slaughter.

WRITER: Brad Radnitz
DIRECTOR: Russ Mayberry

EPISODE 32: "THE TATTLETALE"

The episode Susan Olsen *hates*: Cindy turns stoolie and finks on her schoolmates, her brothers and sisters, and even causes the (temporary) breakup of Alice and Sam when she tattles that she's just seen Alice hugging the mailman.

The mailman? Yep. He'd just delivered a registered letter telling Alice that she'd won a contest and one of five fabulous grand prizes will soon be hers. All she's got to do is sit back and wait for a *second* registered letter that'll contain her winner's certificate, and the details of *what* she's won, and *where* to pick it up. Alice is overjoyed and plants a big bear hug on the mailman.

Cindy, who's on the phone with Sam at the time, rats her out.

We then go to commercial, come back, and find that Alice is all dressed up and ready for a dance date with Sam. The only problem is, the boorish butcher never shows. Alice calls to find out why he's a no-show, and he says that maybe she should "go dancing with the mailman," and hangs up.

Clueless, Alice wonders aloud about Sam's behavior, and an eavesdropping Cindy explains everything.

Annoyed, Mike steps in, lectures Cindy about how wrong it is to be a tattletale, and make her promise never to fink again. She agrees.

At about this exact point in time, Tiger comes barreling through the living room with Marcia's homework clenched in his drooly mouth. "That's it!" bellows Mike with uncharacteristic volume. "If that dog steals just one more thing, I'm gonna ship him off to Siberia!"

A worried Cindy goes to bed.

The next day dawns, and as Alice and Carol go food shopping, the postman rings for the second time. Cindy answers the door, signs for Alice's second registered letter, and watches in horror as—Tiger steals it! She runs after the dog but aborts the plan when she spies the grocery shoppers returning home.

The phone rings.

Alice picks it up, and it's the contest people. They tell her that she's won a hi-fi stereo set, and that to pick it up she's got to take her winner's certificate to Lloyd's Stereo Center by midnight tonight.

"Huh?" asks puzzled old Alice. She hasn't even *seen* her winner's certificate. "Did anyone sign for a registered letter?"

"Yeth," says Cindy. "But that'th all I can thay."

Cutting to the chase, the grown-ups interrogate Cindy and she reveals that Tiger's run off with the thing. One quick search later, they've found it in the doghouse, and Alice is sprinting off to claim her booty.

And that's that.

This episode started causing trouble for Susan the Monday morning after it aired. She went to school and found that none of her friends would talk to her. They'd seen Cindy the squealer on TV and were convinced that Susan was a big rat too.

"I hated catching shit for what Cindy did," says Susan today. "And after *that* episode, I just wanted to strangle the brat."

WRITERS: Sam Locke and Milton Pascal
DIRECTOR: Russ Mayberry

•The reference to "Lloyd's Stereo Center" was a gag aimed at associate producer Lloyd Schwartz.

EPISODE 33: "CALL ME IRRESPONSIBLE"

Greg wants a car. Soooo . . .

1. Greg gets a job with Mike at the architectural firm.

2. Greg loses Mike's important sketches (a theme that would become recurrent in Bradyville).
3. Greg gets fired.
4. Greg's dad goes to bat for the dopey kid.
5. Greg gets rehired, but Greg loses *another* set of plans.
6. Greg gets fired *again*.
7. Greg goes out and finds the second set of plans *anyway*, just to prove what a reliable kinda guy he really is.
8. Greg's *still* fired.

WRITER: Bruce Howard
DIRECTOR: Hal Cooper

EPISODE 34: "THE IMPRACTICAL JOKER"

Jan goes off the deep end (again) and can't stop playing practical jokes. She douses her sisters with rubber spiders, splatters Alice with disappearring ink, and, as a topper, steals Greg's science-project mouse, Myron, and stashes him in a wicker laundry hamper.

Ten minutes later, Myron's chewed his way out of the basket and he's wreaking havoc throughout the house. Alice sees him, does the requisite "Eeeeeeeek!", and calls the exterminator from atop the dinette set.

The kids catch on that Myron's M.I.A. and scramble through the house looking for him—just in time to find that the exterminator's already completed his job. Myron must be mooshed, and Jan learns a hard lesson about taking a joke too far.

But that's not all (we haven't had our "happy resolve" yet). Backyard barking sends the kids running to Tiger's doghouse, where we find—Kitty Karryall? Nope—Myron! Alive, healthy and none the worse for wear.

WRITER: Burt Styler
DIRECTOR: Oscar Rudolph

•This particular story line spawned some real-life practical jokes among us Brady kids, the best of which began when I casually mentioned to a couple of the nosier members of the brood that I had a huge secret. I told them that my secret was *very* private, *very* embarrassing, and that I positively didn't want *anyone* to know about it.

Next, I simply sat back and waited as the news of my deep dark secret spread throughout the Brady kids, tweaking their curiosity and ultimately driving them crazy.

Eve Plumb was first to jump at the bait. The grapevine told me that she was dying to find out about my secret, and for that reason she became the first to know about my . . . glass eye.

With a lot of melodrama and mock sincerity, I told her about how difficult it was for me to carry my burden, and of course she didn't believe me. "Deeply offended" by her lack of trust, I told her that if she really wanted me to *prove* that I had a glass eye, I would gladly pop it out of my eye socket and let her hold it. Suddenly Eve wasn't so skeptical anymore, and she queasily balked at having me "pop out or shut up."

However, over the course of the next couple of days, Eve's fear of seeing a human being pop out an eyeball gave way to an intense and building curiosity. Four and five times a day she'd corner me, ordering that I remove the eye, hand it over, or admit that I was a liar. This went on for almost two weeks, and I knew that my credibility was fast becoming dirt. I'd have to act, fast.

And then it hit me. My dad was friendly with an optometrist, who after some begging lent me a genuine phony eye. I pocketed the prosthesis and practically *ran* to the Paramount set, laughing at the thought of horrifying Eve.

Four o'clock came, and Eve once more charged up to me with her demand: "Gimme the eyeball!"

"All right, all right," I replied, "if you *really* want me to prove it, I will." Hiding a smile, I called over some witnesses, cupped the glass eye in my hand, and reached up toward my real eye. I then asked the now grimacing Eve to hold out both hands, because "sometimes the eye comes out covered in eyeball guts, and I don't want you to drop it." Eve was turning white, but she still hung on, convinced that at any second I'd confess that this whole thing had been a joke.

I didn't, and after a lot of screwing around by my eye socket, a lot of squishy sound effects, and one last exaggerated yank, I dropped the glass eye into Eve's hand. It stared up at her.

She screamed . . . and screamed, and screamed, and screamed some more. She screamed long, she screamed loud, and above all else she screamed in that brain-piercing falsetto that only teenage girls can muster.

Bulls-eye.

•Watch for Oscar Rudolph's Method-acting mouse (see p. 108) *and* Bob Reed's inebriated interaction with the same (p. 69).

•Bob Reed hated this episode so much that it prompted his first-ever scathing memo. Here is what it said:

I want to show you a completely typical example of a problem that occurs with predictable regularity on "The Brady Bunch" and contributes heavily to:

1. downgrade of quality
2. inconsistency in style and performance
3. loss of time due to rewriting and quibbling on the set
4. creation of tension in cast and crew
5. bad performances by frustrated actors

The scene in question is a Tag Scene written for the usual theme tie-up, incorporating the equally usual "ha-ha ending." In this instance, it is dependent upon two pre-set plot ingredients: the child, Jan, having been established as a "practical joker"—now repentant, and, a Teaser Scene involving a gag replica of an ink spot which our young antagonist has placed upon Alice's coat successfully fooling the family into believing it was a real ink stain. Now, read the Tag.
BRADY BUNCH—"Impractical Joker"—Rev. 8/13/70 45.

TAG

FADE IN:

84 (OMITTED)   * 84

85 INT. KITCHEN—DAY * 85

Carol and Jan are peeling and/or cutting up fruit for a fruit cup in a large bowl.

JAN

(peeling a banana)

It's sure a lot easier to peel bananas than it is potatoes.

CAROL

One of these nights we just might try French fried bananas.

86 ANOTHER ANGLE   * 86

Alice enters, carrying a uniform over her arm and some towels.

ALICE

Any more towels for the laundry?

CAROL

(suddenly reacting) Alice—your uniform . . .

ALICE

What about it?

CAROL

There's an ink spot on the pocket.

She looks at Jan knowingly, thinking it another of her jokes.

87 ANGLE FAVORING ALICE   * 87

She investigates, and discovers a large ink spot on the pocket of the uniform she carries over her arm.

88 ANOTHER ANGLE   * 88

as she and Carol look at Jan.

CAROL

(continuing)

Jan, really . . .

ALICE

(a smile)

Couldn't resist one last little joke, huh?

JAN

Mother—I didn't do . . .

ALICE

(interrupts)

I know how to take care of *these* kind of ink spots!

JAN

(protests)

But, Alice . . .

89 CLOSER SHOT—ALICE   * 89

With this, Alice confidently reaches to pluck off the ink spot. But it doesn't pluck off . . . the pocket rips . . . revealing a fountain pen in the pocket with the top off.

90 WIDER SHOT   * 90

ALICE

(sheepishly)

Like you said—there's an ink spot on the pocket.

Carol and Jan laugh, as we—

FADE OUT.

THE END

Problem 1

As was contended three weeks ago, the difficulty in creating a "gag ink spot" to resemble even remotely a *stain* is insurmountable. In the teaser, the onlookers are required to *believe* that the stain is real. Now while the metal gag 'ink spills' may be placed upon a flat non-porous surface such as a floor or a table-top, their lacquered finish shining like a wet puddle, and be remarkably realistic, the same item placed upon a piece of moving, pliant, porous cloth creates no illusion whatsoever. Anything wet would have *soaked into* the material and *dried*.

Well, props couldn't find that kind of "ink spill" anyway, as the magic stores they scouted don't carry them anymore, so they created a plastic pliable gob, that flattened, has the look of a smear of dulled roofing tar about an eighth of an inch thick. It is not smooth on top and is to be applied with double-faced tape.

Assumption: Even viewed from a distance of twenty feet, it resembles exactly what you might expect it to resemble: a plastic gob applied with double-faced tape. Now, if our

Soubrette views this from 18 inches, and our Leading Lady from a few feet and believe it to be real as they are required by the script to do, all credibility is lost or they become cartoon nincompoops—either result undesirable.

Problem 2

In the *Tag,* they spy what we finally learn to be a *real stain* at very close range (it's on a garment hanging on her arm) and believe it is a gob of plastic roofing tar applied with double-faced tape. They believe it to such a degree that Alice plucks at it with such aggressive and purposed confidence, that she rips a tear in the garment! But, that's not all. What does she discover hidden in the recesses of that same pocket strangely unobserved before, but a concealed fountain pen—with the top off! Does it make you wonder?

  a. Couldn't she tell the difference between a gob of roofing tar and a dried ink stain when it's as close as her hand to her face?
  b. Couldn't she see the recognizable outline of a fountain pen before?
  c. Who put a pen in a pocket without the top on in the first place?
  d. If she looks after our children with the same muscular aggression as it took to rip the pocket, we may at the end of the season have buried a few children.

Assumption: It is unactable for Carol and Jan. Alice can either play drunk or an advanced case of glaucoma.

Problem 3

The Tag accomplishes almost none of its requirements. As a tie-up for the theme, it is pitifully poor using an unfortunate continuance of the Teaser which was weak to begin with.

It most assuredly is not funny. Even a laugh machine would

balk. But, worst of all, it requires the actors to present their characters as one-dimensional ninnies with a loss of credibility and solidity and creates a tremendous chasm of inconsistency with previous shows.

Assumption: If you want solely an audience of children under 8 years old, that's one thing. If you want to interest the young parents, we have to be faintly identifiable and empathically solid as well as amusing. So that the parent says "*Our* kids do the same things, and those parents are just like *us*—up to their ears in kids and problems—isn't it *great!* I like them and I like *us!*" But, if they see unreality to such a degree that empathy is lost, then the resultant "Bullshit!" initiates a negative response to the whole show.

The Biggest Problem of All

Whether you give credence to all of the previous assumptions or not, it is clear that the practical incorporation of the "ink spot" business does not work. This was pointed out three weeks prior to shooting—no one said anything. Today, so similar to so many other instances, the following pattern occurred once again.

A discussion with Lloyd Schwartz, an eternal defender of the written word, netted the usual: a justification of why everything was the way it was.

A discussion with Howard Leeds, who after listening to an explanation of the problem, said "I don't see the problem."

Other time-worn utterances are:

1. "Well, if we change this, we have to change something else!"
2. "Well, it's a little late, now!"
3. "Play it—you'll see how it will work!"
4. "Some scripts aren't perfect!"
and
5. "We think it's funny!"
but, mostly

6. "I don't understand the problem!"

Now, invariably this situation develops into a confrontation which has to be pushed to an almost violent level before *any* changes will be offered. By this time, cast and crew alike are weary and stone-faced. The other actors are affected to varying degrees, my metabolism takes two days to adjust and we have lost time and performance. Word changes can be accomplished with less difficulty, but anything more than one speech more often than not ends in hostilities.

The days that follow are also predictable. Assuasion and persuasion from Sherwood. The restoration of at least an outward semblance of amenity with Howard, which has been brought about usually in a moderated conference that ends with Howard echoing in that 'Hail fellow, stalwart comrade' attitude, "When you have any problems, remember our door is always open. And remember, there isn't anything we can't fix."

My thought is, "I'm not so sure I want to pay the price."

EPISODE 35: "A FISTFUL OF REASONS"

Baby talk, baby talk, it's a wonder you can walk.
—Buddy Hinton

Rotten little Buddy Hinton makes Cindy cry by mocking her lisp. Peter tries talking with the little bully but only gets a black eye for his trouble.

When Mike and Carol try talking to Buddy's *parents*, they turn out to be *big* bullies, leaving Mike with only one option: teach Peter the fine art of beating the crap out of a guy.

Pete learns how to fight, runs into Buddy outside of school, levels a perfect haymaker into his puss, and knocks out Buddy's front teeth in the process.

With nothing left but molars, Buddy now lisps just like Cindy. As the episode closes, Peter engages in some truly mean-spirited and un-Brady-like behavior, taunting the now thoroughly defeated and humiliated Buddy with his own dreaded phrase: "Baby talk, baby talk, it's a wonder you can walk." What a catharsis!

WRITER: Tam Spiva

DIRECTOR: Oscar Rudolph

•In this episode (and again in episode 36) you can easily see that whenever a script called for a neighbor's backyard, the Bradys' backyard would simply be redressed (with an extra shrub or phony tree) and filmed as though it were someplace else. It was a money-saving ploy, but it really does look hokey.

EPISODE 36: "WHAT GOES UP . . ."

The Bobster gets a chance to become the youngest ever member of Peter's treehouse gang, but drops out . . . literally.

Bobby falls out of the tree, bounces a coupla times, sprains his ankle, takes a bump, and comes up with a newly acquired fear of heights.

The ever-sympathetic and understanding Bradys try their best to alleviate Bobby's new phobia, and even buy a trampo-

(© Paramount Pictures)

line (watch for Alice's belly-whopper), hoping he'll snap out of it.

It doesn't work, and it looks like Bobby's gonna spend his entire life at sea level . . . until his new pet budgie flies out the bedroom window and into the backyard tree.

Without time to think about his fear, Bobby scrambles up the tree like an orangutan and rescues his yellow-feathered pal. He's cured, and we ring in the closing credits.

WRITERS: William Raynor and Myles Wilder
DIRECTOR: Leslie H. Martinson

•*Brady Mistake!* One of our biggest goofs *ever* shows up in this episode, and it's . . . uh . . . all *my* fault. Watch closely in the scene where all of us Bradys are playing on the backyard trampoline. You'll see Greg turn to Jan and quite clearly say, "Why don't you give it a try, Eve?" We'd blow takes with slip-ups like that all the time, but this is the *only* name gaffe that made it onto the airwaves.

EPISODE 37: "COMING-OUT PARTY"

All nine Bradys (don't forget to include Alice) get invited on a far-out fishing trip by Mike's boss, Mr. Phillips, and the kids are thrilled.

Cindy sneezes.

In the backyard, Marcia practices by casting her line into a bucket.

Cindy sneezes.

Carol appears, brags about being an expert fisherperson, and proceeds to cast *her* line over the fence, and into the Dittmayers' barbecue pit, snagging a five-pound bag of charcoal in the process.

Cindy sneezes again, and the old folks call Dr. Howard. He shows up, takes one gander at Cindy's uvula, and comes to the conclusion that her tonsils need pulling (since when is sneezing a symptom of tonsillitis?). The bad news gets even worse when Cindy's surgery is scheduled for a week from Saturday, the very day of the fishing trip!

But all hope is not lost. Dr. Howard says that if Cindy's tonsils get better by themselves, he *could* postpone the surgery until after the trip (nice set of priorities).

However, when it comes time for Dr. Howard's follow-up visit, Cindy's tonsils not only haven't healed, they've gotten worse. Adding to the misery, when Mommy shows Cindy how to "open up and say 'Ah,'" Doc Howard finds that Carol's tonsils need pulling too! (Notice that the doctor uses the same tongue depressor on *both* Brady women—ugh!)

A full fifteen minutes into the episode, Mike finally comes to the conclusion that he should postpone the fishing trip until a time when the Bradys sport a clean bill of health. He calls Mr. Phillips, explains his predicament, and in no time the trip is rearranged to take place two weeks later. Perfect, right?

Wrong, because while the Brady women's surgery comes off without a hitch, there's trouble brewing come recovery time. Like all tonsillectomy victims, Carol and Cindy are recuperating at home with strict orders to avoid conversation. However, Carol just can't seem to stay off the phone—you know how women are. When Mike calls home from work looking for Alice, Carol defies doctor's orders and picks up the phone. Mike yells at her, hangs up the phone, and then calls back to test her.

Sure enough, after only two rings she picks up. Mike pretends to be Carol's gabby friend Ellie, and when Carol starts to chat she gets yelled at again. Mike hangs up.

A while later, the phone's ringing again, but this time Carol's too smart for Mike. She picks up the phone, and when the voice on the other end says "Hi, Carol, it's Mr. Phillips. How are you feeling?" she replies, "Not well enough to go on that broken-down barnacle barge of yours, you old goat."

Enter Mike, and Carol immediately realizes that she's just insulted the *real* Mr. Phillips! Frustrated, Mike tries to call Mr. Phillips and explain, but gets an earful of phone-slam instead.

Dissolve forward, and Mr. Phillips is inexplicably at the Bradys' front door bearing flowers. He apologizes for being so hotheaded, and explains his rash phone-slamming by saying that "you can insult a man's wife, but never his boat" (beautiful, ain't it?). He also asks if he might interest the Bradys in having their on-again, off-again boat trip officially become on again, and the kids' cheers give him his answer.

In the end, Carol tries apologizing to Mike, until he says, "I guess there's only one way to shut your mouth," and slaps a big wet one on her.

Tag time, Carol's all better and once again is practicing her casting in the backyard. She winds up, flicks her wrist, and sends her line over the fence once more, only this time she hasn't snagged Mr. Dittmayer's barbecue . . . she's caught Mr. Dittmayer.

WRITER: David P. Harmon
DIRECTOR: Oscar Rudolph

EPISODE 38: "THE NOT-SO-UGLY DUCKLING"

Jan's fragile little ego takes yet another beating, when the object of her first-ever crush falls madly in love—with Marcia.

Yep, Clark "Mr. Dreamy" Tyson gets tingly over Marcia, and Jan flips out, blaming her lack of sex appeal on (of all things) freckles! When, after an incognito visit to the drugstore, lemon juice fails to lift the spotty little buggers, Jan becomes even more irrational and invents George Glass, a make-believe boyfriend, to keep her company.

Finally, Marcia finds out that the only reason Clark wasn't crazy about Jan was that she dressed like a frump, and not in the dazzling feminine couture of Marcia.

That does it. Marcia runs her sister through a quick wardrobe makeover, and it isn't long before Clark's tingling returns and points itself straight at Jan.

Is the moral here that you *can* judge a book by its cover?

WRITER: Paul West
DIRECTOR: Irving Moore

•Would you believe, there now exists a New York–based rock band named the Eve Plumbs?

EPISODE 39: "TELL IT LIKE IT IS"

Carol's acting weird . . . which in the Brady house is cause for panic. She's been staying up late, locking herself in the den, and—typing. Oh, my *God!*

Turns out she's writing a story about her crowded house for *Tomorrow's Woman* magazine, a publication that could make Kitty Kelley puke. That's because Carol's honest, realistic portrayal of her chaotic household is rejected by the magazine as "too sensational," but her whitewashed, cleaned-up, extra-double-bland "Portrait of a Perfect Family" rewrite is accepted enthusiastically.

The editors show up unexpectedly at the Brady house with a photographer in tow and are flabbergasted (yes, "flabbergasted") to find the place a madhouse, at least by Brady standards. The house is rocking with such utter pandemonium that they consider dumping Carol's story completely.

But since this *is* "The Brady Bunch," a happy ending is ensured. The magazine's editors decide that Carol's *original* draft was truthful after all, and deserves feature-story status in next month's issue.

WRITER: Charles Hoffman
DIRECTOR: Terry Becker

EPISODE 40: "THE DRUMMER BOY"

The title character in "The Drummer Boy" is Bobby, who's learning how to bang the skins, and driving the Bradys insane in the process. It's a funny little subplot, but it has almost nothing to do with the outing's main storyline:

Yet another sporting superstar pays a visit to the Bradys. This time it's hulking L.A. Rams defensive end Deacon Jones, and he's out to make Peter feel like a "real man." Sounds scary, but it's actually completely innocent.

Y'see, Pete's an enthusiastic member of both the school glee club and the school football team. He enjoys 'em both, but when his teammates start calling him a sissy (ooh, ouch!), he's ready to quit singing for good.

Enter Deacon Jones, who just so happens to be visiting with

**Chris Knight and Deacon Jones.
Check out those pants!** (© 1991
Capital Cities/ABC, Inc.)

Pete's coach. He notices that Pete's upset, finds out why, and
then proceeds to lecture the kid about how "real men" can sing
and play football too. And when Deacon tells Peter that he *himself* loves to sing, Pete is happier than ever to make like a bird.

WRITERS: Tom and Helen August

DIRECTOR: Oscar Rudolph

•Check out the ultra-hip, ultra-ugly bell-bottoms that
Deacon Jones wears. You've got to see 'em to believe 'em.

EPISODE 41: "WHERE THERE'S SMOKE"

This outing stands right up there as one of the two or
three all-time classic episodes of "The Brady Bunch." It's a
simple story about Greg being caught . . . *smoking*
(*aaaaaaaaaaaaaaaugh!!!*).

Once upon a time there was a nice young boy named Greg
Brady, who so desperately wanted to look cool in front of his
hip new musician friends that he caved in to peer pressure,
went against his better judgment, and actually did the
unthinkable . . . he smoked a cigarette.

Thankfully, it wasn't a "reefer" (which would, of course,
have instantly doomed Greg to an irreversible descent into
junkiedom); but when you're a Brady, even one lousy butt is
cause for *big* trouble.

Greg finds that out when Jan and Cindy spy his evil puffing, and Marcia squeals about it to the old folks. They're horrified at the thought of Greg's heinous deed, and they really let him have it with the worst of all Brady punishments . . . a lecture.

They yammer at Greg about the evils of smoking, and when he admits that he wasn't *really* smoking, "just going along with the guys," they let him off the hook with a warning.

Flash forward, and we find that Greg and his musician friends have formed a far-out new rock band called the Banana Convention (cooool) and that they've been spending all their afternoons and weekends rehearsing for their first gig. Everything's going great until . . .

Greg comes home from rehearsal to find that his mom is now the chairman of the PTA's antismoking campaign (ugh). That's embarrassing enough, but Greg's uneasiness quickly turns to horror when he throws his jacket on the couch, and out plops a pack of *cigarettes* (aaaaaaaaaaaaaaaaugh!!! once again). Now Greg's *gotta* be dead meat, yes?

No! Greg tells Carol that he has *no idea* how those cigarettes got into his pocket, and in an absolutely *amazing* show of faith, she actually believes him. But the question remains: where *did* those cigarettes come from?

Alice suggests that reconstructing the crime might unveil the truth. It isn't long before we've rerun the whole sordid little escapade and realized that . . . Greg came home in the wrong jacket!

A Brady reputation is saved, and when we've deduced that the jacket actually belonged to Tommy, the Banana Connection's drummer, we Bradys threaten to rat the guy out to his mom. Crushed, he decides to tell her himself.

WRITER: David P. Harmon
DIRECTOR: Oscar Rudolph

•Unfortunately some of that method-acting from my youth had rubbed off on me. Shortly before this episode was filmed, I tried for the first time to quit my own nasty nicotine habit. However, during rehearsals and filming of the smoking scenes, I didn't fake my inhaling. Soon I was back to my lung blackening pack-a-day.

I had been smoking since I was twelve, but didn't light up on the set in front of the cast and crew. Instead, I'd sneak off to the men's room to be cool. I think my numerous bathroom visits had our staff convinced that I suffered some type of kidney dysfunction.

Happily, after *many* more quitting attempts, my lungs became Marlboro free on September 20, 1984, at 10:00 A.M.

EPISODE 42: "WILL THE REAL JAN BRADY PLEASE STAND UP?"

A scant four episodes after her Clark Tyson breakdown, Jan's self-image suffers yet another neurotic episode. This time she's tired of being a middle child, unhappy about looking just like her sisters, and totally distraught over her perceived inability to stand out in the Brady crowd.

Her solution? In overstated Jan Brady fashion, she runs out to the local department store and buys herself a long brunette wig. She's convinced that it makes her look mysterious and alluring, but as her brother's guffaws hint, it makes her look really goofy (Bobby cracks "she looks like she's got a skunk sleeping on her head").

Jan's final hair-induced indignity comes when she wears the new hair to Lucy Winters's birthday party and gets laughed (literally) right out the door!

Crushed, Jan comes home and wants to die. But wait, en masse, those rotten and ridiculing party kids have undergone a group change of heart. They show up on the Bradys' doorstep, "I'm sorrys" get passed around, Jan's *real* hair receives rave reviews, and that middle Brady gal is happy once more—at least for a *little* while.

WRITERS: Al Schwartz and Bill Freedman
DIRECTOR: Peter Baldwin

•You might recognize Jan's friend Lucy. Her *real* name's Pamelyn Ferdin, and she's got one of those familiar but nameless TV faces, and seems to have appeared at least once on every sitcom ever made. She *is,* however, probably *most* familiar to devoted couch potatoes as Edna Unger, Felix's daughter, on "The Odd Couple," which was filmed next door to "The Brady Bunch" on the Paramount lot.

EPISODE 43: "OUR SON, THE MAN"

Greg at his grooviest.

Sick of being a kid, Greg moves out of the boys' bedroom and into Mike's den, which he turns into a groovy psychedelic bachelor pad (complete with beaded curtains and black lights) almost overnight.

Now a bona fide "man," Greg spends his next school day coming on to an older woman—a *senior . . .* wow!—but ends up getting dissed for a hippie. That does it. Even more quickly than Mike's den became Greg's "far-out space," the Brady big bro becomes the world's cleanest-cut hippie.

Sure, he's got the fringed suede vest, the afro, the headband, the shades, the tie-dyed bell-bottoms. And *sure,* he walks around the Brady house saying things like "I dig your scene, baby" and flipping peace signs at a befuddled Alice. But deep down we all know he's still that same goofy guy we all came to love.

So does that babe-ish senior. She sees right through Greg's hippie disguise, and when he asks her out again, she simply laughs at him.

Smacked back down to earth, Greg realizes the weirdness of his ways, and transforms himself back into a Brady. The fringe and the Afro disappear, and so does the bachelor pad when Greg decides that he actually kinda missed Bobby and Pete, and moves back into their room.

WRITER: Albert E. Lewin
DIRECTOR: Jack Arnold

EPISODE 44: "THE LIBERATION OF MARCIA BRADY"

This time the Bradys take on that hotbed of seventies controversy . . . women's lib!

When a roving news crew bumps into Marcia and asks for her thoughts on the equality of the sexes, she replies with "Anything that a man can do, a woman can do better."

The newscast airs, and when the Brady men get wind of her comments, they laugh heartily (surprisingly sexist, even with the time-warped early-seventies perspective) and challenge her to put up or shut up.

Marcia, of course, puts up, and joins the boys' outdoors club, the elite but rugged Frontier Scouts. That act of forced desegregation drives the Brady boys absolutely *nuts,* and they immediately begin hatching a plan for revenge.

Revenge comes when Peter, in a green dress and matching knee socks, joins *Marcia's* favorite club, the Sunflower Girls. He gamely tries to make a go of his point-proving transvestism, but when he's asked to sell cookies door-to-door (with a sales pitch of "I am a little Sunflower, sunny, brave, and true / From tiny bud to blossom, I'll do good deeds for you"), the public ridicule breaks him. He quits.

However, on the other side of the chromosomal pairing, Marcia gives Frontier Scouting her all, and when she actually pitches a tent, sparks a campfire, and completes their grueling long-distance nature hike, *everyone* is impressed. The guys even admit that maybe, just maybe, women *are* men's equals after all.

WRITER: Charles Hoffman
DIRECTOR: Russ Mayberry

EPISODE 45: "LIGHTS OUT"

Cindy sees a magician do the old disappearing-assistant trick, and freaks. She's sure that the poor woman's been lost in the dark, never to be seen again, and becomes deathly afraid of anything having to do with "magic."

At the same time, Peter just so happens to be working up his *own* magic act for the big pageant at school. (It's amazing how many school plays/pageants/frolics the Bradys appear in.) He too has a disappearing babe trick, which Mike and Carol hope will convince Cindy that there's nothing to be afraid of. Unfortunately, however, the phobic Brady flatly refuses to even look at it.

Finally, the day of the big audition arrives, but disaster strikes when Peter's comely assistant (namely, Jan) twists an ankle at the last minute and can't perform.

Enter Cindy, fully bedecked in a glowing "magician's assistant" costume that Alice hastily threw together ("I pulled the wings off her fairy pixie outfit"). Cindy's loyalty toward her brother has triumphed over her fear. She "disappears" and "reappears" on cue, and once the whole thing's over, even asks to disappear again.

WRITER: Bruce Howard
DIRECTOR: Oscar Rudolph

• The people who play the judges at the school auditorium were actually the stand-ins for Florence and me.

EPISODE 46: "THE WINNER"

Every single Brady has won a trophy . . . except Bobby. That makes the little guy *fanatically* determined to win one of his own. Throughout the episode, he tries to win trophies in a yo-yo marathon, a magazine subscription race, and even an ice-cream-eating contest, failing miserably each time.

It looks like our pal Bobby is just gonna have to adjust to life as a trophy-less loser . . . until the rest of the Bradys joyously present him with his very own gold-plated trophy signifying that he is indeed "the world's greatest Bobby Brady."

WRITER: Elroy Schwartz
DIRECTOR: Robert Reed

• Robert Reed directs his first Brady Bunch episode, and did a *very* credible job.

• *Brady Mistake!* There's a *huge* mistake in this episode, and it's all Lloyd Schwartz's fault. Watch closely and you'll notice Bobby, Mike, and Carol leaving the house in a blue convertible—and then returning in a brown station wagon! I teasingly asked Lloyd how he'd managed to screw up, and after he punched me in the arm, he came up with this story:

"Yeah, it was my fault. The episode called for Bobby to be very excited about going to a cartoon show, and everybody left in the convertible. Now, I was involved in the postproduction of the episode, and I knew that we needed a shot of that car coming *home* from the cartoon show, with the headlights on. I *also* knew that we already *had* that exact shot of the convertible in our stock library, but when we ordered it up, I never really looked at it. So we just slapped it into place without ever noticing that we'd goofed and picked up a shot of the brown station wagon by mistake.

"So we finished the episode, it airs on ABC, and none of us notice the mistake. But then I get a call one day from some guy who says he was watching the show and noticed a mixup with the cars. So he asks me 'Why was that?' and all of a sudden it finally hits me that it was a screw up. And I tell him, 'Well, the truth is, I blew it. I put the wrong shot in,' and I was honest, and thought, 'That's the end of that.' But then a couple of weeks later, there's a big headline in the *National Enquirer* that reads PRODUCER ADMITS, 'I BLEW IT!' Turns out that the 'concerned viewer' who called me was actually a reporter from the *Enquirer*."

EPISODE 47: "DOUBLE PARKED"

Woodland Park is about to be bulldozed, and all the Bradys are up in arms . . . except for Mike. No, he's not hiding a playground-hating dark side; he's been hired to design the courthouse that will ultimately knock out the park.

Uh-oh. It's an odd "Brady Bunch" in that the family members actually take opposing sides on the matter and actually even *argue* with each other. But in the end, with Brady-like simplicity, Mike designs a small park right on the Courthouse grounds. A compromise is reached, and everyone ends up happy once more.

WRITER: Skip Webster
DIRECTOR: Jack Arnold

• Jackie "Uncle Fester" Coogan shows up and appears in a

tiny little cameo, signing a "Save Woodland Park" petition for Alice. He'd play a much bigger (and creepier) role in "Brady" episode 70, playing slimy Harry Duggan, suer of Bradys.

EPISODE 48: "ALICE'S SEPTEMBER SONG"

Here we learn that under all that hair spray, starch, Tang, and Windex, Alice does indeed have a sensuous side.

Briefly, right around the time Sam the Butcher starts taking our favorite maid for granted, Alice gets a paid a visit by a handsome, middle-aged but still-studly old boyfriend named Mark Millard. Sam becomes history, and Alice goes gaga for the guy, until . . .

He tells her about a "hot tip" in the market and says that if she'll give him all her savings, he can *double* 'em in practically *no* time. (Millard must have been really cash-*desperate*. I mean, how much could *Alice* have stashed away?) In a lucky twist, Alice mentions her hot tip to Mike, who quickly checks out both the tip *and* Millard. When he finds out that they're *both* phony, Alice realizes that Mark never really wanted *her* at all. He just wanted her bucks.

She also realizes that even a boring but honest old schlub

**Brady cast photo:
Season three.**
(©Paramount
Pictures)

like Sam is a pretty good catch, and it's not long before the two have kissed and made up, and Sam's slipping her the discount meat once more.
WRITER: Elroy Schwartz
DIRECTOR: Oscar Rudolph

•In what may have been Alice's *only* hot date, she stays out with Mark Millard until (oh my God!) 1:30 A.M.! The Bradys wait up . . . until finally she comes home glowing, mooning about her romantic date but strangely (and uncharacteristically) mum about its details. Could our little Alice have (*gulp*) given up the booty? We'll just have to wonder . . . and hope.

EPISODE 49: "GHOST TOWN U.S.A."

Season three begins when the Bradys get their motor running and head out on the highway, looking for adventure and whatever comes their way.

All right, so the motor was in the family station wagon, and the highway led straight to the Grand Canyon, but it was as close to *Easy Rider* as the Bradys would ever get.

Rolling toward the Grand Canyon at a cautious and sensible fifty-five miles per hour, the Bunch spends their first day on the road singing car songs, and their first *night* on the road camping out in a real Old West ghost town. Once a thriving gold-rush boomtown, this burb has long since outlived its usefulness and fallen into a rundown state of disrepair. It's dusty, grimy, and completely deserted . . . except for its ghosts . . . and Zaccariah.

Zaccariah T. Brown (as played by the fabulous Jim Backus) is a filthy and foul-smelling old prospector who still hasn't given up on pulling a mother lode out of "them thar hills." He's also certifiably nuts.

Zaccariah leaps to the imaginary conclusion that the Bradys are in town to jump his equally imaginary claim. With that in mind, he does what *any* stark raving lunatic who's

Zaccariah Howell III?
(© 1991 Capital Cities/ABC, Inc.)

been out in the desert sun too long would do: he cons the family into touring the town and ends up locking all nine of 'em in what remains of the old town's jail.

Then, ditching his donkey, he steals the Bradys' car and heads for the hills, leaving the family to rot in their cell. Nice guy, huh?

Anyway, Mike uses his architectural ingenuity, and it's not long before he's lassoed the jailer's key ring off its post, opened up the cell door, and sprung the Bunch from the joint.

But they've merely jumped out of the frying pan and into the fire, because the now carless, foodless, and waterless Bradys are stranded in the desert with little hope of surviving the elements.

Mike goes looking for help, but as the episode ends it doesn't look good.

WRITER: Howard Leeds
DIRECTOR: Oscar Rudolph

• You don't have to strain your brain to figure out the connection between Sherwood Schwartz and Jim Backus. What would "Gilligan's Island" have been without Thurston Howell III?

Actually, the Schwartz-Backus bond goes back even further, all the way to Sherwood's first job in TV. He cut his television teeth writing a pretty funny "Lucy" rip-off entitled "I Married Joan," which starred the brilliant Joan Davis as the wacky 1950s sitcom housewife, and co-starred the equally brilliant Mr. Backus as her consistently befuddled spouse.

•The "ghost town" was actually the old "Bonanza" set, formerly used by the men of the Ponderosa. This is the episode we were filming when Governor Rockefeller came to visit.

EPISODE 50: "GRAND CANYON OR BUST"

As the second installment of the Bradys' "Grand Canyon Trilogy" opens, it looks bad for America's happiest family. Mike's off in the desert, aimlessly looking for help, and the rest of the pack is trying to cope with the harsh desert sun.

But then, just when things seem blackest, Mike charges in like the cavalry, not on a galloping steed but in the family's Vista Cruiser (the one that the nutty prospector Zaccariah

The Bunch, effectively blocking the view of the Canyon.
(© Karen Lipscomb)

The mule train.
(© Karen Lipscomb)

stole last week). Somehow (it's never made quite clear) Mike caught up with Zaccariah, convinced the old guy that the Bradys were no threat to his hallucinatory claim, and even talked him into giving back the family land yacht.

Saved from becoming a buzzard buffet, the Bradys clamber into the car and are once again on their way to the Grand Canyon.

This time they make it, and soon, we bump into the classic Brady scene wherein the entire clean-cut clan mule-trains it to the bottom of the canyon. Once there, they pitch camp for the night, get ready to hit the hay, and realize that Bobby and Cindy are . . . missing!

The Bradys wander off in search of the dopey duo, and the cliffhanger hangs for another seven days.

WRITER: Tam Spiva
DIRECTOR: Oscar Rudolph

EPISODE 51: "THE BRADY BRAVES"

Wandering waifs Bobby and Cindy seem doomed. They're hopelessly lost in the Grand Canyon (without even a gift shop or snack bar in sight), and if they don't get help soon, they might even (dum-da-*dum*-dum) . . . DIE!

Enter Jimmy Pakaya. He's a fine young Indian brave who's tired of his Native American heritage and wants to be an astronaut. He wants a life off the reservation, and away from his grandfather's glorious stories of Indian past. He is busily running away from home when he conveniently bumps into our hapless little heroes.

Jimmy makes a deal with his new pals. He'll blaze them a trail back to camp if they'll feed him, keep him a secret, and help him run away. They spit-shake, and in no time they're hugging it up with Mike, Carol, Alice, and every other Brady within squeezing distance. Meanwhile, Jimmy hides behind a tumbleweed.

Later that night, Cindy and Bobby stockpile food (beans in a flashlight) and then clumsily attempt to slip it out to their brush-covered pal. They are (of course) caught, and Jimmy's nabbed in the bust as well. He's angry and uncooperative at first, but one of Mike's patented lectures (entitled "Running Away and Hurting the Ones You Love") is all it takes to start the young brave weeping and thinking about going home.

They make plans to hike to the reservation the next morning, but cancel them when Jimmy's grandfather shows up.

Turns out that Chief Dan Eagle Cloud (played by Jay "Tonto" Silverheels) has been frantically searching for his runaway grandkid. He comes across the Bradys' camp, scares Alice, finds his grandson, and then he *too* is subjected to a lecture from Mike ("That Inescapable Generation Gap and How to Survive It").

After that, it's time to celebrate. The chief bestows "honorary Indian" status upon each Brady; then they all perform Native American dances, and . . . it starts to rain.

Just kidding.

WRITER: Tam Spiva
DIRECTOR: Oscar Rudolph

EPISODE 52: "JULIET IS THE SUN"

In *another* Brady-kid school-play episode (this time it's *Romeo and Juliet*), Marcia lands the lead role and drives the family mad when her head swells up as big as Alice's bottom. She becomes snotty, rude, abusive, and not very ladylike or Brady-like at all. She even revises Shakespeare!

Enter Carol, who's visited the play's dress rehearsal, and seen Marcia verbally cut down her four-eyed, fat-boy Romeo. She becomes thoroughly disgusted with her daughter's star-trippy attitude. With uncharacteristic severity, she pulls the rug out from under Marcia's ego by grounding the girl and yanking her out of the play entirely.

Marcia's crushed, but uses her punishment to reflect upon just how big a jerk she's become. Finally, when the student assigned to play the *much* more modest role of Lady Capulet comes down with last-minute mumps, the thoroughly humbled Marcia offers to play the part.

WRITER: Brad Radnitz
DIRECTOR: Jack Arnold

EPISODE 53: "THE WHEELER DEALER"

A simple episode wherein Greg buys a beat-up old Volkswagen convertible from his sleazy pal Eddie. He hopes to fix it up, but naturally, it turns out to be a clunker (must be a foul-up in the *fahrvergnügen*).

Anyway, Greg finally comes to the conclusion that *this* buggy Bug will *never* get up to speed and that he just may have acted too hastily in his quest to buy a car.

Charles Martin Smith. (© Karen Lipscomb)

WRITERS: Bill Freedman and Ben Gershman
DIRECTOR: Jack Arnold

•Look closely at the guy playing Ronnie and you'll find Charles Martin Smith. He's the nerdy-looking character actor who'd go on to just about steal *American Graffiti* out from under Richard Dreyfuss (he played Toad) and *The Untouchables* out from under Kevin Costner (he played the nerdy G-man accountant). He also starred in the (too) realistic Disney nature film *Never Cry Wolf*—you know, the one about the guy who lives all by himself in the Arctic wilderness eating live mice? Anyway, this was his first acting job *ever*.

EPISODE 54: "THE PERSONALITY KID"

Q: What's for dinner?
A: Pork chops and applesauce.
Brady fans worthy of their bell-bottoms know this episode inside out. Peter goes to a pal's party, ends up a neglected wallflower, and decides that he has absolutely no personality. So, with typical Brady resolve, he slaps on a personality makeover and transforms himself into Humphrey Bogart. Why? I don't know; but when that idea goes bust, our pal Pete invests in a joke book and makes like Henny Youngman. Anyway, Pete gets the idea that his lousy jokes are great and throws himself a bash. He *expects* that he'll be the life of the party but *succeeds* only in being annoying. Finally, Pete's pals can't take it anymore and ask him to quit acting so goofy and just be himself.
Peter finally learns that his *own* personality suits him best.
WRITER: Ben Starr
DIRECTOR: Oscar Rudolph

•*Near Nepotism Alert!* This doesn't qualify as a full-blown alert, but it comes close. Ben Starr (no relation to Ringo) was a very good pal of Sherwood Schwartz, with their friendship dating all the way back to the thirties, when they both wrote gags for Bob Hope.

EPISODE 55: "HER SISTER'S SHADOW"

Jan's gone neurotic *again*. This time she's jealous of her overly perfect sister Marcia. Marcia's teachers love her, Marcia wins awards . . . "All I ever hear is 'Marcia, Marcia, *Marcia*'!" weeps the nearly hysterical Jan. Enter Carol, who probably should've just slipped her a Librium but instead dispenses some motherly advice. She tells Jan that instead of focusing on Marcia's achievements, she ought to try and do something good on her own.

Bad advice. Two days later Jan's tried out for the school pom-pom club, been mercilessly cut, and thrown into an even more desperate funk than before. However, at about the same time that Alice starts hiding the razor blades, Jan's patriotic school essay ("What America Means to Me," no less) wins an award for its high grade of 98.

Uh-oh. Jan scans a closer look at her essay and realizes that her "98" was really *supposed* to be only a "93," and that she really shouldn't have won that award. Crushed again, Jan (being a Brady) refuses to accept her unearned adulation, and during what was supposed to be her acceptance speech she exposes the mistake in front of a cafetorium full of schoolmates.

But happily, the episode ends on the stable side of Jan's mood swings, as she's praised for her honesty, applauded, and just plain thrilled to be alive once more.

WRITERS: Al Schwartz and Phil Leslie
DIRECTOR: Russ Mayberry

EPISODE 56: "THE TEETER-TOTTER CAPER"

The Bradys have to attend ugly old Aunt Gertrude's wedding, but Bobby and Cindy weren't invited ("too little"), and they're not going to take it! Sick of being left out because of their age, the two mini-Bradys set out to show the world that anything adults can do, *they* can do better. They decide to set a world's record, and head to the backyard seesaw, determined to break the current teeter-totter mark of 124 hours.

They fail miserably (actually, they fall asleep at the plank), but a newspaper story about their attempt brings them instant fame. Even Aunt Gertrude calls to invite them to the wedding, but with un-Brady-like vindictiveness, they turn the old biddy down flat.

WRITERS: Joel Kane and Jack Lloyd
DIRECTOR: Russ Mayberry

EPISODE 57: "MY SISTER, BENEDICT ARNOLD"

Okay, this is it! Flip your hair into your face and do the following cheer in an incredibly lifeless monotone, while you're gasping for air like you've got emphysema. Ready? Here we go:

One, two, tell me who are you . . . THE BEARS!
Three, four, tell me who's gonna score . . . THE BEARS!
Five, six, tell me who's got the kicks . . . THE BEARS!
Who's gonna win? THE BEARS!!!
Say it again—THE BEARS!!! YAAAAAAAAAAY,
BEARS!!!!!!

Super-geek Warren Mulaney takes Greg's spot on the first-string basketball team, beats him out in the race for class president, and *then* has the audacity to try and score with Greg's very own sister Marcia. Greg *forbids* her to date the lowlife, but she stabs her brother in the back and, *just* to drive Greg crazy, goes out with Warren anyway.

That means Brady war! Soon, Greg has found Kathy Lawrence, the girl who beat Marcia out for the cheerleading squad, and has her eating out of his hand, even bouncing around the Brady living room doing cheers for him.

Not surprisingly, Marcia hits the roof, and when things blow up, they each end up admitting that they didn't even *like* the person they were dating, and that they were just using them to make each other mad. Then during the commercial, they take off all their clothes and do the wild thing on the orange Formica counter top.

Just wanted to see if you were paying attention. Actually,

in the end, happiness reigns once more at the Brady house, with Greg and Marcia friendly again, and even Kathy and Warren crazy about each other.

WRITER: Elroy Schwartz
DIRECTOR: Hal Cooper

EPISODE 58: "THE PRIVATE EAR"

Peter borrows Mike's new tape recorder, starts eavesdropping on the other kids, and in less time than it takes to sing our theme song, chaos reigns in that cozy suburban-tract Brady house. Each Brady kid suspects another of being the slimy snooper, and when they finally find out that Peter's the culprit, they devise one of those patented Brady-kid schemes to get even.

It starts with a bogus taped message that Mike and Carol are going to throw a surprise party for Peter (for getting a B-plus in geometry). Peter believes it, counts on it, and then is dumbfounded and hurt when nobody shows up. We sensitive Brady kids feel bad.

But not to worry: Mike and Carol have *also* heard the phony message, and they've postponed a weekend ski trip in order to actually *give* Peter that B-plus-in-geometry bash.

WRITER: Michael Morris
DIRECTOR: Hal Cooper

EPISODE 59: "AND NOW A WORD FROM OUR SPONSOR"

The Bradys go to the supermarket and become TV stars . . . almost. Actually, soap magnate Skip Farnum (played by Paul Winchell—the Jerry Mahoney/Knucklehead Smith guy) sees 'em out shopping and decides that they'd be the *perfect* real-life family for his soap commercial.

The Bradys are at first skeptical, then thrilled, then fired after Carol's aspiring-actress friend Myrna (pronounced "Meeeeerna") gives them some horrendous advice about "Method acting." Mike and Carol overact terribly, the kids show up filthy because they know Safe soap will get them

Paul Winchell as Farnum.
(© 1991 Capital Cities/ABC, Inc.)

clean, and Alice shows up in gaudy pincurls because "Safe soap makes doing the laundry so easy, I had plenty of time to do my hair."

Needless to say, corny hippy-cliché Farnum gets one gander at the Bradys' Stanislavskian disaster and gives 'em the boot.

WRITER: Albert E. Lewin
DIRECTOR: Peter Baldwin

•Robert Reed hated this episode so much that he took typewriter in hand, and hunted and pecked out the following memo.

NOTES: "And Now a Word from Our Sponsor" Brady Bunch, August 25, 1971

Once again, "The Brady Bunch" takes an inconsistent literary leap from semi-real situation comedy into thinly motivated farce bordering on slapstick.

It's the old 1930's "Movies enter the lives of Mr. and Mrs. Average America" plot in which our loveable, down-to-earth family is unwittingly hit by a tidal wave of Hollywood lunacy— nearly torn from their middle-class moorings, but thanks to their good humour, stability and unflagging good sense, not only withstand the barrage, but emerge high, dry and unsullied in their victory. Moral: Mr. Average American Man is really the National Hero. (Warm embrace, chuckles and . . . we fade out.)

It's been done a thousand times, and if well written, could probably work again, at least in a dated sense. "And Now A Word From Our Sponsor" is not well written.

Sc. 13
1. In order to elicit some conflict, the author has given Mike an arbitrary skepticism unmotivated by the amount of information he has been given. Carol has had the first-hand experi-

ence and would more probably have cause to doubt Farnum's veracity. The scene would work just as well that way, and the phone call could still be made by Mike.

2. Carol's lines "phony-sincere; sincere-sincere" are ninny lines.

3. Mike's expository speech "Art Emhoff works in one of the biggest advertising agencies in town, etc." is typical of constantly overdone exposition. Cut out the everlasting appositives. Should read, "Art Emhoff is in advertising, and if anybody knows about . . . Skip Farnum, it'll be Art." Over-exposition and appositives almost always create incredulity of character.

4. Mike's phone conversation has no phatic communion in it i.e., normal everyday dialog. He, Art, has been established as a friend. You don't call a friend out of the blue, and go right to the problem without, "How've you been," or "How's your golf game," or "How's your wife," and you don't hang up without the same thing.

Again, this is seemingly small, but it is typical of careless dialog sans transitions. The consequence of which is, we as actors have to spend time on the set searching for something and abandoning time for perfecting performance for which there is no time anyway. This is writing at its simplest level, we have a right to expect someone to know enough or care enough to have it done.

Sc. 14
1. Mike's response to Farnum. "Kooky" is an inapt term. "Oddball," maybe or "Nuts"; "Laughable"; "Ridiculous"; "Cliche," but not "Kooky."

Sc. 16
1. Typical weak scene ending with a limp gag-line.

Sc. 17
1. Needs qualification. The decision to give them money is too easy and unconsidered. Weakens family sense of prudence and responsibility.

Sc. 22

1. Mike: "I can't make heads or tails of this legal double-talk, etc." Nonsense, Mike is an adult in business and capable of understanding contracts.

2. The soap sequence. Carol should introduce the conflict. Again, she has the information, not Mike. To have her overlook the fact that we don't use the product, or to have her say nothing about it, makes her seem thoughtless, careless or stupid.

3. All the soaps are one-syllable names. Sounds phony and is an obvious author's device.

4. The whole soap sequence, i.e., "Help," "Champ," "Best," "Safe" etc. allows Carol to become unreal and cutesy-pooh to no avail. The limpest sort of gag sequence.

5. Mike's speech should read: "Probably not, but I think they should and I think we should. Otherwise, we're frauds."

6. The end of the scene offers too definite and over-positive a course change. Needs qualifying. "I *think* I *ought* to call Farnum, etc.," and "I'll *talk* to them in the morning."

7. The end gag is unplayable. Tearing the contract is out of character and unmotivated—another author's device.

8. In order to make pieces of a contract small enough to flutter like confetti, the business would take far too long and consequently leave a hole as well as place too strong an emphasis on a decision that is not that pressingly important.

Sc. 34–37

1. Desperately needs qualification. It is totally unbelievable that parents would deliberately turn children loose to their own unmonitored devices to purposely dirty and probably damage clothes, if not themselves. Not in a family of nine with some sense of frugality, if not caution. Every middle-class viewer with children would scoff in disbelief. To laugh at a situation is one thing, to laugh at it and believe it could happen is something far more desirable. The things the kids do *could* happen, but not believable the way it's been *given* to happen.

Sc. 40–41

1. Alice's forgetting which pile is which is unbelievable and forces the following scene to become painfully anti-climatic. Should be compressed into one scene.

Sc. 45

1. Mike's line: "We don't know much about acting" is like referring to "movies" *in* the movies. It brings the audience out of the fantasy. Never remind them what they're seeing isn't the truth. Could read: "We've never done this before."

Sc. 49

1. Myrna is the exact antithesis of the author's description. No method actress would spout dialogue like "lots of energy," "bigger than life," etc.

Sc. 50

1. Ludicrous. My God, if Alice has been mopping the floor, as indicated, the mop is *wet!* Yet, she "clasps it" to her breast, "kisses it," etc. Nothing is made of it at all. This is an unfortunate but typical example of how scenes too often get to final with ridiculous inconsistencies or impossiblities.

Sc. 57–etc.

1. Unjustified strain of believability that our "director," when met with failure in one "scene," can immediately without preparation go to another. Should there be a dissolve or a flip or some justification in dialog?

Sc. 63

1. Mike's line should read: "This *is* my house,"—take the edge of sarcasm off.

Sc. 64

1. Carol: "I guess we'll just have to wait until Mr. Brady gets home, etc." Ninnyism. Once again, Carol becomes a nincompoop. If Carol can read a grocery list, she can look up a given reference.

The Character of Skip Farnum

Skip Farnum, our foil, is a paper thin, one-dimensional version of the old pot-boiling cliche of the Hollywood director, updated by someone's version of the 'mod' dialect. In 45 speeches, he has been given almost as many cliches ranging from "like real," "rap" (twice), "flip" (twice), "lay it on," "cool it," "squares," "gig," and the inevitable theatrical labeler of the au courant young,—"dig" (twice).

The theory seems to be, if a little bit of character dialog will help the character, a whole lot will make him.

An old tenet of the theater is that comedy character is based upon *behavior* aided by plot involvement and sometimes, though not always, dialog.

This performance will entirely depend on what the actor and director can bring to it, while being severely hampered by dialogue and aided by no behaviour at all, with the exception of framing a scene through his hands.

We are led to believe he is "one of the biggest directors in TV commercials," and yet, we never see him really direct. What a disappointment! In his big scenes, he does little but react to us and respond with one-liners. Meanwhile, the comedy-burden of the scene is left to us, the family, and in the case of Mike and Carol, by severely over-acting which if done to the height it is written will cause suspension of belief and character. We are not that dumb.

Think of the funnier, or at least more real and consistent situations we could have been given.

Myrna is written as "definitely a method actress." Mike and Carol under tutelage could end up doing a "method" approach to commercials, or even improvising, or *trying* to. This could be far funnier, less predictable and certainly more consistent with the character.

Farnum says he wants us "natural" "unrehearsed" and yet he gives us *scripts* to learn and we are seen to go through it *three* times without variation except heightening of the "Ham." It's too much. We can only get broader which is no surprise by the third time, *and* endangers the believability of our characters. If he gives us no scripts at all, and we *have* to make it up, then it falls right in with Myrna's approach, improvisation and ultimate conflict with what *he* sees as "realistic"—which obviously isn't.

This way Farnum could actually *direct* us, show us how he wants it, *do* it for us. He's the broad character, give him a chance to use it instead of just saying it.

In short, it seems to me, the problem with this script is not in the plot situations. It could all happen. Where the rub comes is in *how* it is brought about. The troubles are: totally unmotivated behavior; as ever—weak dialog; and over-written cliched characters. The script reads as if it were put together by a committee, with each guy responsible for a different area . . .

ROBERT REED

EPISODE 60: "CLICK"

Mike and Carol actually disagree about something . . . Greg. Seems that Greg wants to join the high-school football team, and while Mike's all for it, Carol's afraid he'll get hurt. Finally, after Mike and Greg give her a long song-and-dance about the relative safety of organized scholastic athletics, Carol okays Greg's participation.

Uh oh, just after Greg joins the team, and goes to practice, he busts his ribs. Carol does an "I told you so" routine, and Greg *stops* taking gridiron hits and *starts* taking gridiron snapshots as the team's official photographer.

I *still* think that was a wimpy compromise.

WRITERS: Tom and Helen August
DIRECTOR: Oscar Rudolph

EPISODE 61: "THE NOT-SO-ROSE-COLORED GLASSES"

Well, Jan's gone whacko yet *again*! She needs glasses but

is just too neurotic about her appearance to wear them. Blurry eyed, she leaves school on the wrong bike, squints as her grades start to go south, and finally crashes her bicycle through the kids' group portrait that Mike had taken for his and Carol's wedding anniversary.

After that, the glasses stay on, and the kids sneak out. They have the picture retaken and swap it for the busted one, but eagle-eyed Mike realizes the switch when he notices Jan's wearing her glasses in the new shot—she had refused in the original.

WRITER: Bruce Howard
DIRECTOR: Leslie H. Martinson

EPISODE 62: "BIG LITTLE MAN"

Puny little Bobby has had it up to *here* (my hand is under my chin) with people goofing on him because of his height. So when Sam absent-mindedly calls him "Shrimpo," he goes off the deep end and starts hanging from his closet rod in the hope of stretching himself out.

One day later, Bobby's thrilled, and convinced that he's grown a full inch and a half. That shrinks to an inch when Marcia admits that she moved the height mark on his bedroom wall down a half-inch, to help him feel good about himself. That drops to zero when Jan and Cindy each fess up that they did the same.

Bobby bums, but then his tiny stature ends up saving the day.

Helping Greg close up Sam's butcher shop, Bobby proves that his brain is *also* tiny when he locks himself and his brother in Sam's zero-degree meat locker. All looks lost until Greg busts the locker's small window and only little Bobby can fit through the opening, saving both of their lives.

This is another one of those episodes that people seem to remember especially fondly.

WRITER: Skip Webster
DIRECTOR: Robert Reed

EPISODE 63: "GETTING DAVY JONES"

This may be possibly the most popular "Brady Bunch" episode of all.

Marcia is the president of the Davy Jones Fan Club at Fillmore Junior High, and she's made her pals a solemn vow that she can get Davy to appear at their prom.

Marcia's completely clueless as to how she'll actually go about fulfilling that pledge, but gamely gives it her best shot. She tries to catch up with Davy at the local TV station . . . and fails. She dresses up like a bellboy, with Greg in tow, hoping to surprise him in his hotel room (probably not the first girl to do that), and even chases the Monkee to the local recording studio.

Twice more Marcia bites it big-time, and gets unceremoniously tossed out of both establishments on her can. However, as she whines about her predicament to the recording studio's sound engineer, Davy just happens to catch her entire whiny, moany sob story on his headsets.

Before long, it's time for another celebrity to pay an unexpected visit to the Brady pad. Davy shows up, explains overhearing Marcia's tale at the recording studio, agrees to play the prom, asks her to be his date, sings to her; and as the episode closes, he's swapping spit with the gal. (All right, so maybe it's just a coupla pecks on the cheek.)

Anyway, if the Museum of Broadcasting ever calls looking for a "Brady" episode to put on display, this may be the appropriate choice. Either this or the "Oh, my nose . . ." thing (Episode 90).

WRITERS: Phil Leslie and Al Schwartz
DIRECTOR: Oscar Rudolph

•Here's an odd little slice o' trivia. *Listen* closely to this episode and you'll realize that Marcia Brady has the same schoolteacher as that evil Brady twin . . . Bart Simpson! Yep, Marcia Wallace (who'll always be best known as Carol Kester Bondurant, the red-haired secretary from "The Bob Newhart Show") played Marcia's teacher Mrs. Robbins. She now supplies the voice for the equally creepy Mrs. Crubopple, thorn in the side of American pop icon, Bart Simpson.

EPISODE 64: "DOUGH RE MI"

What can you say about this particular episode except "Ay-Yi-Yi-Yi-Yi"?

We enter the Bradys' half-hour universe to find Greg holed up in his room, hard at work writing the song that he hoped would "really break" his recording career. It's called "We Can Make the World a Whole Lot Brighter," and he assures us it's *great!*—The only problem is that Greg doesn't have the hundred and fifty dollars that it's gonna take to get his masterpiece recorded.

Peter then hatches a plan wherein *all* of the Brady kids will sing on the recording and split the costs six ways. Sounds great, . . . until the other five kids get a load of Peter's awful voice (which is funny, because even in real life Chris Knight can't sing worth a lick). Turns out Peter's voice is in the pubescent process of changing, and is uncontrollably jumping from octave to octave.

At this point the loving Brady siblings get together and decide to dump the dead weight from the group. Peter's crushed—until an extra-sensitive Greg figures out a way to keep everybody happy. He locks himself back up in that room of his, sits down, and creates an equally awful song called "Time to Change," all about growing up and finding yourself (sounds like Springsteen), and showcasing the wretched voice of Peter Brady.

WRITER: Ben Starr
DIRECTOR: Allan Barron

•Both "We Can Make the World a Whole Lot Brighter" and "Time to Change" would appear on the second Brady Kids record album entitled *Meet the Brady Bunch* (I wonder where we got *that* idea).

EPISODE 65: "THE BIG BET"

Greg makes like a *real* older brother and verbally abuses

Bobby, belittling his puny stature and lack of muscle power. He also declares that he could do *twice* as many chin-ups as his teeny-tiny brother. Bobby snaps, and challenges Greg to make good on his boast or spend one week as his personal slave.

Greg laughs, accepts, and forgets about the whole thing, while Bobby goes the Jane Fonda route and exercises like a man possessed. Come contest day, Bobby kicks butt, and Greg unhappily spends the next seven days as his indentured servant.

WRITER: Elroy Schwartz
DIRECTOR: Earl Bellamy

•*Nepotism Alert!* Sherwood's daughter Hope makes the first of her three appearances as Rachel, main squeeze to Greg. Working with the boss's daughter, I was on my absolute *best* behavior.

EPISODE 66: "JAN'S AUNT JENNY"

The Bradys spend the weekend happily (we did *everything* happily) cleaning junk out of the attic, and come across a decades-old photograph of Carol's aunt Jenny. Incredibly, the photo looks exactly like Jan!

At this point, Jan (who we've already learned is insecure about her looks) figures that if she could get hold of a current photo of the old gal, she'd have a good idea of what *she* will look like forty or fifty years down the line.

A couple of weeks later the photo arrives, and Jan learns that she'll someday grow up to look just like . . . Imogene Coca! YIKES!!! Surprising no one, Jan goes off the deep end (again) and gets thoroughly bummed about her future face. However, after she *meets* Aunt Jenny, Jan's mood swings 180 degrees (again), because it turns out that the old bag is really a pretty cool chick. She travels the world, is totally hip, and even gives the Bradys something they've always needed—an authentic Eskimo totem pole.

WRITER: Michael Morris
DIRECTOR: Hal Cooper

Henderson, Plumb, and Imogene Coca. (© 1991 Capital Cities/ABC, Inc.)

•Everybody knows how brilliant Imogene Coca was with Sid Caesar on "Your Show of Shows," but she was also terrific in "It's About Time," Sherwood Schwartz's sci-fi sitcom, in which she co-starred with another comic genius, Joe E. Ross (best known as Car 54's Gunther Toody).

•This show introduces a couple of grooming changes in the Brady kids. First, we'd recently done a show about Jan getting glasses, and from this episode forward, you'll notice that she wears them in every show. That's because *Eve* ended up nearsighted, too. Also, this episode marks the beginning of my totally frustrating and vain attempts to keep my rapidly curling hair straightened and under control. It looks goofy, and over the next few shows, it got a lot worse before I finally gave up.

EPISODE 67: "CINDY BRADY, LADY"

Cindy's sick of being a little kid, and miserable that she can't do anything to speed up her aging process. Enter Bobby, who comes to the conclusion that Cindy would feel more grown up if she had a secret admirer. So, trying to cheer the kid up, he starts sending her anonymous gifts.

The monkey wrench gets tossed into the works when Cindy tells her secret admirer (it's Bobby disguising his voice on a pay phone) to visit the house and say hello. That's it; Bobby's sure he's a goner.

Desperate, he comes up with a plan to save his neck, and bribes his buddy Tommy with a "gen-yoo-ine Kennedy half-dollar" to pose as the elusive secret admirer. Mike finds out about the scam and nearly blows a blood vessel, but things turn out fine because Tommy decides that he really *wants* to see Cindy again, and even gives Bobby's four bits back.

WRITERS: Al Schwartz and Larry Rhine
DIRECTOR: Hal Cooper

•The kid who plays Tommy in this episode is a familiar-faced actor named Eric Shea. He can be seen on "The Odd Couple," in *The Poseidon Adventure,* and you've heard his voice a million times in "Peanuts" cartoons as Linus.

EPISODE 68: "THE POWER OF THE PRESS"

A "high concept" episode. Peter gets his own column in the school paper, starts calling himself "Scoop" Brady, neglects his studies, gets a D minus on his science test, writes an extremely flattering column about his science teacher in hopes of upping his grade, gets turned down flat, and in the end learns a lesson about hard work and the power of the press.

WRITERS: Bill Freedman and Ben Gershman
DIRECTOR: Jack Arnold

EPISODE 69: "SERGEANT EMMA"

When Alice goes on vacation, we Bradys mope around wondering how we'll survive a week without her. That is until Alice's identical cousin Emma shows up, takes charge, and proves that "looks" are perhaps the *only* thing the two have in common.

Alice is wonderful, Emma's a beast. Alice is a sweetheart, Emma's unbearable. Alice is sweet, Emma's Butch. Actually, Emma has spent her entire adult life in the army, and in no time has the Brady house reeling with her strictly enforced military regime. Six A.M. workouts, chipped beef on toast for "chow," bedroom inspections, and an early-evening lights-out leave the Brady civilians worn out and depressed.

They endure Emma for Alice's sake and even turn their "Welcome Home, Alice" party into a going-away party for Emma when the old gal stumbles on to their preparations and misinterprets. Needless to say, the Bradys would never hurt Emma's feelings, and when the Sarge is moved to tears by their (misinterpreted) kindness, everyone learns a lesson about tolerance and loneliness.

In the end, Alice lets the Bradys know that she's thrilled they liked Cousin Emma so much. She explains that Emma has a hard time making friends and (for some inexplicable reason) usually rubs people the wrong way. However, since the Bradys were so crazy about her, she'll be back for three weeks when Alice goes on her *next* vacation!

You may not be surprised to learn that Ann B. Davis plays *both* roles.

WRITER: Harry Winkler
DIRECTOR: Jack Arnold

•As odd as this may seem, in real life Ann B. Davis does little or no cooking (although I think she knows how to make toast). Believe it or not, she also admits to being "not very good with children."

EPISODE 70: "THE FENDER BENDERS"

Uncle Fester's back, and Carol's crashed into him. Actually, Jackie Coogan isn't playing Uncle Fester but rather a money-grubbing slimebag named Harry Duggan.

The plot has Carol backing into Duggan's car in the supermarket parking lot. The damages are minor, and they both agree to take care of it by themselves. However, a couple of hours later, Harry storms the Brady house, clad in a huge neck brace and carrying a cane. Now he's claiming that Carol smashed into his car, maimed him, and had better give him a *lot* of money to cover the damages.

The Bradys don't buy his act. They toss him out the door, and it isn't long before Duggan's doing his "Owww, my neck!" routine in court. Things look grim bad for the Bradys until our hero Mike throws his briefcase onto the floor behind the dastardly Duggan. The crash startles the fortune hunter, he cranes his neck around to check out the noise, and an entire courtroom full of gawkers (not to mention the judge) find out that he's phony.

WRITER: David P. Harmon
DIRECTOR: Allan Barron

EPISODE 71: "MY FAIR OPPONENT"

In a hybrid of *Pygmalion* and *Frankenstein,* Marcia makes over Molly, the school's stereotypical geeky ugly-duckling type, and helps her run for the maniacally coveted position of Fillmore Junior High School Banquet Night hostess. However, Marcia's creation soon turns on her, becoming an unbearable, cliquish, nose-in-the-air jerk.

Things really start to boil when Marcia attempts to stop the monster by beating it out for Banquet Night hostess. But when Molly swipes Marcia's brilliant campaign speech, she *also* swipes the election out from under her.

As we near the end of our episode, however, Molly is hit with one of those miraculous only-on-"The Brady Bunch" changes of heart. She apologizes, fesses up about the stolen speech, and fixes it so that they can *both* go to the banquet as *co*-hostesses.

Then we all packed up and went to Hawaii.

WRITER: Bernie Kahn
DIRECTOR: Peter Baldwin

•Banquet guest of honor "Colonel Dick Whitfield" gets his character name from the real-life husband of Frances Whitfield, our on-set teacher.

EPISODE 72: "HAWAII BOUND"

Year four starts off by placing the Bradys in paradise.

There's really . . . uh . . . not much plot to the next three episodes, but who cares.

The Bradys are flying off to Hawaii. Why? Simple. Mike has

**The Big
Kahuna...about
to wipe out.**
(Barry Williams)

designed a high-rise that's currently being built in Oahu, and his architectural firm has decided that he and his whole family should drop by and check it out (wow, that's *some* firm!).

Anyway, we get there, and the Bradys walk you through an eleven-minute travelogue touring Hawaii. Bobby finds a tiki on the beach, laughs when he's told that it's cursed, but then changes his tune when big brother Greg enters a surfing competition, wipes out on a wicked wave, and disappears into the tropical foam.

Did Greg drown?

Tune in next week and find out.

WRITER: Tam Spiva
DIRECTOR: Jack Arnold

•If you've read pages 719 through 84, you know all about how that wave nearly drowned me for real, how a monster outrigger nearly drowned *all* the Bradys, and how the tropical ambience helped me finally lock lips with Maureen.

EPISODE 73: "PASS THE TABU"

Okay, you guessed right Greg doesn't drown but Bobby is

Large livin' at the luau. (© 1991 Capital Cities/ABC, Inc.)

now convinced that his tabu tiki is indeed a harbinger of really bad luck, and heaves the thing into the sea.

Enter Jan, who's strolling along the sand when she comes across . . . the tiki! She picks it up, pockets it, and, thinking he'd lost it, returns it to Bobby.

Once the tiki's back, Bobby wants no part of it; but Peter, convinced that maybe it *is* harmless after all, starts wearing it on a string around his neck. The necklace lasts about seven hours. Halfway through the night, Greg wakes up to find Pete's pajamas covered by the tiki . . . *and a giant poisonous wolf spider!!!* Yikes!

Mr. Spider gets tossed, but the tiki's not so easily disposed of. The mysterious island native Mr. Hanalei tells the boys that the only way to remove a tiki's curse is to return it to its original burial ground.

WRITER: Tam Spiva
DIRECTOR: Jack Arnold

•The "poisonous spider" wasn't deadly, but it *did* have *large* fangs. In fact, when it came time to shoot the bug scenes, our "spider wrangler" held up shooting until he could place a tiny piece of styrofoam over each pointy little fang.

Even *with* the foam "caps," that thing made me shudder.

EPISODE 74: "THE TIKI CAVES"

Here, the Bradys borrow the plot of their Grand Canyon adventure and transplant it to the tropical climes of Hawaii.

First, the boys make a trek through the Hawaiian rain forests in search of the sacred ancient burial cave where they can put the evil tiki to rest once and for all. Miraculously, they find it, but once they're inside, it's Grand Canyon all over again. Let us count the parallels.

Zaccariah, the psychotic prospector, is gone, but he's been replaced by Professor Whitehead, the psychotic archaeologist—played with a kitschy zeal by legendary big-screen scary guy Vincent Price.

Zaccariah irrationally believed that the Bradys were out to jump his gold claim; Professor Whitehead irrationally believes

In the "Tiki Caves." From left, a crew member, Chris Knight, Vincent Price, Mike Lookinland, Barry Williams, Lloyd Schwartz.
(© Karen Lipscomb)

that the Brady boys are out to steal the credit for *his* important archaeological discovery, the burial cave.

Zaccariah imprisoned the Bradys by locking them in the ghost town jail; Professor Whitehead imprisons the Brady boys by tying them to giant-economy-sized tikis.

Mike caught up with Zaccariah, gave him one of his surefire lectures, and convinced him that the Bradys were his friends; Mike catches up with Professor Whitehead, lectures *him*, and convinces him that the Bradys are his friends.

Zaccariah apologized for his evil doings and let the Bradys go. So does the professor.

In fact, Mike's thorough talking-to shames Professor Whitehead so badly that he decides to simply *donate* his find to the Honolulu Museum.

In the end, the evil tiki's put to bed, the Bradys' bad-luck streak is over, and the grateful Honolulu Museum tosses them a swinging Brady beach bash, wherein everybody blows the ceremonial conch shell and (in a thinly disguised reprise of their Grand Canyon "Indian dance" scene) shakes their grass to the strains of a hula.

WRITER: Tam Spiva
DIRECTOR: Jack Arnold

EPISODE 75: "TODAY I AM A FRESHMAN"

People seem to remember the subplot of this particular

episode more vividly than they do the main story. *Nobody*, it seems, paid much attention to Marcia's anxiety over finally taking that giant step out of childhood and into high school. They forget how she begs Greg (Big Brady on Campus) to introduce her around, and how she tries to make friends by joining every single club in school. There's scuba (watch for Maureen in that wetsuit—ooof!), ceramics, yoga, even karate. But *most* important to Marcia is her pending acceptance into the snootiest of all high-school cliques/clubs, the Boosters. They fancy themselves as the grand high exalted creme de la creme of upper-educational babes.

What people *do* remember is the episode's goofy little subplot, wherein Peter builds a volcano. It's an insignificant little story line, which was written at the last minute and sprang from that television writer's treasure trove . . . complete and total desperation.

This episode of "The Brady Bunch" was getting dangerously close to its first day of shooting with *no one* having written a decent subplot. The clock was ticking, and tensions were rising. With his state of mind somewhere in between manic and panic, Lloyd Schwartz pounded his fist on the writers' table and said, "If we don't nail this thing soon, I swear I'm going to *explode!*"

And that was it. When Lloyd yelled the word "explode," he remembered building a model volcano in high school, and our subplot was born. As an added bonus, he came up with a way to have his volcano subplot affect the episode's main story line (that's the elusive ultimate goal for most sitcom writers).

Anyway, those Booster snobs come over to Marcia's house in order to make sure they approve of her life-style. Marcia's doing her best to kiss up, but when Pete's volcano goes kablooey, spraying gray mucky "lava" all over the gals, they go nuts. Marcia laughs and realizes what a bunch of geeks the Boosters really are.

WRITERS: William Raynor and Myles Wilder
DIRECTOR: Hal Cooper

•By the way, if you want to know how to make that highly volatile Peter Brady volcano, its easy. Just get yourself three prop guys, some explosives, a special-effects man, and a pyrotechnician. Pay them obscene sums of money, and from there it's a piece of cake.

EPISODE 76: "CYRANO DE BRADY"

I like this episode a lot, because it marked one of the few times that Peter and Greg were allowed to appear really close on-camera.

The story was simple, but fun. Peter gets a major crush on Jan's pal Kerry but has no idea how to break the ice with her. Greg, being the quintessential early-seventies suburban babe-magnet, comes to the rescue, and it isn't long before Peter's outside Kerry's window with Greg hiding in a shrub, feeding him sure-fire pick-up lines.

Things go awry when Kerry gets the message—but falls for Greg!

WRITER: Skip Webster
DIRECTOR: Hal Cooper

EPISODE 77: "FRIGHT NIGHT"

The episode where the Bradys are scary . . . on purpose!

The boys pull spooky pranks on the girls (like having a slide-projected "ghost" terrorize them in the night), the girls seek revenge (their cellophane-wrap monster scares the P.J.'s off Peter), and things keep escalating until Alice smashes Mr. Brady's head to bits with a Louisville Slugger.

The head in question here is not *la cabeza del señor Brady* but the hideous ceramic bust Carol's sculpted of her man. It has just come home after winning third place at an exhibition when Alice, spooked by an extra-scary Brady-kid prank, takes bat in hand and cracks the skull of that lurking ceramic figure in the living room.

WRITER: Brad Radnitz
DIRECTOR: Jerry London
•Watch for the bedroom scene, wherein you'll find Carol

in a poofy pink nightie and Mike in his ultimate mod sleep-wear, Nehru pajamas. Who said the Bradys weren't hip?

•Also look closely at the bust of Mike: it looks *exactly* like show-biz enigma John Davidson.

EPISODE 78: "CAREER FEVER"

Greg's gotta write an English paper about what he wants to be when he grows up. Problem is, he has no idea what that might be. So Greg does what all young American students do in situations like this: he lies, and comes up with a fabrication about wanting to be an architect, just like good ol' Dad.

Mike gets wind of Greg's career decision, believes it, and it isn't long before he's guiding Greg toward a lifetime in architecture. Miserable, but not wanting to hurt Mike's feelings, Greg hatches a plan. He tells Mike that he wants to design a house all by himself, and then proceeds to sketch out the most hideous home imaginable, complete with moat and drawbridge.

Mike takes one look at the drawing and realizes that Greg's no architect, right? Wrong. Like most dads, Mike's blind to the failings of his son, decides that Greg's disaster was based solely on the fact that he needs better drafting utensils, and remedies that situation by supplying Greg with an expensive set of professional tools.

Greg realizes that he's trapped and tells the truth? Sure. He simply takes his tools, sits down, and creates a house even more horrendous than the first. Mike finally gets the message, Greg finally tells the truth, and all is once again joyous in Bradyland.

WRITERS: Burt and Adele Styler
DIRECTOR: Jerry London

•This is the episode wherein the Bradys' normally bizarre wardrobe went absolutely berserk! From Jan's shocking-pink velour bell-bottom hip-huggers to Peter's daShiki, we're out of control.

EPISODE 79: "LAW AND DISORDER"

Bobby becomes a safety monitor at school and is quickly

transformed into a power-mad, swollen-headed rules freak whose activities are so by-the-book that *no one* can stand him anymore. At school he's reporting his friends for chewing gum, and he even rats on Cindy when she commits the major indiscretion of running in the halls.

That's not all. The overzealous youth brings his new attitude home and starts finking on his brothers and sisters over things like missed chores and curfews. In short, he's turned into a real little dork.

But then the troubled Brady learns a lesson. In this case, Bobby is forced to ignore a "condemned" sign in order to save a classmate's kitten from an abandoned house, ruining his good suit in the process. Bobby sneaks home and tries to secretly launder his suit, but succeeds only in burying the laundry room under five feet of suds. Finally, after a thorough mopping and a thorough speech from Mike, Bobby learns that "rules are made to be broken."

And then it's time to launch the S.S. *Brady,* a rowboat salvaged and restored by those ever resourceful (and "ever in search of a subplot") Bradys.

WRITER: Elroy Schwartz
DIRECTOR: Hal Cooper

EPISODE 80: "JAN, THE ONLY CHILD"

The Bradys are going to yet another corny/goofy/unbelievable party (this time the whole brood is busily prepping for a square dance), and Jan is going mental again. This time, she's not only sick of being the middle Brady kid, she wants to be the *only* Brady kid. Jan wants her siblings dead!

At the same time, Alice and Carol are competing to see who makes the best preserves. (Why? I don't know.)

Anyway, the rest of the Brady kids make Jan's wish come true by ignoring her completely, and it isn't long before Jan learns about the downside of being an only child and gets her overalls ready for some foot-stomping and promenading.

WRITERS: Al Schwartz and Ralph Goodman
DIRECTOR: Roger Duchowney

EPISODE 81: "THE SHOW MUST GO ON??"

Mike and Carol *both* get conned into performing with a kid at the annual Westdale High Family Frolics. Carol and Marcia perform a duet ("Together" . . . you know, from *Gypsy*), and Mike is asked to read a sensitive poem . . . Oh, *no!!!*

Anyway, rather than appear square, Greg and Mike sabotage the poem, adding visual gags, bad puns, and a rubber chicken . . . it's *real* hip.

WRITER: Harry Winkler

DIRECTOR: Jack Donahue

•In what may be the grossest event ever to occur in the Brady house, Alice spends a good minute-and-a-half sublimating her sexual tensions by . . . squashing flies on the orange Brady counter. Her swatter takes out a good half-dozen before the carnage is over. Yuck. Maybe she needed more days off.

•Watch this episode and look for the nerdy bald-headed, little man with the accordion. He's Frank DeVol, and he wrote the "Brady Bunch" theme music. You may also recognize him from his more familiar—and much funnier—role as "Fernwood 2-Night"'s one-nostriled bandleader, Happy Kyne.

•This is Maureen McCormick's favorite episode. She says, "I had a really great time rehearsing, singing, dancing, and doing the song with Florence. I wish we could have done one every episode."

EPISODE 82: "YOU CAN'T WIN 'EM ALL"

As another beautiful day dawns on the Brady house, we get the good news that *both* of the littlest Bradys have become semifinalists who might just appear on a real-live TV game show. All they have to do is pass a simple eligibility test. Cindy's thrilled and starts boning up for the big quiz. Bobby, on the other hand, is relaxed, and cockily assured that he'll become a contestant without any trouble whatsoever.

The test comes and goes, with Cindy acing the quiz and

Bobby learning a lesson about overconfidence. He's depressed, but worse is that Cindy believes she's about to become a TV superstar!

The snotty little Brady spends *hours* fixing her curls and trying on outfits . . . only to fail miserably when the cameras start to roll. She chokes, with stage fright leaving her speechless, answerless, and ultimately prizeless.

She returns home expecting the other kids to make fun of her, but unlike kids in the *real* world, we Bradys are extremely compassionate. Even Bobby goes out of his way to help pick up Cindy's spirits, telling her that she was really a winner and that *he,* having failed his eligibility test, was the *real* loser.

What a weird moral.

WRITER: Lois Hire
DIRECTOR: Jack Donahue

•*Nepotism Alert!* Game-show host Monty Marshall is played by an actor named Edward Knight, who just happens to be Chris Knight's father.

EPISODE 83: "GOODBYE, ALICE, HELLO"

A series of miscommunications have us Brady kids convinced that our pal Alice is really a squealing, tattletale-ing fink. We start ignoring her, and before long she's whimpering and packing her bags. Her replacement arrives, and while she's a very nice woman, she has *absolutely* no personality. Soon the kids realize what a mistake they made in squeezing Alice out the back door.

So it's off to Alice's new job (she made up a story about taking care of a sick aunt, but her replacement spilled the truth about where she *really* was). She's waitressing in a diner, and in no time (after refusing to let the kids order chocolate—pimples, ya know) she's convinced to come back home. "I've got my old job back!" she gleefully cries. "And I'm never gonna leave it again!" (She wants to be a maid forever?)

WRITER: Milt Rosen
DIRECTOR: George "Buddy" Tyne

EPISODE 84: "LOVE AND THE OLDER MAN"

Marcia at the height of her babe-itude gets the hots for a dentist! He's Dr. Stanley Vogel, and he's flattered, but unlike *most* red/hot-blooded American males of the 1970s, he's only interested in her teeth.

The whole thing gets under way when that goofy Jan reads an article in a teen magazine that says much older men make *perfect* boyfriends for teenage girls (must have been *Playboy*). That makes sense to Marcia, who gets her hormones all in a knot, and goes wild for Dr. Vogel. He, on the other hand, somehow manages to stay completely oblivious to Marcia's shameless man-chasing.

So oblivious, in fact, that he calls Marcia and asks if she's free Friday night (because his kid needs a baby-sitter). This being a television sitcom, Marcia completely misunderstands and begins to imagine herself as "Mrs. Marcia Dentist," an ultrasatisfied, ultrahappy doctor's wife.

But since Marcia has to return next week, she *can't* run off with an older man, and the older man absolutely *positively* can't bag Marcia.

Marcia's dreams all come tumbling down when Jan finds out that Dr. Vogel's . . . gulp . . . married! And it's only as Marcia tries to dump the guy that she realizes he never wanted her in the first place. It was all just one of those kooky sitcom mixups.

WRITER: Martin A. Ragaway
DIRECTOR: George "Buddy" Tyne

EPISODE 85: "EVERYBODY CAN'T BE GEORGE WASHINGTON"

The Bradys have school-play problems yet again. They survived Marcia's big-headed Juliet debacle, and muddled through Mike's poetry at Westdale High's Family Frolics, only to run smack into the Peter Brady/Benedict Arnold dilemma.

In a nutshell, Peter tries out for his school play hoping to audition well enough to land the part of George Washington. He succeeds . . . too well. He's too good to merely play the father of our country, and instead lands the play's most difficult part . . . Benedict Arnold.

Once that's established, Pete spends the rest of the half-hour trying to weasel his way out of the role, until finally he realizes how important Benedict Arnold is to the play, and how his classmates are depending upon him.

The stage play fills out the episode, and it's pretty funny, especially Peter's/Benedict's deathbed schtick.

WRITERS: Sam Locke and Milton Pascal
DIRECTOR: Richard Michaels

•*Nepotism Alert!* Barbara Bernstein, Florence Henderson's daughter, is back again, *this* time playing a gal named Peggy.

EPISODE 86: "GREG'S TRIANGLE"

Greg's hanging with this extra-curvy cheerleader named Jennifer who's just plain *throwing* herself at him. Turns out she's paying attention to Greg only because he's judging the head-cheerleader competition and can snag her the position she's always wanted.

Trouble brews and Marcia stews, because *she* wants to be head cheerleader too. She disses Jennifer to Greg, thus becoming the second hopeful looking to take advantage of her relationship with the head judge.

Finally, when push comes to shove, Greg makes like a Brady and does the right thing. He *doesn't* vote for Jennifer, *doesn't* vote for Marcia, and instead votes for Pat, the girl who's . . . the most talented.

WRITERS: Bill Freedman and Ben Gershman
DIRECTOR: Richard Michaels

•Pat is played by a young actress named Rita Wilson, who'd one day grow up, fill out, and marry a guy named Tom Hanks.

EPISODE 87: "BOBBY'S HERO"

Bobby unexplainably decides that Jesse James is now his hero (he was originally supposed to worship a skyjacker, but the network nixed it as "too real"). Mike, Carol, and Bobby's teachers unanimously hate the idea; but books about Mr. James and even a movie about the bad guy fail to dissuade Bobby's enthusiasm. Only a visit from an old geezer named Jethro Collins, whose entire family was wasted by James, and an eerily realistic nightmare in which Jesse James offs the Bradys (to the delight of every TV critic in America) slaps the deranged Brady kid out of his infatuation.

WRITER: Michael Morris
DIRECTOR: Leslie H. Martinson

•During the "mass murder of the Bradys" scene, look closely at Mike Lookinland's face. You'll notice that he seems genuinely horrified at the cartoon-style carnage taking place around him. That's because Lloyd Schwartz took the kid off into a corner right before the scene and basically just scared the hell out of him. Lloyd tells it this way:

"I knew that the family was going to die funny, but I wanted genuine horror to show up on Bobby's face. I knew those two things would work against each other, and that was the effect we were going for.

"First we did the scene with no rehearsal for Bobby. We rehearsed the 'funny dying,' but he had no rehearsal for the actual shooting. So I took Michael outside and proceeded to discuss with him things like having his dog run over, or his parents being shot, lying in the street with blood oozing out of them and maybe their brains splattered on the sidewalk, and I just filled his head with these horrifying gory images, because I wanted him to think about those things while the whole shooting scene was taking place.

"I told him, 'You're not to see the Bradys dying funny. You're to see Jesse shooting your real parents, and they're really dying.' That's why when you watch that episode, you'll see real terror in Bobby's face. The whole thing worked really well.

"And then I had a debriefing with Michael right after."

•Burt Mustin, who played Jethro Collins, owned one of those familiar but nameless TV faces and was often referred to as "that old guy." He was past eighty-eight when we shot this episode, but he kept right on performing (he had a recurring role on "All in the Family" as the guy Edith sprang from the old folks' home) until his death, in 1977, at the ripe old age of ninety-three.

EPISODE 88: "THE GREAT EARRING CAPER"

Carol lends her favorite antique earrings to Marcia, and they promptly come up missing in action. Why? It's simple. Cindy stole 'em, then proceeded to lose 'em.

Desperate, the youngest, blondest Brady sucks up to Peter and begs him to employ his new detective kit in searching for the earrings. Twenty-two minutes go by, and they fail . . . miserably. It's only after Cindy confesses and the entire Brady brood "re-enacts the crime" that the earrings show up safe . . . but unsound. Turns out they ended up in the washing machine, where one earring survived untouched, but the other got mangled.

The Bradys' only unhappy ending.

WRITERS: Larry Rhine and Al Schwartz
DIRECTOR: Leslie H. Martinson

EPISODE 89: "GREG GETS GROUNDED"

Greg is rubber necking sidewalk babes while driving and nearly cracks up the family wagon. He swears Bobby to secrecy, but the little guy blabs almost immediately. Mike and Carol are justifiably pissed off, and they take away Greg's car privileges for a week.

Oh no, not that—not when Greg's got rock-concert tickets! Hmmmm . . . Greg ponders his punishment, and with the bug-like dexterity of a divorce lawyer, chews himself a loophole. Y'see, Mike took away Greg's *family* car privileges for a week, but if he could get a buddy to *lend* him some wheels, he could *still* take a date to the concert without ever *really* breaking a single rule!

So that's what he does. Mike's angry about this sneaky behavior, but realizes that there's nothing he can do about it.

Then he hears Greg promise to take Peter, Bobby, and their enormous toads to the "big frog-jumping contest." When Greg later tries to back out of the deal (he's got a hot date with Rachel) Mike makes *sure* that he keeps his word—after all, wasn't that what their car argument was all about?

Flash forward and we find that Greg's reluctantly driven the boys to their contest, brought them home, tossed them out into the driveway, and peeled out of the driveway to pick up his date. Jump cut, and we find Greg at the drive-in, cuddled up with Rachel, while Bobby and Peter's boxful of frogs lies unnoticed in the back. Now, before you can say "Quick, get me the Compound W," the biggest, fattest, slimiest toad of all has leapt out of the box, over a bucket seat, and onto Rachel's head.

The date goes downhill from there.

WRITER: Elroy Schwartz
DIRECTOR: Jack Arnold

•Susan Olsen remembers that in between shots, the younger Brady kids spent a lot of the week chasing Maureen McCormick around the set, making her scream by threatening to put our special-guest frog on her head.

EPISODE 90: "THE SUBJECT WAS NOSES"

Jack Arnold wins the prize for capturing on film the most memorable Brady visual *ever!* Pigskin meets pug nose.

Over and over again I'm asked how we faked bashing Marcia's face with that football, and the answer, I'm happy to report, is "We didn't." Mo just stood on her spot and the propman lobbed the thing into her face. Later, with slo-mo added, and some sound effects ("Oh, my nooooose!") Maureen really looks like she's been given a free rhinoplasty. Fortunately we only needed to shoot it once, and Mo recovered quickly.

Marcia makes a date for the school dance with nice but unspectacular Charley, then dumps the poor geek for school superjock Doug Simpson. She cuts Charley loose with a rude, yet effective, "Something suddenly came up" (Greg's all-purpose surefire date buster), and vainly primps for her big date.

Enter that football, exit Marcia's WASP-Y little proboscis.

Enter Doug Simpson, who gets one look at Marcia's new Karl Malden look and promptly cancels their date, saying that "something suddenly came up."

Marcia's crushed, hurt, and embarrassed—not only about her looks but also about how she treated good ol' Charley. She calls the guy, apologizes, reinstates their date, and another Brady's learned another life lesson.

WRITERS: Al Schwartz and Larry Rhine
DIRECTOR: Jack Arnold

EPISODE 91: "HOW TO SUCCEED IN BUSINESS"

Peter Brady begins a lifelong tendency toward messing up every career opportunity that comes his way. Here, he lands a job fixing bicycles at Mr. Martinelli's bike shop, where his enthusiasm is overflowing, but his plodding work habits and lack of mechanical aptitude get him fired in just three days!

He comes home dejected and, after dinner, prepares to discuss his business bust with the folks. Problem is, just as Pete's about to drop the bad news, Alice shows up sporting an absolutely humongous cake (did ya ever notice how much cake we Bradys ate?) complete with "Congratulations Peter" scrawled on top. That takes the wind out of Pete's sails, and he just can't bring himself to fess up.

Pete keeps trying to wriggle out from under his dishonesty, but somehow, with the rest of the Bradys so proud of his budding business acumen, he just can't. Instead, he passes his "work hours" by sitting in the park and feeding the pigeons (watch for Pete to actually pick up and pet one of those disgusting little rat-birds).

Enter Mike and Carol . . . on brand new *bikes*. Uh-oh. They pedal their cycles toward Pete, flick their kick stands, and tell him that they've just come from Mr. Martinelli's store, where they bought new bikes and found out all about Pete's predicament. Mike tells Pete that losing a job is nothing to be ashamed of, and that "heck, I've been fired *lots* of times."

Somehow the news of his father's ineptitude makes Peter feel a whole lot better. Everybody hugs. Then, after a long dissolve and an even longer camera shot of the Brady brood on cycles (Alice's bike comes equipped with training wheels), we coast once more into our closing credits.

WRITER: Gene Thompson
DIRECTOR: Robert Reed

•Even in Brady reunions, Peter's pretty much a total failure. He's a struggling, unhappy Army corporal when the Brady girls get married (Chris Knight says he believes Pete *had* to enlist after placing a bun in the oven of a local girl . . . yeah, right) and a struggling, unhappy businessman throughout *Brady Christmas* and "The Bradys." I guess Pete's as close to a black sheep as the Brady family will ever get.

EPISODE 92: "AMATEUR NIGHT"

WARNING! WARNING! RUN! RUN! The Brady kids are singing again!

This time around, we've entrusted that dumbhead Jan to purchase a silver platter for our parents' anniversary, but her misunderstanding over the cost of engraving (it's eighty-five cents *per letter,* not "altogether") leaves the six of us $56.23 in debt.

Our solution? Get jobs? Borrow? Steal? Nope, we Bradys decide to secretly form a musical group and win first prize on a local TV talent show!

We audition for the show by belting out another one of those headache-inducing Brady pop classics. This time we warble a groovy, overly optimistic ditty called "It's a Sunshine Day (Everybody's Smilin')," and it's good enough to get us on the air.

Come showtime, we're calling ourselves the Silver Platters, and we're loaded for bear. We've got our vapid little song down pat, we're outfitted in ultra-seventies/ultra-cool blue-and-white bell-bottomed outfits, and we've got choreography cheesy enough to make Paula Abdul cry. Sadly though, despite our brilliance, we lose to Pauline's Prancing Poodles.

No need to worry, though, because Alice, Mike, and Carol all just happen to catch our act on live TV and hear our explanation of why we need the prize money.

By the time we get home, the platter's been purchased (Mike picked it up), the problem has been solved, and the Bradys are smiling once more.

WRITERS: Sam Locke and Milton Pascal
DIRECTOR: Jack Arnold

•Hal Peary, who played "The Great Gildersleeve" on radio—the guy who pronounces the word "yes" as "muhhh-yeeeeeesss"—appears as the bank manager, Mr. Goodbody. He's a genius!

EPISODE 93: "YOU'RE NEVER TOO OLD"

Carol's grandma Connie (Florence Henderson under gobbed-on latex wrinkles) pays a visit, and so does Mike's *great*-grandpa Hank (Robert Reed under even gobbier goo).

Grandma's a real swinger. She shoots hoops, jogs, even uses the newest and grooviest expressions like "far out" and "whatever turns you on." Great-Grandpa, on the other hand, is pretty much dead from the neck down. He *looks* like a cadaver, and basically, he hates *everything* . . . especially Grandma Connie.

The Bradys set the old folks up on a date, and the results are predictably disastrous . . . until the old geezers have a change of heart and end up eloping to Las Vegas (*somebody's* gonna break a hip), thus turning Mike and Carol into brother and sister, or something like that, and all six Brady kids into cousins . . . I think.

WRITERS: Ben Gershman and Bill Freedman
DIRECTOR: Bruce Bilson

EPISODE 94: "A ROOM AT THE TOP"

Greg starts acting like a normal human being and decides he wants out of the Brady house. He's sick of sharing his bedroom, sick of putting up with geeks like Peter and Bobby, and *really* sick of having no privacy. He wants to move in with a college pal, but Mike says "not until you're eighteen." As a compromise, Mike also suggests that with a little effort, Greg could fix up the attic and turn it into a pretty cool bachelor pad.

At the same time, Marcia's *had* it with trihabitation. Jan and Cindy have driven her *nuts*, and she wants out of the babe-filled bedroom. Carol's solution? "Why not fix up the attic and move in?"

Predictably, the sparks fly, Greg and Marcia butt heads, and all appears hopeless.

However, the half-hour ends on a happy note. Marcia lets Greg have the room, at least until he goes away to college the following year.

In the tag, Cindy whines that since she's the youngest, *she* won't get to sleep in the attic until 1980!

WRITERS: William Raynor and Myles Wilder
DIRECTOR: Lloyd Schwartz

•*Nepotism Alert!* This episode was *directed* as well as produced by Lloyd Schwartz. It was taped at the high point of the romance/grope-athon between me and Maureen, and shooting was tense (see pp. 101-105).

EPISODE 95: "SNOW WHITE AND THE SEVEN BRADYS"

By episode 95, we had *really* begun having to stretch for story lines. In this case, Cindy somehow manages to talk the entire Brady family into appearing in her production of "Snow White and the Seven Dwarfs" (with Sam the Butcher

**Waking up
"Snow White."**
(© Paramount
Pictures)

as Dopey . . . ouch!). The results are humiliating.
WRITER: Ben Starr
DIRECTOR: Bruce Bilson

•As the Bradys are embarrassing themselves onstage, look
closely at their audience. In the first row, smiling a broad
smile, is a handsome, white-haired older woman. This is
Frances Whitfield, who served as teacher/legal
supervisor/referee to the Brady kids throughout the run of
the show. We loved her like crazy.

EPISODE 96: "MAIL ORDER HERO"

Season five premiered with a sports star and a fashion
statement. Joe Namath in a leisure suit? Sounds unbelievable, but it's true, and on display in the dead center of this
episode.

In a reworking of the "Marcia meets Davy Jones" story,
Bobby brags to his friends that he's best pals with
Broadway Joe. They demand that he put up or shut up, and
Bobby gets desperate. Finally, Cindy comes up with a plan,
and writes a letter to Joe that portrays Bobby as a near-
death basket case, and good-hearted Joe decides to pay a
visit.

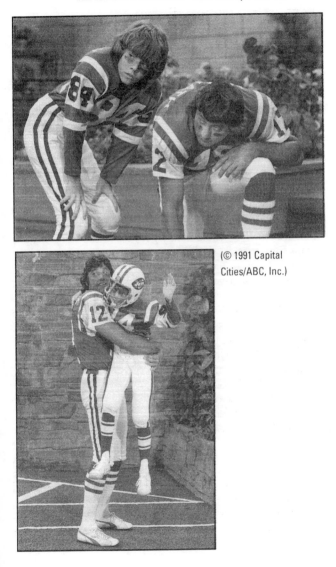

(© 1991 Capital Cities/ABC, Inc.)

Despite the plot, this was one of the most enjoyable episodes we ever filmed. Joe was terrific. I already mentioned that Florence Henderson was nuts about the guy, and in the end threw herself at him in the Bradys' Astroturf backyard (see p. 95). He let us kids take advantage of him too, and tossed about a hundred and eighty thousand passes to Chris, Mike, and me.

WRITER: Martin A. Ragaway
DIRECTOR: Bruce Bilson

EPISODE 97: "THE ELOPEMENT"

The Brady girls drop a bomb: Alice is getting married!!! They know it *has* to be true because they overheard Alice on the phone talking to Sam about elopement. When Alice asks for Saturday off, and Sam calls Mike asking about where a newlywed guy might find nice affordable housing, that seals it. The whole family goes crazy and starts making plans for a surprise wedding reception.

Oops! Come Saturday, the Bradys all jump up, yell "Surprise!," nearly scare Alice and Sam into early strokes, and find that the whole thing was a mistake. Alice's cousin Clara was eloping (she had called asking if Alice would serve as her witness), and she needed Saturday off because she and Sam had a big bowling match to attend.

The Bradys decide that they'll never jump to conclusions again . . . at least until next time.

WRITER: Harry Winkler
DIRECTOR: Jerry London

EPISODE 98: "ADIOS JOHNNY BRAVO"

This week, we Brady kids are polluting the airwaves yet again, this time singing on something called "Hal Barton's TV Talent Review." I wear plaid pants and a leisure suit jacket, but the rest of the kids don't look quite so . . . hip.

Enter wily and va-va-*voom*-ish talent agent Tami Cutler, who's seen our act and wants to make Greg—and *only* Greg—a superstar. She tells him that he's "totally cosmic and happening," which her brown-nosing lackey/assistant

On "Barton's TV Talent Review." (© Paramount Pictures)

Buddy affirms with an enthusiastic "Righteous!"

Greg mulls over the offer, weighs the alternatives, and does the right thing . . . he dumps the rest of the group. Tami gives him a sparkly/spangly, nearly Elvisian costume, and when he performs again, he gets mobbed by a swarm of wild young babes. His head swells, he changes his name to Johnny Bravo and decides to blow off college and become a full-time show-business legend.

But it all caves in when Greg finds out he's really just a precursor of Milli Vanilli: Tami's been mechanically "sweetening" (i.e., fixing) his voice.

That's it. Greg keeps his artistic credibility, kills Johnny Bravo, and once again becomes that nice, normal, level-headed, Vanilla kid that we've always known.

WRITER: Joanna Lee
DIRECTOR: Jerry London

•Claudia Jennings, who plays Tami Cutler, was the 1970 *Playboy* Playmate of the Year, and went on to appear in *loads* of cheesy car-chase B movies.

EPISODE 99: "NEVER TOO YOUNG"

Against his better judgment, Bobby gets himself kissed by a *girl* (Melissa Sue Anderson from "Little House on the Prairie"), sees fireworks (quite literally, thanks to the special effects guys), and goes wild for more. Problem is, after a second smooch (and more skyrockets), Bobby finds out that the object of his osculation *may* have given him a sexually transmitted disease . . . the mumps.

Uh-Oh . . . if Millicent comes back *positive,* the whole family could catch Bobby's mumps and have to miss out on Saturday's gala Roaring Twenties party.

WRITERS: Al Schwartz and Larry Rhine
DIRECTOR: Richard Michaels

EPISODE 100: "PETER AND THE WOLF"

There's this girl, Sandra, and Greg's crazy about her, but she can't go out with him unless he can find someone to double up and keep company with her visiting cousin, Linda. "Uh-oh," Greg thinks. "Visiting cousin? Can't get her own date? Heeeeere, poochy, poochy, poochy."

Greg's pals all feel the same way, and (since men are scum) *none* of 'em will touch *this* blind date with a ten-foot pole. Finally, desperate to snag Sandra, Greg turns to Peter and asks *him* to make the supreme sacrifice and date the dog.

Celebrating our one hundredth episode.
(© Paramount Pictures)

Peter, who's never had a date of *any* kind, agrees, and it's not long before he's sporting a phony mustache (to look older) and trying desperately to act as cool as Greg.

Date night comes, and as it turns out, Linda's even hotter than Sandra! Peter's thrilled, but terrified, and soon his nervousness, not to mention his detachable mustache, clues the girls into the fact that Peter's a phony.

They don't let on. Instead, they make a plan that's sure to drive Greg crazy, and it works like this. The foursome heads off to a pizzeria, where *both* girls throw themselves all over Peter, kissing it up big-time.

Pan around the room, and we've got trouble, because seated in the corner are Mike, Carol, and Mike's "clients from Mexico," the Calderons. They see the improper osculatory behavior and are outraged. Finding out that the offenders are Brady kids only makes it worse.

Finally, Peter fesses up, tells the whole story, apologizes to the Calderons, and smooths over the bumpy Brady brouhaha.

WRITER: Tam Spiva
DIRECTOR: Leslie H. Martinson

•I always looked forward to the episodes where Greg had dates, in the hopes that I'd get to work with someone "hot." However, I had a rival in Lloyd Schwartz who'd cast those parts, beat me to the punch, and generally did most of the post-episode dating himself.

EPISODE 101: "GETTING GREG'S GOAT"

Greg hooks up with Raquel, and then hides her in his room overnight. Sounds more like an episode of "Three's Company" than "The Brady Bunch."

Actually Raquel's a goat, and the mascot for the Coolidge High School football team. Greg's stolen her to avenge the theft of Westdale's bear-cub mascot. With no place safe to stash the ill-gotten goat, Greg tucks her away in his attic bachelor pad, where he hopes she'll lay low until the coast is clear.

She doesn't. She eats Greg's clothes, smells terrible, and

Greg and "Raquel."
(© Paramount Pictures)

when Mike overhears Greg yelling "C'mon, Raquel, stop it," he jumps to the extraordinarily un-Brady-like conclusion that Greg's got a *girl* in his room! They then have an exchange that seems like something lifted directly from Jack Tripper and Mr. Roper:

> MIKE: Greg, I think we need to talk about Raquel.
> GREG: Yes, sir?
> MIKE: I know you're seventeen years old and you do have a right to privacy, but did you really think you were going to get away with this?

The music swells and they kiss.
(© Paramount Pictures)

GREG: I don't know, I brought her up there last night, and thought I'd sneak her out in the morning.
MIKE: She was up there ALL NIGHT?!?!?!
GREG: Yeah, but to be honest with you, I can't *wait* to get rid of that beast.
MIKE: Greg, that's a terrible way to talk about a girl, no matter *what* she looks like!

The misunderstanding gets cleared up, Mike helps Greg keep the goat under cover (turns out Mike's an ex–mascot swiper too, and sensitive to Greg's cause), and things work out fine . . . until:
Carol hosts an emergency meeting of the PTA aimed at getting to the bottom of this recent epidemic of missing mascots. The meeting, led by Mrs. Gould (played by Sandra Gould—Gladys Kravitz from "Bewitched"), gets under way just in time for Raquel to bust out of Greg's room and run amok all over the house.
WRITERS: Milton Pascal and Sam Locke
DIRECTOR: Robert Reed

•Robert Reed directs his third "Brady" episode and does a pretty good job tackling the frantically farcical tale on film. The only thing I can't figure out is how come he let himself wear a plaid Qiana shirt and mismatched plaid bell-bottoms throughout the show. I mean, that was unfashionably ugly even by seventies standards.

EPISODE 102: "THE CINCINNATI KIDS"
You already know about what a heinous time we had in filming this episode, and how we nearly ended up headless on the roller coaster (see p. 121–123).
The story: Mike's designed a large-scale addition to a midwestern amusement park, and he's drawn up some very important sketches to illustrate his ideas. He sets up a "sell" meeting at the park and decides to bring the whole family along, thus turning the trip into a fabulous vacation in . . . Cincinnati?

The Brady mob descends upon this poor man's Disney World, and it isn't long before Mike's sketches are lost. With no time to spare, the Bradys fan out, frantically searching the park, desperate to find those sketches and save the day.

Finally, Jan gets lucky and plucks them out of a canoe. Now, however, comes a mad dash, with the Bradys passing off the sketches pony-express style until they get back to Mike (and the park's board of directors) just in the proverbial nick of time.

WRITERS: Al Schwartz and Larry Rhine
DIRECTOR: Leslie H. Martinson

•*Nepotism Alert!* There's also a subplot in which Greg needs to borrow a cartoonish bear suit in order to impress a local girl. The guy who's *originally* in the suit is Lloyd Schwartz, the show's associate producer.

EPISODE 103: "QUARTERBACK SNEAK"

Marcia dates another jerk. This time he's Jerry Rogers, the sleazy all-star quarterback of Clinton High's football team—the hated archrival of the Bradys' glorious Westdale. To Marcia he's extra-dreamy, and she's soon gone mad for the boy—so mad that she doesn't believe her brothers when they tell her what a slimeball the guy really is.

Greg tells Marcia that the reason Jerry's been hanging around the Brady house isn't to steal Marcia's heart but to run off with Greg's football play book. Marcia's miffed, but she agrees to help set up a sting operation that she's *sure* will prove hunky Jerry innocent.

It doesn't. Jerry takes Greg's play book (actually, it's just a phony that the guys have left as bait) and dumps Marcia faster than he can stuff it into his pants. He makes up a story about being late for a team picture and says to Marcia, "I hope you understand."

And as the mood music builds, Marcia lowers her eyebrows, tosses her hair back twice, glares at the geek, and says, "I understand . . . perfectly."

At this point, her dramatic stare tosses us into a commercial.

Two and a half minutes later, we return to find the Brady boys laughing about how they've put one over on Jerry. Mike, however, puts a parental halt to the boys' fun when he lectures to them that they haven't just put one over on Jerry but on all of Clinton High, and that what *they've* done makes them just as bad as Jerry.

Suitably crestfallen, Greg phones Jerry and explains the switch. The only problem is . . . Jerry's not buying it. He's sure that Greg's honesty is just some sort of desperate last-ditch attempt to recover the book (he don't know the Bradys very well, do he?).

Anyway, Westdale clobbers Clinton (20–6), Jerry gets benched when the coach finds out about his theft, and justice reigns supreme once more in the perfect parallel universe that the Brady Bunch calls home.

WRITERS: Bill Freedman and Ben Gershman
DIRECTOR: Peter Baldwin

•This episode also offers us a look at Carol's college sweetheart "Tank" Gates. He runs football plays in the Brady living room, constantly calls Carol "Twinkles," and wears an incredibly stupid Donald Trump-ish hairdo. It should be obvious to any Bradyphile that Carol's college days must have been spent trolling for beefcake.

•Chris Beaumont appears in the last of his four episodes— a guest cast record. He had previously shown up in "Our Son the Man," "The Wheeler Dealer," and "A Room at the Top." Now, of course, he's that playbook-stealing snake Jerry Rogers.

EPISODE 104: "MARCIA GETS CREAMED"

Haskell's Ice Cream Parlor gets a brand new afternoon manager . . . Marcia Brady. She's a fabulous worker and fanatically ambitious about her minumum-wage career.

Her boss, Mr. Haskell, recognizes Marcia's exemplary

work habits and responsible nature, and he uses them to his full advantage: he retires. That leaves Marcia with more work, more pull (no raise), and an assistant to hire.

Enter Peter, who gets the job, screws up, and loses the job in record time.

Enter Jan, who gets the job, excels, and ends up taking Marcia's place when Mr. Haskell returns, bored nearly to death by retirement.

"Marcia," says the truly creepy Mr. Haskell, "you're a wonderful worker. But Jan is a little bit better, and since I can only keep one of you, I'll have to keep her."

Major dork! Marcia is rightfully aghast, but then, when she gets a call from David Cassidy look-alike Jeff, she decides that getting fired was a blessing in disguise, because *now* she'll have plenty of free time to devote to her dreamy new boy-toy.

WRITERS: Ben Gershman and Bill Freedman
DIRECTOR: Peter Baldwin

•Henry Corden, who plays Marcia's jerky boss, Mr. Haskell, is today the voice of Fred Flintstone, but he'd probably like the world to forget that he made his acting debut in one of the most hilariously inept movies ever made. Entitled *Blood Feast* and released in 1963, it was the very first slasher/gore flick, and was made by the "Grandaddy of Gore" himself, Herschell Gordon Lewis.

EPISODE 105: "MY BROTHER'S KEEPER"

Greg's up on a ladder painting the bedroom shutters a godawful shade of puke-ish green. Peter holds the ladder, Bobby shows up underneath, and (you guessed it) the whole thing comes tumbling down.

Greg hangs onto the windowsill, the ladder takes a header, and Bobby yanks the slow-reflexed Peter out from under an enormous falling planter—and gets drenched with that green paint in the process.

The boys clean up, Alice serves up a nice big tureen of

Hungarian goulash, and Pete makes a solemn vow that since Bobby saved his life, he will from this day forth become the little Brady's personal slave.

Pete does all of Bobby's chores, shines his shoes (we Bradys were *major* shoe shiners), cleans up after him, and, in general, just lets the kid treat him like dirt.

Finally, Peter gets fed up and can't stand anymore. He quits his job as slave and even refuses to share his room with the little geek. (They even employ that standard sitcom cliché wherein the feuding parties do that white-line-down-the-middle-of-the-room thing.)

But all is soon forgiven. Bobby manages to lock himself into a closet, gets a little claustrophobic, and when Peter finally springs him, they make up, and a happy ending is had by all.

WRITER: Michael Morris
DIRECTOR: Ross Bowman

EPISODE 106: "TRY, TRY AGAIN"

Jan takes ballet lessons—Jan's a clod.

Jan takes tap-dance lessons—Jan's a clod who drives her family crazy with her tapping.

Jan tries baton twirling—Jan's a clod who breaks the rec room window.

Got the idea? This time Jan's insecurity shifts from her appearance to her competence. Having tried and failed at all the above activities, Jan's ready to throw in the towel and accept her role in life as a no-talent slob.

But then the school play (*another* school play?) beckons. Jan tries out for the lead, and *this* time . . . she fails miserably again.

But it all works out okay, because in trying out for the role of a struggling artist, Jan realizes that *nothing* in life comes easily, and that to be really good at *anything* you've got to practice, practice, practice.

Yeeeeesh.

WRITERS: Al Schwartz and Larry Rhine

DIRECTOR: George "Buddy" Tyne

•They let us kids pick out our own wardrobe for this episode, and we did an okay job—except for the shoes! I inexplicably wear blue-and-white suede saddle shoes (no, I'm not kidding), Maureen's in orange clogs, and Eve spends most of the episode wearing an *enormous* pair of red patent-leather platform pumps.

EPISODE 107: "KELLY'S KIDS"

In an attempt to land Sherwood Schwartz a prime time spin-off, the Bradys generously gave up their weekly half hour of fame and handed it over to their squeaky clean new neighbors the Kellys.

The Kellys are thinking about adopting a child; and since *nobody* knows more about kids than the Bradys, they drop in on their friends bearing dessert. They break out the coffee cake, and when Mike and Carol give parenthood a *glowing* review (you would *too* if your kids were perfect) the Kellys run out the very next day and pick up Matt, a healthy eight-year-old blond boy, at the local orphan mart.

They get the kid home, and everybody's ecstatic . . . except the kid. Turns out he desperately misses Dwayne and Steve, his two best pals from the orphanage. That starts the Kellys thinking, and (whoosh) they swing back down to the work-house, scoop up the extra coupla kids, and bring them home too!

Enter the Kellys' nasty neighbor Mrs. Payne (subtle, huh?). She *hates* children and makes it quite clear that she'll be spending the foreseeable future as a Gladys Kravitzian thorn in the Kellys' side.

And there you have it: three adopted kids, two goofily white-bread parents, and the prerequisite annoying neighbor. Sounds okay, but maybe a little bland. Perhaps it needs one more twist.

How about *this?* In an achingly seventies plot device, Matt's white, Dwayne's black, and Steve's Oriental. Throw in Mrs. Payne's barely concealed bigotry and you've got the makings of a hit show.

But no. The network got a look at this spin-off pilot and promptly passed, leaving the fates of the Kellys trapped forever in video limbo.

WRITER: Sherwood Schwartz
DIRECTOR: Richard Michaels

•The attempted spinoff starred Ken Berry ("F-Troop," "Mama's Family") as Ken Kelly and Brooke Bundy (best known as Diana Taylor from "General Hospital"'s late-seventies glory days) as Kathy Kelly. That familiar-looking kid who played Matt was none other than Todd Lookinland, Mike's brother.

EPISODE 108: "THE DRIVER'S SEAT"

Marcia's finally old enough to take her driver's test, and she's *really* excited about it. First comes the written exam. She passes, but when Greg realizes that he passed that same test a year ago, with a much higher grade, he teases his sister bigtime.

Before long, Marcia's fuming, and proposing yet another one of our fabulous Brady bets. This time, Marcia bets Greg that she'll beat his *road* test score or do his chores for a month (we used chores the way prisoners use cigarettes). They shake, and the deal's sealed.

Now, Marcia's *really* nervous; trying to pass your road test is gut-wrenching enough, but throw a month's worth of chores into that equation and you're talking *major* pressure. Jan suggests that to calm down, Marcia try out a technique from her debating club: seems that whenever a debater feels nervous, they're coached to imagine their opponent *and* the audience clad *only* in their underwear. That makes them both seem a lot less imposing, and results in increased self-confidence for the debater.

Makes sense to Marcia, so when push comes to shove and "park" goes to "drive," she pictures her driving instructor in *his* underwear (and he, in all likelihood, pictures Marcia in *hers*), doesn't get nervous, and passes with flying colors. But . . .

She doesn't beat Greg's score; she merely ties it. Does that mean the bet's a "push"? Not in Bradyland, we've still got half an episode to kill. Now before you can say "bell-bottoms," an auto-obstacle course is set up and Marcia's practicing, prepping to battle it out with Greg, in a winner-take-all, sudden-death drive-off.

Greg, on the other hand, is completely cool and taking his opponent *very* lightly (I guess he didn't learn anything from that chin-ups debacle with Bobby). In fact, he's so sure he'll win his showdown with Marcia—she is, after all, just a girl— that he doesn't even *look* at the homemade Brady test track.

Bad idea. Marcia breezes through the course, while Greg . . . well, let's just say that he laundered a lot of groovy polyester dresses that month.

WRITER: George Tibbles
DIRECTOR: Jack Arnold

EPISODE 109: "MISS POPULARITY"

Jan tries to give her low self-image a shot in the arm by competing in her school's "Most Popular Girl" contest. Driven to win at all costs, Jan makes campaign promises that she has no intention of keeping, lies to her classmates, underhandedly smears her opponent's name, and in general acts like a real politician.

The student body gets one look at Jan's slimy modus operandi and promptly . . . elects her.

Scan your VCR forward and when Jan's pals start asking her to fulfill some of her grandiose campaign pledges, and she can't deliver, they're not pals anymore.

Fast forward one more time and Jan's apologizing for her sleaziness in a speech to the whole school, and promising to uphold every single one of her campaign promises.

She is, after all, a Brady.

WRITER: Martin A. Ragaway
DIRECTOR: Jack Donahue

The Bunch with astronaut James McDivitt and "Kaplutians" Frank and Sadie Delfino. (© Paramount Pictures)

EPISODE 110: "OUT OF THIS WORLD"

Peter and Bobby have suddenly become UFO fanatics, even going so far as to corner real live Apollo 9 commander James McDivitt—he believes that he saw a UFO while in space—after his appearance on a local talk show. They ask him about his close encounter, ask for his autograph, tell him to keep up the good work, and then head home for some of Alice's famous pot roast ("It's out-of-this-world, too!" guffaws Alice).

After supper, the two would-be Carl Sagans decide to sleep outside and monitor the night sky for "visitors." The other kids make fun of them, but Bobby and Pete are undaunted, and before long they've spotted a genuine UFO. At least that's what they *think*.

Actually, it's Greg playing a (rather childish) trick on the overactive imaginations of the stargazers. With a flashlight, a clothesline, some plastic sheeting, and a sound-effects whistle, he's created a fairly believable UFO.

They buy it—and photograph their find as proof of its existence. After a lot of yelping and excitement, the boys hit the sheets and nod off. (In a far-out dream sequence, Bobby meets some tiny little extraterrestrials.)

Come morning, Carol develops her boys' UFO pix and

finds that they really *did* get shots of *something*. She shows 'em to Mike, and things get out of hand when he calls in . . . the Air Force.

Things get even crazier when Greg comes home and realizes that his prank has now gained national military significance. He immediately confesses, but while Greg's upstairs, demonstrating his homemade UFO to Mike, he unwittingly causes the Air Force's Captain McCarthy to believe that he *too* has had a close encounter of the third kind.

Chaos ensues and multiplies, until finally the air is cleared, the dust settles, Peter and Bobby are disappointed, Captain McCarthy is outraged, Mike's embarrassed, and Greg is grounded.

WRITERS: Al Schwartz and Larry Rhine
DIRECTOR: Peter Baldwin

•Bobby's Martians (actually, they say they're from "Kaplutia," so I guess "Kaplutians" would be correct) are played by Mr. and Mrs. Frank and Sadie Delfino, the two "little people" who spent five years acting as stand-ins for Bobby, Cindy, Peter, and Jan.

Why not just use *kids?* Lloyd Schwartz explains it:

"From the beginning of the show we used little people as stand-ins for the kids and we did it for a couple of logical rea-

Mike Lookinland and Frank Delfino.   **Susan Olsen and Sadie Delfino.** (Courtesy Sherwood Schwartz)

sons. They didn't have to worry about school, they could work longer hours, they did a good job, and they became very valuable members of the crew. But the problem was that as the kids grew, Frank and Sadie didn't. It finally got to the point where they had to walk around the set with customized boxes which they'd stand on, to approximate the kids' height. For example, Frankie had a "Bobby" box, and a "Peter" box that was a little bigger. Sadie had the female equivalent. But they couldn't move around the set on these boxes, and that caused all sorts of problems whenever we had to rehearse any action scene.

"Finally, during the third or fourth season, somebody from ABC came up to me one day and said 'Fire them,' and I said, 'Fuck off, we'll put up with it, they're part of the family.' Every once in a while, if you look very closely at an episode, you'll find them as extras in a scene. But the really *perfect* part for them was in this episode, playing the friendly 'Kaplutians.'"

And by the way, if you're at all interested in couch-potato-type trivia, Frank's line "One small step for spacemen, one giant leap for Kaplutians" was ad-libbed by Frank as we shot. So was Sadie's "C'mon, honey . . . let's go." They threw 'em in to break up the crew, and were so successful that they left 'em in.

•All through this thing, you'll notice that Greg's got a Band-Aid draped over his bottom lip. Zit? you ask. Chapped lip? Hickey? Nope, it was none of those things; I had merely put my face through the front window of my Porsche, and needed the bandage to cover up my unsightly (not to mention painful) stitches. Ouch!!

We rehearsed this episode just before Thanksgiving in 1973, and when we had the thing up to speed, we all said our goodbyes and headed home for a gluttonous holiday.

Come Thanksgiving day, I got up bright and early, got into my brand-new speed wagon, and not a mile later had a head-on collision with a station wagon . . . piloted by a young woman who was driving toward me while facing *backwards* and *talking* to her *dog!*

After the crash, me ... and my car.
(Barry Williams)

I hit my brakes. She hit my front bumper. I split my lip on the steering wheel, then cracked the windshield with my forehead: one split second, one rearranged face. (By the way, just *try* being seventeen years old, and explaining to the cops that *any* accident wasn't your fault.)

Ninety-six hours later, Monday rears its ugly head once more. I'm patched up and on my way back to work, *afraid* that they'll have to write me out of the show, or hopefully come up with a story line to explain my disfigurement.

Once I got to the lot, Lloyd Schwartz took one look at my lip, promptly squealed "*Eeeee!* Yuck!" and decided that Greg had cut himself shaving. "What does Greg shave with?" I wondered. "A lawn mower?" Anyway, they slapped a band-aid on my head and that was that.

Two scar-removal surgeries later, that "shaving cut" is *still* noticeable on my lower lip.

EPISODE 111: "TWO PETES IN A POD"

Pete's got a double, and we've got a story line.

Rushing through the school hallways one day, Peter bumps (literally) into a kid who looks exactly like him (only with nerdy black glasses). Together, they team up for what can best be described as "Brady pranks aplenty." The matched pair are yukking it up and reveling in their ruckus, until . . .

Uh-oh. Mike's set up a blind date between his boss's daughter and Peter on the same night that our pal Pete has made a date with Michelle, "the grooviest, most absolutely far-out chick in school!"

When date night finally arrives, *phony* Pete hooks up with the blind date, while the *real* Peter hooks up with that ultra-babe Michelle. Paths cross, befuddled double-takes abound, chaos rules, and an extra-wacky time is had by all!

WRITERS: Sam Locke and Milton Pascal
DIRECTOR: Richard Michaels

•This episode marks Robbie Rist's *real* first appearance as the Bradys' cousin Oliver. Episode 112 is all about Oliver's moving in with the Bradys, but we *shot* this episode first and aired the two in reverse order.

The role of Cousin Oliver was a brainchild of Paramount president Doug Cramer. He felt that the Brady children had become somewhat ancient by TV-kid standards and that someone younger should be introduced into the cast to appeal to the five-and-under crowd. Sherwood resisted but finally gave in.

Robbie Rist first came to Sherwood's attention when he was asked to interview for the attempted Brady spin-off, "Kelly's Kids." Although the role he auditioned for ultimately went to Todd Lookinland, Robbie had made a good impression on the casting types at Paramount.

Most everyone agreed that the addition of Cousin Oliver was unnecessary, and he had a tough time trying to fit in with "the family."

EPISODE 112: "WELCOME ABOARD"

There's gonna be an obnoxious new addition to the Brady family . . . Cousin Oliver. Apparently, Oliver's parents have been sent off to a South American jungle/architectural site, and the round-headed little guy has nowhere else to go.

The Bradys welcome the remarkably untraumatized little Oliver with open arms and shouts of "Welcome to your new family!" But it isn't long until he wears out his welcome and convinces the kids that he's a jinx.

First he splatters Greg with ketchup; then it's off to the backyard, where Bobby's busily mowing the Astroturf. Oliver tries to lend a helping hand but succeeds only in tripping our pal Bobby and launching him headfirst into the backyard flower pots. "Hmm," the Brady kids surmise, "maybe this kid is bad luck."

The next twenty-four hours see Oliver completely unravel Carol's newly knitted afghan, smash Marcia's ceramics project, and ruin Mike's architectural mock-up. Now the kids are convinced! He *is* a jinx.

We break for commercials, but come back to find that

Oliver *too* now thinks he's bad luck—so bad, in fact, that he's refusing to come along with the family when they visit a real live movie studio. However, after some more of the Bradys' patented "reverse psychology," Oliver reluctantly agrees.

Good thing, because the Bradys' party of nine (including Alice, but minus Mike, who supposedly had to work) makes the last one through the gate the park's one millionth customer! Oliver was the lucky millionth, and because of that his entire party gets to appear in a real movie!

The "movie" turns out to be little more than a turn-of-the-century-flavored pie fight, wherein you'll find us in period costumes and really, truly heaving pies at each other (another reason why there's no Bob Reed here). Watch closely and you'll see me accidentally slamming a pie into Mike Lookinland's head, and Eve cramming a nice banana cream into Maureen's nose.

But in the end, Carol locks her sights on Oliver, aims a coconut custard squarely at his head, once more yells "Welcome to the family!"—and with a gleeful yelp, pops him one in the mush.

WRITERS: Al Schwartz and Larry Rhine
DIRECTOR: Richard Michaels

•*Nepotism Alert!* Lloyd Schwartz shows up in a cameo once again. This time he's clapping the slate on the movie set.

EPISODE 113: "THE SNOOPERSTAR"

I remember thinking, "Gee, this would have been a good script if we'd done it four years ago."
—Susan Olsen

An embarrassing episode for Cindy and the rest of the Bradys as well, it starts with the gal eavesdropping on a conversation between Peter and Bobby.

"You're not talking about *me*, are you?" she asks awkwardly.

"Uh, no."

Next, Cindy heads inside, sneaks up behind Greg, and listens to his scintillating telephone conversation of "Far out. That's wild . . . *absolutely* wild . . . really far out."

"You're not talking about *me*, are you?" she asks even *more* awkwardly.

"Uh, no."

Cindy's dissed again, but instead of getting the idea that she's a royal pain in the butt, she comes to the conclusion that the family is hiding something from her. Determined to get to the bottom of this imaginary Brady conspiracy, she launches an all-out snoopathon, with her first stop being Marcia's diary.

Cindy swipes the book out from Marcia's underwear drawer and gives it a quick, illicit read . . . at least that's what *she* thinks. Turns out that Marcia and Jan are lurking just behind the bathroom door and watching her every move.

"Let's surprise her in the act," says an agitated Jan.

"No, let's teach her a good lesson," says the scheming Marcia.

Together, the Brady babes come up with a plan. First, they write a bogus entry in Marcia's diary, all about a famous Hollywood talent agent who's coming to the Brady house hoping to sign Cindy to a contract as "the next Shirley Temple." And second, they leave the diary in plain view.

Cindy (of course) reads the entry, and before you can say "hackneyed," she's tapping around the house singing "On the Good Ship Lollipop."

Enter Penelope Fletcher. She's a rich and impossible old woman who's contracted Mike to design her Penelope Fletcher Cultural Center. She's already nixed his first ideas, and now she's stopped by the house to check out his revisions.

Enter Cindy, embarrassingly clad in full Shirley Temple regalia. She's *convinced* that Ms. Fletcher is the cryptic Hollywood talent scout, and immediately she lays on the charm. The now pubescent Cindy launches into a mortifying rendition of "On the Good Ship Lollipop" while tapping up a storm.

Ms. Fletcher is at first taken aback, but then really gets into Cindy's Shirleymania, even joining in with her songs and offering up some tap-dance suggestions of her own. Then, as can *only* happen on TV, she accepts Mike's new plans sight unseen, and dances off into the night singing "Animal Crackers in My Soup."
WRITER: Harry Winkler
DIRECTOR: Bruce Bilson

•Penelope Fletcher is played by the fabulous Natalie Schafer—Lovey Howell herself. Her Brady appearance would be immediately followed by the second from her island hubby, Jim Backus.

EPISODE 114: "THE HUSTLER"
Guess what—the big boss at Mike's architectural firm is Thurston Howell III. He calls himself Mr. Matthews, but with Jim Backus playing him, you could close your eyes and swear you were back among the bamboo and coconuts, just waiting for Gilligan to do something dumb.

Instead, we spend most of this episode in the Brady garage, waiting for *Bobby* to do something dumb. It all starts when a couple of apelike moving men drop off a humongous crate in the Bradys' driveway.

Question 1: What's inside?

A: A deluxe pool table.

Question 2: Who sent it?

A: Mr. Matthews, as a reward for Mike's plans winning the company a very lucrative contract.

Question 3: What would the Bradys want with a pool table?

A: Good question.

Turns out that the only Brady who cares anything about the gentlemanly sport of billiards is Bobby. It also turns out that he's great! He soundly crushes his siblings, and when Mr. Matthews pays a visit, he beats the pants off *him* too (much to Mike's consternation).

Fortunately Mr. Matthews turns out to be a good sport. He pays off on his gambling debt (276 packs of gum), and the Bradys are once again content . . . at least till next week.

WRITERS: Bill Freedman and Ben Gershman
DIRECTOR: Michael Kane

EPISODE 115: "TOP SECRET"

This time Bobby's the booby. When Mike needs official clearance to inspect a top-secret government construction project, he's visited by an agent of the FBI. Bobby eavesdrops on the meeting, and jumps to all sorts of erroneous conclusions. He then becomes convinced that this FBI guy is some kind of double agent, out to *steal* Mike's plans.

While this is going on, Sam's trying to figure out a way to expand his store without upsetting his landlord (or tipping off his competition). He asks for Mike's help, and together they come up with the blueprints for Sam's "secret project."

Bobby's youthful little brain mangles the truth so badly that when he hears about Sam "getting ready to show the blueprints to Gronsky," he's positive that his pal the butcher is gonna sell Mike's top-secret prints to a no-good Russian spy named Gronsky.

In the end, we find out that Bobby's completely misguided and that Gronsky is *really* just Sam's landlord.

However, none of that comes out until *after* the kid's locked them both in Sam's meat locker.

WRITER: Howard Ostroff
DIRECTOR: Bernie Wiesen

EPISODE 116: "THE HAIR-BRAINED SCHEME"

We Bradys limped through our final episode with a plot Robert Reed found so unbelievable and stupid that he flatly refused to appear in it. He *did*, however, hang around the set while the episode was being shot, grumbling about its idiocy.

You be the judge.

The setup goes like this. Bobby hooks up with a mail-order company in an attempt to become a millionaire hair-tonic salesman. At the same time, Greg's getting ready to graduate from hallowed Westdale High, and Cindy's off on the service porch trying to breed rabbits.

Got it? Good. Now Bobby launches an all-out sales blitz upon the neighborhood. He tries his best to peddle his hair goo but, alas, comes up a total failure.

Our miniature Willy Loman comes home depressed, frustrated, and ready to quit until Greg takes pity on the little guy and actually coughs up two bucks for a bottle. Bobby's thrilled . . . until Greg actually uses the stuff, and it instantly turns his hair a shocking, nearly Day-Glo shade of orange.

Greg freaks, and when five separate shampoos only make the color *worse*, he submits himself to the humiliation of . . . the beauty parlor.

One simple dye job later, Greg's hair is back to black, and ultra-groovy once more.

At home, Bobby's dumping the rest of his hair tonic inventory down the drain when he slips and accidentally spills some on Cindy's rabbits. The result sets off a brainstorm (well, a brain *drizzle* anyway), and Bobby's quickly planning to make his million by selling orange bunnies.

In the tag, Greg returns home from graduation (with honors), and Carol lets him know just how proud she is of him, and says that "it's just too bad your father is out of town and had to miss it."

On the set, thirty feet away, under a gaffer's ladder, "Dad" was grimacing.

Several weeks later, with "Sanford and Son" clobbering us in the Nielsens, "The Brady Bunch" was executed. Little did they know we'd live forever in syndication, and in the hearts of our fans.

WRITER: Chuck Stewart, Jr.
DIRECTOR: Jack Arnold

•*Three Final Nepotism Alerts!* Florence's daughter Barbara and Sherwood's daughter Hope have teamed up to play the girls Greg runs into at Carol's beauty parlor. Look *very* closely and you'll find Sherwood's wife, Mildred, in the scene, smiling happily under one of those enormous old space-helmety kind of hair dryers.

Child Actor . . . To Be or Not to Be

ne of the most nagging questions I have had to face in the years since growing up on the Brady set is, "Do I think kids in show-biz is a good idea?"

Having been headstrong and determined as a toddler, it is only in recent years, with the benefit of hindsight, that certain things have become apparent. Without question putting a youngster in that environment is risky. There are lots of temptations, insecurities, and rejections. Of course many of those same things come with just good old everyday growing up. Still my experience leads me to this understanding: There is one chance to be a child. A lifetime to be an adult.

Is it worth the price of foregoing childhood interests and activities to get a start on a career? In some businesses an early start can be an advantage. Not so in show business. The demands and expectations for an actor are completely different for kids than adults. Kids are basically expected to be energetic, natural, adorable, reliable, and most importantly, directable.

On "The Brady Bunch" we were essentially required to be ourselves. The difference of course was that we were not a real family, and the situations our characters found themselves in were designed more for entertainment than reality. We were actors, balancing our workload, who spent the better part of five years growing up on a soundstage.

I consider myself and our group extraordinarily lucky. Lucky to have a producer and a studio teacher who insisted we be allowed to remain kids, and a studio that supported the notion. Lucky we had a TV mom and dad who were sensitive to the inherent problems of our circumstances. Lucky that without exception, we all had the kind of families and home life that provided the stability so crucial to growing up with healthy attitudes. Lucky we had each other to hang with, to share with, and to relate with. And incredibly lucky to have been part of a TV show that has generated a tremendous amount of viewer loyalty and several generations of friends. But does all this luck and experience help prepare you for a career as an adult? Does this credit provide the kind of foundation on which a career can be built? Not for the child actor.

Ironically, the more successful you become as a kid, the more difficult it is to break the stereotype mold. If you're branded a "kid actor," even a "good kid actor," the struggle to become accepted as an adult can be insurmountable. Almost without exception any kid who has made it as an adult has done it *despite* being known as a young actor—not because of it. Which means that even if time is taken later to break it all down and learn the craft and study the art of acting, there are precious few chances to actually get a shot at credibility. The stigma that follows early identification is constant.

The acting demands are considerably more complex on adults than kids. The requirements for making an insightful, creative contribution to a movie, or a play, or yes even a television show, are very different for an adult. You must pull from life experience, understand and recreate reality, and bring subtleties to a role that kids, lacking that experience, can only approximate or hit on by accident.

Child actors I've known both while they were active and

after they retired (at around age 22!), found themselves woefully unprepared for an adult life as an actor. Accustomed to having things come their way, they knew little about the business side, the unemployment side, or the devastating effects of adolescent typecasting. Additionally, used to getting by on looks or youth, they knew little about their own craft. The most compelling actors have techniques for using their life experience in bringing their roles to life—the kind of experience kids often sacrifice.

This can come as a huge shock to a young person cruising into their teens, or in my case early twenties, who find themselves with real-life responsibilities, out of work for the first time in years, and with prospects drying up. What happens when that "special quality" that once worked so well, doesn't work anymore?

Salaries for sitcom actors have changed considerably since the seventies. In our fifth and final year the highest salary among us kids was $1100 a week. Not bad for a teenager. But take into consideration agent commissions, taxes, and the fact that some of the kids were expected to contribute to their families. It was enough to indulge in toys, but hardly enough to carry you through the slow periods that inevitably followed. In addition, residual payments for subsequent airings of the show dried up shortly after we finished filming.

A side effect of all of this is that it can also alienate you from your peers and even shake up the family. It is difficult for even the most well-adjusted family to be comfortable when one of the siblings is getting a disproportionate amount of attention from people, studios, magazines, not to mention full-time baby-sitter, Mom. While the other teenagers in the house are worried about whether or not they can afford movie tickets and popcorn, the kid TV star is financing his new BMW, vacationing in Oahu, and scamming front row Madonna tickets. On top of that they have absolutely no adult responsibilities to get in the way of their fun!

For classmates at school it is nearly impossible to be comfortable with this extra attention. So you learn to be comfortable in the adult world of the workplace. But it is not a natural environment for a kid to be in all the time. They can learn the grown-up banter, the humor, the pressures, and the expectations, but with so many authoritative figures around, it can be overwhelming.

Nobody ever said growing up was easy. But not having the opportunity to play with, compete with, study with, and relate to others your own age creates a serious handicap. So serious, many never recover from it. It's easy to point to the more publicized examples of child stars gone awry like Danny Bonaduce, Adam Rich, Dana Plato, or Todd Bridges. But how many lesser known actors have struggled unsuccessfully with reintegrating into life after a fling with fame, even though it may not have made the headlines?

I am not for an instant suggesting that show business is to be blamed when people behave irresponsibly. After all the business doesn't owe you anything. It is a major influence, but my belief is that people who have problems in life are going to have them whether or not they were ever in a hit TV series. Let's face it, merely being famous is not going to fundamentally change *who* you are. To suggest otherwise is simplistic and a cop out. I am saying that together with other factors, especially the quality of the family environment, being a young professional inhibits rounded growth and interrupts natural development.

If you're sequestered on a soundstage as a child, the outside world is relatively foreign and difficult to relate to. And that is intensified if the previous several years have been in the coddled, spoiled world of temporary fame or earning power. For many, like myself, the teenage rebellion is delayed and comes later, at a less desirable and less appropriate time.

This phenomenon also applies on a larger scale. For example, professional athletes or Olympic hopefuls who train exclusively from their pre-teen years on. When there is always another practice to attend, or a new move to learn, or an interview to go on, how much time is spent on emotional development?

"The Brady Bunch" experience could have had a very different or even negative impact. It did create obstacles that had to be overcome. However, we survived, and lived to tell about it.

Epilogue: So Where Are They Now?

know, I know, you're not gonna let me close this thing out until I answer "Whatever happened to the Bradys?" However, I should preface this whole section by saying that while some of us ex-Bradys have remained more involved in "the business" than others, it's also true that quite often, just when you least expect it, a job offer that you simply can't refuse comes up and bites you in the behind. So even though some of us are now living perfectly contented "civilian" lives, at any moment, with the right project or timing, they may once again rejoin the land of make-believe. But for now:

Susan Olsen is a freelance graphic designer. She's designed a line of custom-painted sneakers, does a great deal of silk-screen work, and is currently attending college, where she's learning to develop artistic techniques for computer applications. She also played bass in a band named Light Sweet Crude. "The name," she says, "describes the band perfectly."

Eve Plumb continues to work on television, on stage, and in motion pictures (most recently in Keenan Ivory Wayans' *I'm Gonna Git You Sucka*). She's also studied

330

Lookinland, through the lens. (© 1990 Paramount Pictures)

and performed improvisational comedy with L.A.'s most esteemed troupe of lunatics, the Groundlings. She paints in acrylics and watercolors on canvas and paper, and holds the dubious distinction of being the first Brady kid married, and the first divorced.

Maureen McCormick devotes most of her time these days to her husband and young daughter Natalie, but she also owns the rights to several stories that she's trying to get produced either as feature films or TV movies.

Michael Lookinland lives with his wife, Kelly, and young son, Scott Michael, in Salt Lake City, Utah. He currently works behind the scenes for independent movie production companies filming in his area. He's worked as a production assistant and camera assistant, but has his eye on one day becoming a camera operator or director of photography.

Chris Knight worked for a few years as a casting director but now claims to be happily out of show business for good. He is married and currently the general manager of a software development company. His company works toward broadening the marriage between creativity and computers.

Ann B. Davis lives in Pennsylvania as part of a Christian household community. She is happy, healthy, and has devoted her life to doing the Lord's work. She also continues to work on stage and screen throughout the world.

Florence Henderson is very much in demand in several venues. She's constantly onstage performing her musical act, hosts "Country Kitchen" for cable's Nashville Network, and is active in various charities including Chidhelp U.S.A. She is also recognizable as TV's foremost proponent of Wessonality.

Robert Reed continued to work as the well-respected actor he was up until he passed away in the spring of 1992. He was a regular on several non-Brady TV series, appeared in numerous movies of the week, and often hit the road to appear in stage productions. When at home in Los Angeles, he enjoyed teaching Shakespeare at UCLA.

As for me . . . thank God for the theatre! In the years since the Bunch, I have played in musical and stage productions virtually everywhere in the country and even landed on Broadway a couple of times. I haven't turned my back on TV and occasionally appear on the tube in the weekly guest spot. Recently my wife Diane (who is also a singer) and I have put our acts together and hit the road with our version of AN EVENING WITH. . . .

And of course, lurking around every corner is always the possibility of another *Brady reunion!*

So as you can see, we all turned out fine, and there's not a bad banana in the Bunch.

Index

333